painting by Brigette Cheyrou

DAVE "POPS" MASCH:

FEARED BY FISH...

LOVED BY MANY...

KNOWS IT ALL!

©2012 On The Water, LLC

All rights reserved. Published in 2012

No part of this book may be reproduced in any manner without the express written consent of the publisher, except in the case of brief excerpts in critical reviews and articles. All inquiries should be addressed to: On The Water • Suite 2 • 35 Technology Park Dr. • E. Falmouth, MA 02536.

www.OnTheWater.com

Printed in the U.S.A.

ISBN-13: 978-0-9706538-7-1

ISBN-10: 0-9706538-7-5

10 9 8 7 6 5 4 3 2 1

Written and illustrated by Dave Masch

Chris Megan, Publisher
Neal Larsson, General Manager
Kevin Blinkoff, Executive Editor
Jimmy Fee, Editor
Andy Nabreski, Cover Photography
Ksenia Pryme, Design

Cooking The Catch Two

Written and illustrated by
Dave "Pops" Masch

An **On The Water** Publication

about the author

I was born in 1937 in Detroit, Michigan, and came to Massachusetts in 1955 to attend Harvard College, kind of by accident.

I saw the ocean in 1955 and have not yet recovered from it. After Harvard I was in the biology department at the Woods Hole Oceanographic Institution for ten years, spending time at sea. I worked as a counselor, cook, instructor and "professional father figure" at the Penikese Island School for 29 years.

Since retirement ten years ago, I spend my time reading, writing, cooking, eating, telling lies and some truths, and I fish.

Dedication

I dedicate this book to my friend, Dick Backus, first a hero to me, then a boss and finally my dear friend. I have always wondered where the expression "He knows his onions" originated. Well, Dick knows both his onions and his fishes.

I would not have done this but for my lovely wife, Jeanne.

Acknowledgement

· ·

I wish to thank Catherine Cramer, who hired me to write the cooking column in On The Water magazine, and Neal Larsson, who first suggested that we turn the columns into a book.

Publisher Chris Megan made this possible, and Andy Nabreski made this book and the first one presentable with the help of George Clondas. This could not have been done without the efforts of these fine people. Thanks again.

Thanks also to "Predator" Phil Stanton, who keeps me in fish and friendship, and to my son-in-law, Scott Britton, who inspires my cooking.

Introduction

● ●

I want to thank all of you who purchased my first cookbook and hope to thank you for buying this one. The first book, now in its second printing, is still selling. These sales inspired all of us to produce this second book.

Someone wrote that the only reason to write a cookbook was "to add to the pleasure of mankind." There is one other reason, and this is money, though adding to the measure of happiness of mankind cannot be discounted.

My competition in the kitchen with my son-in-law, Scott, continues to inspire me, as do the protein donations of my good friend "Predator Phil." You will hear more about these guys in the text of the book.

Thanks to all of you, my friends!

David "Pops" Masch

Chapter One:
JANUARY

I almost never make New Year's resolutions, but this year I am going to make one. I have resolved to eat even more seafood. This may not be a great idea in an ecological sense, but I do not think the increase in consumption by one old guy who already eats an excessive amount of seafood will make a hell of a lot of difference. I do intend to consult the Monterey Aquarium's recommendations for what seafood to avoid, but everything else will be fair game.

Sea Scallop

The recipes in this chapter led me to think of the wonderful packaging in the natural world. Name a finer package than a bird's egg. What could be an improvement on the shell of a quahog or an oyster?

I think the only packaging devised by man that even comes close is the use of intestine for containing sausage stuffing. How could form better follow function?

Enough idle thoughts, let us get on with the preparation of some delicious meals and celebrate seafood in the kitchen and dining room.

Pops,

Could you explain and demonstrate the best way to open quahogs? I often run into a few stubborn ones and can't remember if cold water and ice helps or hinders opening them. Thanks a lot.

Rick Smith

The quahogs should be chilled, calm and content – in other words, "chilled out." If you jostle them too much or treat them roughly, they will "cross their legs," as my friend Rocky Bartlet says, and you will have a helluva time opening them. This chilling advice applies to oysters, as well.

If you are right-handed place the clam in your left hand with the rounder end to the right and with the clam knife in your right hand align the blade between the clam's lips. Your right thumb should be on the hinge of the clam or not touching it at all. Now squeeze with your left hand until the knife forces the shells apart. Cut the adductor muscles, the muscles that hold the shells together, and twist. The shells should part. Run the knife along the bottom shell to free the clam, and there you have a quahog on the half shell, one of nature's great gifts to humankind!

If you still have trouble opening some, put the shy ones in the microwave and zap them for about 15 seconds and they will change their minds.

Dear Pops,

We recently ventured out to do some cod fishing out of Plymouth, Massachusetts. Every place we tried was loaded with dogfish (sand sharks), hundreds of them, following the hooked fish right to the boat. A cod did not have a chance to get near our baits. They tell me this species is endangered. Is that true? They have no predators that I know of. Any tips on fishing around them? And, can they be used for lobster bait? Thanks!

Mike Caffrey

The only thing to do when besieged by dogfish is to move and try again.

The spiny dogfish is not an endangered species but was at one time overfished by gill-netters. They have recovered and often show in huge numbers in some areas, as you know. Dogfish do have predators, particularly larger sharks. If you use only cod jigs, you will catch fewer dogfish than when you use bait.

Dogfish can be used for lobster bait but do not fish as well as oilier baits such as herring, bluefish, mackerel and butterfish. Dogfish make good eating if you skin and fillet them soon after catching them; they make up most of the fish in England's fish-and-chips shops. Give them a try, and you will be a happier fisherman.

Hello, Pops,

Could you please explain the proper way to fillet a tuna to maximize the amount of high-grade meat available? What is sushi-grade tuna and should this meat be kept separate from the loin or toro?

Derrick Hill

Tuna is cut into four major pieces. The cuts are made lengthwise and both vertically and horizontally down the midline of the fish — the vertical cuts leave the backbone behind. The two slabs, one from each side of the tuna, are split lengthwise, making four pieces. The stomach flaps, or toro, are cut from the two ventral fillets and dealt with separately.

Sushi (raw fish with rice) and sashimi (raw fish) grade tuna merely means tuna that has been handled with great care from the moment it was caught and bled until it reaches the consumer. Japanese standards for grading tuna are much more stringent than ours. Toro is sold for the highest price.

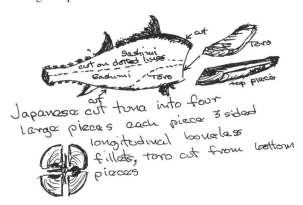

Bivalve Beatitudes!

Here we are in the shortest days of the year, months from when the striped bass return to open yet another season of warm-weather piscatorial pleasure. Except for the brave ice fishermen and a few intrepid smelters, not many of us will catch fish in winter, but before the harbors freeze, we will have access to shellfish or to people who have such access and "owe" us or love us. Sometimes this nets us shellfish without braving the cold.

In the past two weeks, I have been rewarded for teaching shellfishing to kids 35 years ago. Shannon, the widow of my young friend, Seth, who died recently (I often mentioned his cooking in this column), brought me a mess of oysters. I taught Seth where to find them and how to find them and hide them until they reached legal size.

Another shellfishing protégé of mine, Liz Prete, rewarded me with two pounds of bay scallops. The best scallops on earth!

My son-in-law brought me oysters, also. Maybe now that I have reached my declining years, I will be able to rely on friends and family for shellfish. None of them are much good at quahogging; my daughter Amanda is, but unfortunately she is not currently fishing.

Several delicious meals grew out of my students' largesse. I feel I am reaping rewards from seeds sown long ago, and I am very pleased!

OYSTERS AND EGGS (for 2)

12 oysters, shucked
4 eggs
1 scallion (optional)
Salt and pepper
A dash of Tabasco
Parsley for garnish
1 Tbsp. butter

Melt butter over medium heat, add drained oysters, and sauté until edges curl or tighten. Add eggs and optional chopped scallion, Tabasco, and salt and pepper. Stir until eggs are done to your choice of degrees of dryness. I like mine slightly runny. Garnish and serve. Accompany this with toast and a green salad and you have a gourmet light dinner for two.

This is good. The next recipe may be better. Dry white wine goes with both.

HANGTOWN FRY (for 4)

10 eggs
24 oysters, shucked
8 slices bacon
½ cup flour
Salt and pepper
1 cup fine cracker crumbs
4 Tbsp. cream
6 Tbsp. butter
A dash of Tabasco (optional)

Cook bacon until crisp, set aside. Beat two eggs, drain oysters, roll in flour, dip in egg, and roll in cracker crumbs to coat. Beat the rest of the eggs with the cream and seasonings.

Melt half the butter over medium heat and sauté the oysters on both sides until lightly browned. Melt remaining butter, add beaten eggs, and stir until beginning to set. Now fold the omelet over on itself while still slightly runny in center. Serve garnished with bacon strips. This is very, very good.

You can, if you wish, skip breading the oysters and lightly sauté them directly in the bacon fat. Add butter to pan before scrambling eggs. You can also crumble the bacon into the beaten eggs before scrambling.

This is another great light supper dish – try it soon!

CREAMED SCALLOPS AND PEAS (for 2)

1 lb. bay scallops
1½ cups tiny frozen peas
1 cup milk
3 Tbsp. butter
Salt and pepper
A dash of nutmeg
A dash of Tabasco (optional)
1 Tbsp. flour

Make a cream sauce (béchamel) by stirring 1 Tbsp. of flour into 1 Tbsp. of melted butter over medium heat in a small saucepan. Now stir constantly for two minutes. Add 1 cup of hot milk to butter and flour mixture; do this off heat and whisk until smooth. Return to low heat and simmer gently. Salt and pepper to taste and stir in a dash of nutmeg. Put thawed, barely cooked tiny peas into sauce and keep hot as you sauté the scallops.

Put a Tbsp. of oil and 2 Tbsp. butter in a heavy-bottomed frying pan. Heat oil and butter until butter just begins to color, then put in scallops, shake pan, and leave alone until scallops have lightly caramelized. Now turn them over and do second side. Sprinkle with salt and pepper. Turn heat to low and pour peas in white sauce over scallops. Scrape bottom of pan to loosen browned bits into sauce.

Serve the creamed peas and scallops over rice, toast or biscuits. You will not be sorry – I promise!

Last evening daughter allowed as she was going quahogging on the morrow, which is today as I write this. If she goes, I think she will bring me some. If she does, as a good daughter should, I will make the following dish.

SPAGHETTI WITH VONGOLE CLAM SAUCE (for 4)

3 strips bacon
1 lb. spaghetti
2 Tbsp. olive oil
1 small chopped onion
2 cloves garlic, minced
2 dozen or more littlenecks
1 cup dry white wine
½ cup minced flat-leaf parsley
Pinch of red pepper flakes
Freshly ground black pepper

Cook bacon in large skillet with a lid. Drain crisped bacon on paper towels and crumble. Leave bacon fat in pan.

Boil spaghetti to al dente state. Add olive oil to bacon drippings and sauté onions and garlic gently until golden, about five minutes. Do not burn garlic. Add the washed clams, pepper flakes and wine to skillet and cover. Cook until all the clams open, about five minutes. Throw out clams that do not open. Put drained spaghetti, parsley and crumbled bacon into the skillet with the clams and stir. Add pepper to taste and there it is – joy in a skillet.

I like lots of pepper, and, although it is considered heretical by many, grated cheese (Parmigiano-Reggiano) with mine.

A green salad, some crusty bread and butter, and a bottle of chilled, crisp, dry white wine, and you have a meal you could serve proudly to anyone on earth! ◄━►

Squid Sausage? C'mon!

My lovely stepdaughter and her husband, Scott, contender for leading cook in the family, took my wife Jeanne (also lovely) and me to New York City for a weekend of elegant and ethnic dining in honor of our celebrating eight decades on the planet. We interrupted our dining with cultural excursions and glorious sightseeing; we visited the newly redone Museum of Modern Art and the never redone Katz's Delicatessen.

On our first night in town, our generous sponsors took us to the beautifully understated Chanterelle Restaurant, a world-class restaurant of elegant simplicity. There I had the good fortune to try one of the best seafood concoctions (there is no negative connotation here) I have ever tasted, a seafood sausage created by David Waltuck. This sausage, which resembles a large bratwurst, is composed of a fish mousse of striped bass, egg whites, seasoning, and cream, along with shrimp, scallops, lobster, pinenuts, cayenne pepper, brandy, and port. The whole works is piped into a casing, then gently poached and finished under a broiler. It is served as an appetizer with a simple, elegant beurre blanc sauce flavored with a fresh herb. Glorious is an understatement – I only had one mouthful and was blown away!

I have no recipe for you yet, but I hope to come up with one by collaborating with my kitchen rival, Scott. I figure that if you can't beat them, join them, or at least collaborate with them.

This may seem sophisticated for this cookbook, but the ingredients are common enough, and the resulting product is so good that we "simple folk" should not be deprived of this great, attainable culinary experience. I promise a future recipe that will be grand, if not glorious. I will even acknowledge Scott's contributions.

The former statement may be pretentious, but I intend to follow through. Here is a very simple, somewhat exotic recipe by my current culinary idol, Mark Bittman, whose column "The Minimalist" appears in the "New York Times" food section every Wednesday. I look forward to it eagerly.

This is a good dish for mid-winter, when most of us are catching nothing. Squid freezes very well, is fairly cheap and is always available. You can buy it pre-cleaned or clean it yourself: time consuming but not difficult.

I always say that squid should be cooked for less than a minute or more than an hour; anything in between leaves you with rubber bands. Mark Bittman agrees, and the following recipe takes only two minutes to cook.

SQUID WITH BLACK PEPPER, VIETNAMESE-STYLE (serves 4)

2 Tbsp. cooking oil
1 ½ lbs. squid, cleaned and cut into rings
1 or 2 Tbsp. chopped garlic (2 for me)
2 Tbsp. fish sauce (nam pla or nuoc cham) or more to taste
Salt if needed
Freshly ground black pepper (at least a tsp.)
Chopped fresh coriander (cilantro), an optional but delicious garnish
Cooked white rice for serving

Put oil in a large wok or skillet and heat over a high flame for one minute. Add squid, stirring frequently until it just becomes opaque, about 30 seconds.

Taste; the moment the rawness is gone, add garlic and stir. Add the teaspoon of black pepper, stir in the fish sauce, cook 10 seconds and taste. Add more sauce and salt if necessary. Remove from heat, garnish and serve.

This is simply outstanding. Fish sauce is available in the foreign foods section of your supermarket.

I bet this simple recipe could make even those "fake bay scallops" from God knows where – the ones that sell for about $5 a pound in supermarkets – edible and possibly good. I haven't tried it yet, but I might if I can bring myself to buy any of those things that remind me of pale pencil erasers.

Scallops, like squid, freeze very well, but freezing is usually unnecessary unless you harvest your own; fresh sea scallops are almost always available here in New England. Bay scallops, perhaps the finest shellfish on earth, can be prohibitively expensive – about $25 per pound on the Cape and $30 to $40 a pound in New York and Boston. If you find them for less than $20 a pound, they are not bay scallops of New England origin.

The following recipes are for sea scallops, seemingly raw, but actually cooked by the acid in citrus juice, which causes chemical reactions in seafood similar to those caused by heat. These recipes make wonderful appetizers or luncheon dishes. They too are courtesy of Mark Bittman, taken from his award-winning cookbook, "Fish."

SCALLOP SEVICHE, VERSION 1

1 lb. bay or sea scallops
Juice from ½ lemon, ½ lime, ½ orange
4 scallions, minced, both green and white parts
2 Tbsp. fresh cilantro or parsley, chopped
½ tsp. cayenne pepper
Romaine lettuce leaves

Cut bay scallops in half, or cut sea scallops into chunks or four slices. Combine the cut scallops with all the other ingredients except the lettuce. Cover and refrigerate for at least two hours, stirring a couple of times. Serve on lettuce leaves, fajita style, or with bread or crackers. This serves 6 to 8 people as an appetizer or 3 as a luncheon. I can eat a half-recipe myself with joy.

SCALLOP SEVICHE, VERSION 2

½ lb. sea scallops
Juice of one large lemon
¼ cup extra virgin olive oil
Salt and freshly ground black pepper to taste
3 Tbsp. minced fresh basil

Cut the scallops into ½-inch thick slices horizontally; divide among four plates. Drizzle ¼ of the lemon juice and olive oil on scallops on each plate, sprinkle a little salt and pepper. Top with the chopped basil, let rest for 5 minutes, and serve. Fame awaits you!

Sea Scallop

These seviche recipes can be used with fresh fluke, scup, or sea bass fillets cut ½-inch thick, and they will produce wondrously good results. Start with scallops now and look forward to next summer's fish.

An Ecumenical Recipe Pairing

I have a clam chowder in my refrigerator that I made yesterday afternoon in preparation for the local Woods Hole annual chowder competition held at the Landfall Restaurant. I made the chowder yesterday because a chowder develops greater depth of flavor with an overnight aging. My wife and I had the newly prepared, not-yet-cooled chowder for dinner last night and found it to be very good; by this evening, after reheating, I hope it will be delicious.

Every couple of years, I feel called upon to write a diatribe about what passes for clam chowder in many, if not most, local restaurants. What is served is often a thick white paste containing canned clams and – horror of horrors – chopped canned or frozen potatoes, along with a few onions and a sprinkling of stale paprika. Some boast of their chowder being thick enough to stand up a spoon. Any chowder that will stand up a spoon is not worth eating, in my not-so-humble opinion. I find these concoctions to be abominations unfit for man, only maybe fit for beasts.

In France, you are not allowed to label any loaf as "bread" if it contains anything beyond these ingredients: flour, yeast, salt and water. I would like to see a similarly restrictive list of ingredients for any soup called clam chowder. The ingredients should be limited to clams, potatoes, onions, salt pork, butter, flour, some form of milk, and seasonings.

I recently heard a lady from Nantucket on the radio expressing her outrage at people putting adulterants like celery and leeks in their chowder. She even found the use of cream in a chowder to be pretentious. Chowder has been a mainstay of the diets of Nantucket's denizens for centuries. In Herman Melville's classic novel of the whaling trade, the protagonist, Ishmael, and his cohort and harpooner, Queequeg, board at an inn on Nantucket before sailing. The men were offered two dishes, both chowders. The only choice was clam or cod. You can bet that you couldn't stand a spoon up in either one of these. If you could, you would have had mutiny on your hands.

I don't want to discuss the clam-flavored tomato soup served in Rhode Island and points west to Manhattan, and I don't refer to them as chowder at all. It can be a fine soup, but it is not a chowder in my world.

Here, once again, using the ingredients I have listed, is my recipe that my old, now dead, friend Captain Gene Crocker, tugboat man, described as "clam chowder the way God meant it to be."

CLAM CHOWDER

2 cups clam meats, ground
2 lbs. potatoes
1 medium onion, minced
4 oz. salt pork, diced
2 Tbsp. butter
1 ½ cups whole milk
1 can evaporated milk (or one cup cream)
Salt, pepper, and a pinch of thyme
¼ tsp. Tabasco

Clams, Potatoes, onions
salt pork, and milk

I like to steam the clams myself so that I have clam broth in which to boil the potatoes. If you do not make your own clam broth, use bottled clam broth.

In a heavy kettle, render salt pork over a medium flame until opaque. When enough fat has been rendered, add minced onion and sauté until opaque. If you like a thickened chowder, now is the time to add flour to your salt pork and onion mixture to make a roux, stirring at least two minutes to cook away any floury taste.

While you have been doing the above, you should have your potatoes boiling in clam broth. Add your boiled potatoes and the broth they cooked in to the roux and stir until the broth is smooth, then add the ground clams, pepper, and Tabasco. There you have your chowder base.

I like to thoroughly cool this base and refrigerate it overnight, adding the milk and pinch of thyme just before serving. Be careful not to boil your chowder, as it might (will) separate.

I like to serve the chowder in a warm bowl to which I have added a pat of butter, sprinkled with a bit of paprika.

I was saddened to read recently that Maine sea biscuits, which are thick, round crackers, are no longer being produced. These crackers were added by the diner to thicken a chowder, but alas – they are no more. Oyster crackers or saltines can partially fill the void left by the sinking of the sea biscuit.

In the current trend toward seeking national unity under a new political regime, I think publishing a recipe for Manhattan clam soup, often erroneously called chowder, is in order. This recipe can be found in "The Silver Palate" Cookbook by Rosso and Lukins.

MANHATTAN CLAM SOUP

4 Tbsp. sweet butter
2 cups finely chopped yellow onions
1 cup chopped celery
5 cups chicken stock
1 ½ tsp. thyme
1 bay leaf
Salt and pepper
1 large can Italian tomatoes, chopped after draining
1 cup chopped Italian (flat-leaf) parsley
2 medium-sized boiling potatoes, peeled and diced
3 dozen small clams (about 2 cups clam meat)
Grated orange zest (optional garnish)

Melt butter in a large pot. Add onions and celery and cook covered over low heat for about 20 minutes, or until lightly colored. Add all remaining ingredients except clams and orange zest, and bring to a boil. Reduce heat and simmer for 30 minutes until potatoes are very tender.

Meanwhile, scrub your clams and steam open; use about an inch of water in the bottom of a pot just big enough to hold them. Drain pot, saving clam liquid for future use. Remove clams from shells and grind, mince, or process until desired texture is achieved.

Add clams to other ingredients, taste for seasoning (I like to add a little hot sauce), and serve with orange zest on the side for optional garnishing. Crackers are also appropriate here.

I wonder if Captain Crocker is turning in his grave, having been mentioned in a column alongside Manhattan clam chowder!

Alas, my chowder did not win the Woods Hole chowder competition, but that is a problem not of the recipe but of the cook. Perhaps I should apply my efforts to clam soup and look for a contest in Manhattan, or maybe New Jersey.

Clams In Michigan

My wife, who grew up by the sea, promptly became ill upon arriving in Michigan and remains in the hospital with a mysterious abdominal ailment a week later. Could this be because she is too far from the sea? I don't believe this is so, but it has come to mind.

This situation has taken me far from my library of cookbooks and my collection of natural history books, so I have to wing it on the columns of this month, which may make them briefer and slightly less accurate, but I do intend to still be at least 80 percent accurate.

I am writing this in the hospital room of my wife, who is off having a test involving a light and a submersible camera which will probe her depths much like a remote control submarine probes those of the ocean looking for points of interest. I hope that whatever the sub finds in my wife will be benign and easily fixed so that we can return to our home by the sea.

I brought a half bushel of chowder clams and four-dozen "topnecks" to share with and expose my family to. The chowder was a success, but there was little interest in raw clams on the half shell, in fact none. I consider raw clams among the finest bits of seafood in the world. It is interesting at how forbidding new foods are to people; this probably had great survival value in early human history in preventing poisoning. I remember offering my father a lobster, which brought this comment: "Dave, if that thing lived in the bushes, you wouldn't touch it with a stick!" Needless to say we didn't eat it.

My brother-in-law, a clergyman, has spent his entire life in and around farms in the Midwest and was fascinated by the quahogs, their sometimes partly blue shells, and the way they fit in their perfectly designed shell homes. He removed them from their shells after they had been steamed open, a new experience and one I think he enjoyed. The quahog shells have all been saved for nature and art projects at the local Lutheran school.

I made some well-received stuffed quahogs using leftover sage-and-onion turkey stuffing as the foundation. I suggest that you try this. You could even start with packaged stuffing using diluted clam juice as the moistening agent.

LEFTOVER STUFFED QUAHOGS

2 cups sage, onion, and bread stuffing
1 cup (or more) ground or chopped clams
¼ cup diced onion
¼ cup diced green or red sweet pepper
¼ cup diced celery
1 scallion, minced (optional)
Red pepper or Tabasco (optional)

Gently sauté vegetables in butter until nearly clear. Mix in all the other ingredients. Stuff shells with the mixture. You may close with a second shell or leave uncovered.

You can heat your "stuffers" in a microwave or in a 350 degrees F oven. The uncovered ones will form a crust on top in a conventional oven, which many people like. This can also be achieved under a broiler.

Serve these delicious morsels as they are or with melted butter and lemon. You will be locally famous, especially if you do this in Central Michigan.

I have often been surprised by how many people on the East Coast think that littlenecks, cherrystones and chowder clams are different animals or species; they are not. They are all hard-shelled clams (Mya mercenaria) but of different sizes. A 2- to 2¼-inch clam is a littleneck, a 2¼- to 2½-inch clam is a topneck, a 2½- to 3-inch clam is a cherrystone, and any clam larger is a "chowder." The first three sizes are often eaten raw on the half shell or broiled as in clams casino; the "chowders" are always ground for clam sauce, chowder, or cakes.

A delicious way to prepare clams broiled on the half shell is to cover the clam meat with a piece of bacon, cut to fit, and broil until bacon crisps. Everyone you can get to try one of these will be delighted. I suppose there might be exceptions, but I have yet to run into one.

I am going to try these on my Michigander family this evening.

I have driven by several restaurants offering all-you-can-eat fish fries. I was curious about what fish were being served, hoping I would find walleye or yellow perch, two of my favorite freshwater fishes. The first place I asked said they were serving pollock, a sea fish common yet seldom used in New England, delicious especially when fresh. I was given several pounds by my generous editor, Kevin Blinkoff, a few days before coming to Michigan. I ate it for breakfast and dinner with gusto; for breakfast I coated it with seasoned flour and sautéed it briefly on both sides. I had to cut the thick end of a large fillet crosswise into cutlets of equal thickness.

I used the thinner end of the fillets to make pollock meuniére, almost as good as sole, but since sole in unavailable in North America except at an astronomical price, a fine substitute in this classic dish.

SAUTÉED POLLOCK MEUNIÉRE

½-pound pollock fillets per person, (between ¼- and
½-inch thick each)
Seasoned flour to coat
Milk to moisten
A liberal amount of butter to sauté the fish in and
   make the sauce
1 Tbsp. lemon juice or ¼-cup dry white wine
A sprig or two of parsley, minced

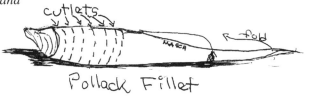

Moisten the fish with milk and coat the fillets with seasoned flour (I use a plastic bag for this) and set aside. Meanwhile, melt butter over medium heat until bubbles subside. Brown fish in butter until brown on both sides (2 to 3 minutes per side). Remove fish to warm platter and keep warm in the oven at 175 degrees F while you finish the sauce.

Add wine or lemon juice to butter and cook until butter darkens. Add parsley and pour over warm fillets. Decorate with additional parsley and serve with sliced or quartered lemons. Peas and rice are also good with this dish.

I did find a place that served an all-you-can-eat walleye meal on certain nights. I did not think that they were a legal commercial species, but apparently Native Americans are still allowed to take them for sale.

We are waiting to hear what the exploratory sub found in Jeanne, my wife, and hope to return to New England, home-range of the quahog, soon. ◄

How Can You Do This? Watch!!

I remember when many kinds of fish were considered food for the poor — preserved fish, salt cod, herring and mackerel were particularly cheap. This is certainly no longer true; fish is now more expensive than most meat and poultry. It may not be long before only fishermen and the rich will be able to afford fresh seafood.

A few years ago I wrote a column about canned fish, or "tinned" fish as the Brits say, that was well received, and now that fresh fish is even more costly, it is time to write another one. Canned fish is still fairly inexpensive and can be tasty and even delicious. If you look hard enough, especially in gourmet shops, you can find ridiculously expensive canned seafood if you are too proud to eat the moderately priced canned seafood from the supermarket.

I enjoy a tuna salad sandwich on (dare I say it?) a soft roll. I have written "serve with a crusty bread" so often I am afraid to mention soft bread. My favorite tuna salad must have a little sweetness; I always include sweet pickle relish in mine.

MY TUNA SALAD SANDWICH

1 5 oz. can tuna
1 Tbsp. pickle relish
2 Tbsp. minced celery
1 Tbsp. minced green onion tops
1 Tbsp. chopped parsley (optional)
A grind or two of pepper
2 Tbsp. mayonnaise or to taste

Tuna Sandwich

Mix the whole works together and "Bob's Your Uncle," tuna salad my way. You can make this with leftover fish of any kind. If you do, add a little salt. You can also use canned salmon, tiny shrimp, sardines, crab meat, or whatever. You will not be sorry.

I like it made with sardines with melted American cheese on top.

A GREAT ANTIPASTO LUNCH (FOR 4)

Bag of lettuce (baby mixture) or baby spinach
Large can 16 oz. sardine or herring in tomato sauce
4 hard-boiled eggs, halved
¼ lb. sliced salami
¼ lb. sliced cheese (your choice)
Some sliced red onion
1 pint grape tomatoes, whole or halved
Salt and pepper
Vinaigrette sauce for greens
¼ lb. sliced ham, rolled

Antipasto Stuff

Dress your chosen greens with vinaigrette and arrange on platter. Arrange all other ingredients artfully on greens. I put fish and sauce as they come on each end, the cheese and meat in the center, with a necklace of tomatoes and hard-boiled eggs. This is beautiful and satisfying. It is good on a gray winter Sunday.

You can add or subtract ingredients. I like to add a few anchovies and olives or use tuna for the fish. Serve this with warm, crusty bread and butter, and life will be good. It is even fairly healthy.

THE EASIEST WHITE BEAN AND TUNA SALAD

1 lb. can white beans (Cannellini or Great Northern) drained
1 5 oz. can tuna, drained
¼ cup commercial Italian vinaigrette
1 minced scallion
1 Tbsp. minced parsley
Salt and pepper

Mix drained beans, tuna, minced scallion and salad dressing. Salt and pepper to taste. Garnish with chopped parsley and serve.

This is nice in a pita pocket with tahini dressing or all by itself, a personal favorite.

THE EASIEST CANNED SHRIMP AND RICE EVER

1 4 or 5 oz. can shrimp
½ cup spicy salsa
¾ cup Arborio rice
2 cups vegetable broth or bouillon
2 chopped scallions or green onions

Canned Fish, Rice

Combine rice and salsa in a saucepan and heat gently. When warm pour in broth and heat to boiling, reduce to simmer, and cook for 20 minutes.

Remove from heat and stir in shrimp and green onions. Presto! Add salad and bread and dinner is ready.

I have so many recipes in mind that we may have to have another month of canned fish recipes unless I hear too many complaints. Canned fish are easier to clean than fresh.

I often try to picture the people who shell those tiny canned Norwegian shrimp or fillet anchovies and then roll them up. They must be gnomes, or the 'little people' as the Irish say, or a bunch of watch repairmen with their loupes. It's a mystery to me.

CRAB CAKES WITH SPICY MAYONNAISE

3 cans crabmeat (4 oz. ea.)
2 Tbsp. tomato paste
¼ tsp. cayenne pepper
1 tsp. lemon juice
2 green onions, finely chopped

1 Tbsp. chopped cilantro
1 egg lightly beaten
2 Tbsp. Parmesan cheese
3 Tbsp. cornmeal, divided
1 Tbsp. butter
1 Tbsp. olive oil

Mix the crabmeat in a bowl with the next seven ingredients and 1 Tbsp. cornmeal. Mix until well combined and form into four cakes or patties. Dredge in the remaining cornmeal. You may need more than 2 Tbsp..

Melt butter and olive oil in a frying pan over medium-high heat until bubbling. Turn heat down to medium and place patties in pan. Flatten them slightly with a spatula. Cook for three to five minutes on each side until nicely browned.

Mix mayonnaise (1/4 cup) and cayenne (1/2 tsp.) together and serve on the side with lemon wedges.

The last two recipes are based on a cookbook called "The Tin Fish Gourmet" by Barbara-Jo McIntosh. The crab cake recipe is as good as any canned fish you can get.

Is a crab a fish? Is an oyster a fish posing as a stone? These are philosophical questions I can't get into now. It is time to open a can and make dinner. I guess I will never be a true gourmet.

Chapter Two:
FEBRUARY

I would rather have my stock in the refrigerator or freezer than in the market. I try to keep chicken, beef, and fish stock on hand at all times. This is fairly easy for me, but since I have little money, it is equally easy not to invest in the market.

There are few things more rewarding than a hot fish or clam chowder on a "Farch" day. Farch is a name coined by a friend for the gray, damp, cold and windy season here on Cape Cod that runs from sometime in February to sometime in April.

One dark day in February, my wife Jeanne took our six-year-old grandson Cooper out to lunch at a seaside restaurant in Woods Hole. They ordered clam chowder. When Cooper swallowed his first spoonful, he leaned back, crossed his hands over his belly and said, "Oh,

Fish stock

Grandma, there is nothing better than that first taste of clam chowder." Now, nearly 20 years later, Cooper is a cook in a restaurant and a true gourmand, possibly a gourmet.

I think you may quote Cooper if you try the simple chowder recipe in this month's menu.

Dear Pops,

There was a time when my husband Andy used to tell me that I "lost fishing points" whenever I would fish with him and catch the dreaded skate. Well, wouldn't you know that the other day on television, Emeril was "bamming" with delight some fillets of skate. Hmm . . . seems like my husband may just have been jealous of the gourmet delight that I had caught. Anyway, I am wondering if you could explain to me how to fillet a skate. It doesn't look fun, but perhaps you have an easy way of getting the job done. Also, have you eaten them yourself and is there a recipe that you would recommend? Thanks for your help!

Susan Nabreski

Skate are delicious but a pain to skin; you do not fillet them.

Cut off the wings, and with a sharp knife cut between the skin and white flesh until you can get hold of the skin with a pair of pliers. The skin is rough and will abrade your skin. Raise the skin and pull, and use your knife as if you were skinning a larger animal. With a sharp enough knife you can skin them like a fish fillet with your knife, parallel to the skinning board, or you can poach the wing and easily remove the skin afterward.

Poach wing in stock or water with white wine or white vinegar added (1/2 cup to a quart of water), one bay leaf, and one cut onion. After 10 minutes remove skate and skin it, remove meat from central cartilage, arrange on a hot platter, top with a Tbsp. of crushed capers and chopped parsley.

While skate is poaching, heat a half-stick of butter until nut brown (do this over medium heat). Pour this over skate. Salt and pepper to taste. Rinse butter pan with a Tbsp. of vinegar and pour on skate. This is outstanding - you will never regard a skate with disdain again.

Dear Dave,

I have every copy of On The Water *ever printed, beginning in 1996.*

In all of your "Cooking the Catch" columns, never once have you done any recipes for escargot using different snails found on the Cape. Since after all these years you must be desperate for new ideas, I figured this would be a big help. I'm thinking of moon snails and periwinkles.

Thank you,

Jim Dudac

At times I have thought quite a bit about moon snails and periwinkles... odd things to think about. I think of moon snails eating my treasured quahogs and of periwinkles coming over with the Pilgrims on the Mayflower, the former on the bottom and the latter on deck.

I have also eaten both species and found that both are good. However, moon snails are tough and periwinkles are tedious to work out of their shells. Anyway, if you're feeling adventurous, the easiest way to enjoy snails is to tenderize them by boiling them in seawater until the operculum (the little trap door) falls off. Work out the meat with a pin, dip in butter, eat, and smile.

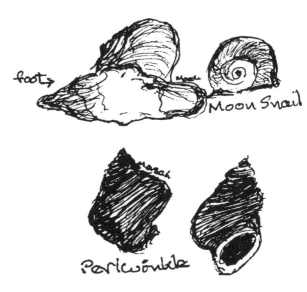

You Can Put Stock in These

Maybe February is the cruelest month for nonmigratory fishermen, other than the hearty souls who venture out onto the ice. We cannot catch any fish, so it is to the pantry for canned seafood or to the freezer where last summer's fish have not quite lost their flavor entirely. If you are wise, as I have been on only a few occasions, you will have frozen clam juice or fish stock in your freezer. These elixirs can go a long way toward relieving the February funk I find myself in. There is nothing like a good chowder or fish soup to warm a dulled spirit. We should have done this last fall, but since we did not, we must make some clam broth or fish stock. The hardest thing about the process is getting the fish racks or heads and shelling out to get chowder clams (large quahogs). The supermarket will not be able to help you with fish skeletons, but your local fish markets will if you are polite. Avoid salmon if possible; cod heads or bones are great, so are halibut bones. Just wing it; you cannot go far wrong.

FISH STOCK (1 gallon)

4 lbs. fish heads and bones
4 quarts water
4 crushed garlic cloves
3 halved medium onions
1 cup chopped parsley (can be left whole)
1 stalk celery
1 carrot
2 cups dry white wine (or 3 Tbsp. vinegar)
½ tsp. basil
½ tsp. thyme
½ tsp. pepper
4 tsp. salt to taste
1 sliced lemon (optional)

Fish Stock

Put all ingredients in a stock pot and bring to a boil; reduce heat to a rolling simmer and cook for 30 minutes and no longer – fish stock, unlike beef stock, does not benefit from longer cooking. In fact, I think it develops off-flavors.

If you are going to use this stock in a dish that will contain shellfish or crustaceans (paella, cioppino, etc.), you may cook them in the simmering broth; they will only make it more delicious. If you cook shellfish (mussels, oysters, clams), omit salt, for the bivalves will release their own. Check for salt at end of cooking period.

Skim the foam that surfaces during cooking. After 30 minutes, remove pan from heat and drain. Some people go as far as straining through cheesecloth, but I don't bother.

Your stock is now ready for use. This stock freezes very well and lasts for at least six months.

If, God forbid, you cannot make your own stock, there are adequate fish bouillon cubes available, but you will not be as pleased with yourself if you use them, nor will you have bragging rights: "Oh no, I make my own stocks!" Go for it.

CLAM (OR MUSSEL) BROTH, PLAIN

Clams
Water

Put ¼ inch of water in bottom of whatever covered container you use, put in clams, and boil covered until all clams open. The liquid you have remaining is pure, very salty broth.

CLAM BROTH, FANCY

Clams (or mussels)
Water
A sliced medium onion
A sliced carrot
A handful of parsley
A stalk of chopped celery with leaves
A crushed clove of garlic
6 peppercorns

Put ¼ inch of water or white wine in whatever vessel you choose, add all ingredients but clams, and simmer gently for 5 minutes. Now add your shellfish, cover, and steam until all are open. If a clam does not open, put it aside and open away from stock; it may be full of mud – yuck!

Strain this ambrosia and there you have a lovely, but salty, clam stock.

You may use these stocks as a basis for soups, jambalaya, spaghetti sauces, gumbo, and chowders. You will probably have to dilute the clam stock a bit because of its saltiness. A little dry white wine in the stock cannot hurt a bit.

SIMPLE FISH CHOWDER

2 quarts fish (or diluted clam) stock
2 lbs. white–meated fish (cod, haddock, pollock, hake, whatever)
1 medium onion, minced
¼ lb. salt pork or fatback, not lean
2 Tbsp. butter
3 or 4 lbs. of potatoes, cubed (a Yankee might use 5 pounds)
½ tsp. thyme
2 cans evaporated (not sweetened) milk
Dash of Tabasco
Whole milk (or not)

Pollack

You can use unpeeled potatoes if you like, but a Yankee may not eat them in chowder – that could be O.K., too.

Cut potatoes in pieces of whatever size you prefer and cover with stock; boil until just tender. Meanwhile in a separate pot, maybe the one you will finish the chowder in, melt the butter and gently sauté the minced salt pork until it reaches a light tan color. Add chopped onions and gently sauté until opaque (nice word).

If you wish to thicken your chowder a bit, add up to 3 or 4 Tbsp. flour to fat and onions and sauté gently for 2 to 3 minutes, stirring to cook, but not to burn, the flour.

Now add either the stock and potatoes to the fat and butter mix or the other way around, and stir thoroughly. Place whole fish fillets in pot with potatoes and simmer until fish is white throughout.

Now pour canned milk and as much bottled milk as you wish into the pot, stir without breaking up fish, add dash of Tabasco and pinch of thyme, mix in gently, heat until steaming and "Bob's your Uncle."

You can eat the chowder now or bring it to room temperature and refrigerate it until tomorrow.

The fish fillets are cooked whole so you can serve chunks of fish in every guest's bowl.

Serve this with crackers and sweet pickles, and people will be willing to wrestle you for your recipe. That is a promise! ◀━🐟

Fighting Farch

The most dismal season, the most oppressive and demoralizing here on Cape Cod, runs from February until early April. There is usually little sunshine, plenty of rain, and a few bright snowfalls to relieve the boredom. The few brilliant days after the snowfall all too soon turn back to low clouds overhead, mud underfoot, and dirty snow sludge along the roads. A friend, which friend I have forgotten, coined a name for this season. He calls it Farch, an ominous word fitting a gray season. When I went to sea as a young man, I usually managed to get to tropical climes during this season, callously leaving my family at home to cope. I no longer have that option – so what to do to pass through Farch?

I know I could go ice fishing, but the ice around here has been unsafe in recent winters, providing me with an excuse to sit at home and brood. I am not good at brooding for very long, so I light a fire, get out my 50-plus seed catalogs and spend too much money on too many seeds and plants for next summer's fantasy garden. I also read fishing magazines, look at gear catalogs, and muse about fishing to come, if we survive Farch once more.

This musing about fishing leads to thoughts of eating fish and cooking them. I experiment with new ways to make frozen swordfish steaks good rather than merely edible and with new, to me, seasonings for farm-raised salmon, fish I feel ambivalent about using because salmon farming does so much harm to estuaries and other fisheries. A salmon farm in the mouth of a river will almost always destroy sea-run trout fishing in that river, but alas, that type of aquaculture is here to stay. The salmon are available and I will eat them, but before we get to the salmon, we will discuss a delicious breakfast or lunch.

Two members of my family, one generation down, have provided me with shellfish once again; this time it was a half-dozen large oysters and a gallon of scrubbed mussels.

The breakfast I made this morning was a variation of an old-time dish called, for some reason unbeknownst to me, "Hangtown Fry."

SCRAMBLED EGGS WITH SCALLION AND OYSTERS

6 large oysters, shucked
4 eggs
2 scallions (green part only, sliced thinly)
A dash or two of Tabasco
Salt and pepper
2 Tbsp. butter

Oysters and eggs

Melt the butter in your favorite skillet; meanwhile, put the oyster meats (cut in half if really large) in a bowl with the sliced scallions, eggs, Tabasco and a couple grindings of black pepper and mix as for scrambled eggs. The butter should be bubbling nicely in the skillet. Pour in the egg and oyster mixture and cook gently until the eggs are set the way you like them, taste for salt and serve as-is on toast or on a buttered muffin. If you like oysters, these will be some of the finest scrambled eggs you have ever eaten!

If eaten late at night this dish is said to help prevent a hangover. If eaten in the morning it is said to be a cure. Give it a try, you will not regret it!

I made a dinner this week centered on the suspect farm-raised salmon. Wild salmon is better, but not always available and often wildly expensive. Farm-raised salmon is good, and often excellent when carefully prepared. I sautéed a 1½-pound salmon fillet coated with sesame seeds and anointed it with a parsley, lemon, butter and caper sauce. The slightly sharp sauce contrasted very nicely with the unctuousness of the slightly undercooked salmon, making a delicious dish.

SAUTÉED SESAME SALMON AND SAUCE *(for 3 or 4)*

1½ to 2 lb. salmon fillet
Sesame seeds to coat
4 Tbsp. butter or light olive oil (or both combined)
Salt and pepper

Salmon + Sesame Seeds

Pour sesame seeds on a plate and push fillet down on them. I leave the skin on the fillet, believing it holds more flavor unskinned, but you do not have to. The salmon should be sticky enough to hold a coat of sesame seeds without being dipped in egg or milk. Salt and pepper the fish on both sides.

Melt the butter, butter and oil, or whatever, and sauté the coated fillet on both sides until lightly browned and nearly cooked through. I like it to remain red-pink in the center. This should take a scant five minutes a side over medium heat. Remove from skillet and keep warm on a heated platter placed in a 170 degrees F oven.

BROWNED BUTTER, CAPER AND LEMON SAUCE

4 Tbsp. (1/2 stick) butter
1 Tbsp. chopped parsley
1½ Tbsp. lemon juice (from 1 lemon)
1 lemon cut in wedges
2 Tbsp. rinsed capers
¼ cup white wine (optional)

De-glaze sauté pan or skillet in which you cooked the fish with ¼ cup of white wine. The de-glazing is optional. Melt the butter and cook over medium heat until it begins to turn brown, remove from heat, add lemon juice and capers and pour over the salmon upon which you have sprinkled the minced parsley. Garnish with quartered or sliced lemon and serve, proudly!

STEAMED MUSSELS PORTUGUESE

3 to 5 lbs. mussels
1 cup dry (cheap) white wine (vinho verde or pinot grigio)
6 peppercorns
¼ pound sliced linguica or chourico
¼ stalk sliced celery
1 small onion sliced
2 cloves garlic crushed
4 sprigs parsley

Put everything but the mussels in a pot big enough to hold all the mussels and bring to a boil. Simmer about one minute, dump in the mussels, cover the pot, and cook until the liquid nearly bubbles over. Turn down heat and steam for about a minute longer, and there you have it, lovely mussels, a delicious broth to serve them with, and a feather in your culinary cap.

Serve the mussels with broth, melted butter, crusty bread, a green salad and more wine, and Farch will begin to lose its depressing dreariness.

Grateful for Gifts from the Sea!

I worked for 29 years at the Penikese Island School, located on one of the Elizabeth Islands, 14 miles south-east of Cape Cod and 1 mile from Cuttyhunk Island, right in the midst of what is perhaps the best striped bass fishing on earth. From the window above the kitchen sink, you can see Canapitsit Channel between Cuttyhunk Island and Nashawena Island, where Frank Church caught his record striper, and from a second-floor window, you can spot Sow and Pigs Reef, where many record fish have been caught.

Our school at Penikese served delinquent and otherwise troubled teenaged boys. While at the school, I served as a counselor, teacher, cook, father figure, fishing guide, pig-gelder, enforcer of the rules, and keeper of the peace. Those were great years!

The school, founded by George Cadwalader, continues to positively influence the lives of young men, and does so with more success than most.

A couple weeks before Christmas, the school's office called to tell me that a student from 25 years ago was looking for me and also for a tape of a TV show produced in 1985 by The National Geographic Society that focused on Penikese and in which he appeared. When I called him, I learned that he felt his time at Penikese had not only changed his life but probably saved it as well.

He remembered learning to fish, dig clams, and gather mussels and periwinkles. He said these experiences led him to his career in the wholesale seafood business. He is now the manager of the shellfish department of a large wholesaler in Boston.

I told him I had written a seafood cookbook and that I would send him a copy. He insisted on paying me, but I refused. He said he would "take care of me" nonetheless. If this statement had come from one of our many other graduates, it might have frightened me, but it did not in this case.

I sent him a book, and a day or so later a foam shipping container was resting on my front step. It contained a 4-pound salmon fillet, two-dozen prime Duxbury oysters, and 2 pounds of bay scallop meat (worth a small fortune). All together this gift was worth far more than my book, at least in dollars. My book would last longer, but his would bring far more immediate enjoyment.

I could not use this bounty all at once, and since scallops freeze well, I froze them. The oysters will keep for weeks or even longer if stored cup-side down, so the salmon had to be used first. I cut a 1½-pound piece off the tail end and sautéed it, coated it with sesame seeds, then cut the remaining 3-pound slab in half lengthwise to make gravlax to serve at a large party as an appetizer. If someone gives you a large salmon side, you might (and probably should) do the same.

Scallops, Eggs, Scallions

SAUTÉED SALMON AND SESAME SEEDS (for 2)

1 lb. fillet of salmon (about ½-inch thick)
Sesame seeds (black or white, or a mixture)
3 Tbsp. peanut oil
Lemon
Parsley
Salt and pepper

Heat oil in sauté pan to nearly smoking. Oil will shimmer slightly on the surface when ready for the fish.

Salt and pepper the salmon liberally on both sides and roll in sesame seeds. If seeds won't stick, moisten fillet with milk or milk mixed with a little egg. Egg Beaters, the yolkless egg product, are good to keep on hand for when you need just a little egg.

Sauté the fish skin-side down in the hot oil for about 2 minutes, then turn the fillet over and sauté for as long as it takes to get the salmon nearly cooked through. I like mine nearly raw at the middle. Sprinkle with parsley and lemon juice and serve proudly.

Salmon cooked in this way is good to serve on a bed of spinach, dressed with lemon and olive oil. The spinach can be raw, wilted or cooked. They are all delicious.

GRAVLAX A LA BITTMAN (SALT-AND-SUGAR CURED SALMON)

3 to 4 lbs. salmon fillets, skin on, in two pieces
3 Tbsp. salt (5 Tbsp. if Kosher)
2 Tbsp. sugar
1 Tbsp. freshly ground black pepper or less, to taste
1 good-sized (supermarket-sized) bunch of dill, roughly chopped, stems and all
1 or 2 Tbsp. spirits – (e.g., gin, vodka, brandy)

Lay fillets skin side down and sprinkle with salt, pepper, and sugar. Spread the dill over them and splash on the booze – I use two Tbsp. Sandwich the fillets together, flesh to flesh, and wrap with plastic wrap. Cover the sandwich with another plate and put a weight on the top plate. I use a brick, though canned goods will do – anything to compress the salmon. Refrigerate for two or three days. Open the package every 12 hours and baste contents inside and out with the accumulated juices.

After two days (three is better), remove fillets from wrapper, wipe off the dill, and thinly slice the fillets on the bias as you would smoked salmon. Serve on pumpernickel, rye bread, or crackers with a side of lemon wedges.

QUICK SAUCE FOR GRAVLAX

3 Tbsp. French's Honey Dijon Mustard
1 Tbsp. lemon juice
3 Tbsp. dill leaves, chopped

Mix and serve. Delicious. You can make this same dish (or one very similar) with bluefish next summer.
We ate the beautiful oysters raw with a choice of black pepper, Tabasco, cocktail sauce, or lemon. They were splendid!

One day for lunch, I opened four large oysters and ate them each accompanied by half a traditional pork breakfast sausage. This taste combination was learned from my culinary hero, James Beard, and is magical and splendid. You really don't need more than ¼ sausage per oyster. You must try it!

I still have two pounds of precious bay scallops to use. Some will go into a seviche, some will be sautéed with ginger and garlic, and since I got them free, some of them I will use in the following recipe.

CHINESE SCALLOPS AND EGGS (for two-plus)

¼ lb. bay scallops
2 Tbsp. peanut oil
1 Tbsp. dark sesame oil
¾ cup chopped onion
1 Tbsp. soy sauce
6 scallions, thinly sliced
4 eggs, lightly beaten

Soften onion in heated peanut oil. Add scallops and cook for 3 minutes. Add soy sauce and sliced scallions to beaten eggs and pour over scallions. Cook gently, stirring until eggs are set. Sprinkle with dark sesame oil and serve.

I am proud to have received these gifts from a student, just as I am proud to have my own children and young friends bring me gifts from the sea, things I taught to them to find or catch more years ago than I care to remember. They should keep up the good work!

Is Anything Better Than Pasta with White Clam Sauce?

Despite my recent run-in with overconsumption of clams, in this case quahogs, I remain addicted to them, especially in white clam sauce, so I have decided to fill this column with recipes for my potentially fatal passion.

All white clam sauces need at least four basic ingredients – clams, garlic, olive oil and Italian parsley – though in a dire emergency you could omit the parsley. I always carry a head of garlic with me when I travel both for personal security and happiness and in case I run into some clams and olive oil.

We will start with the simplest, and some say best, recipe.

WHITE CLAM SAUCE (for 4)

2 dozen or more littleneck quahogs
1/3 cup chopped Italian parsley
2 large cloves of garlic sliced
¼ cup virgin olive oil
Freshly ground black pepper

Hardshell   Surf

Gently sauté the garlic over medium-low heat until it is soft, add the well-washed clams to the pot, cover, and steam after adding half of the parsley. Be careful not to burn the garlic.

After about 10 minutes, all the clams should have opened. Grind in a generous amount of black pepper and "Bob's your Uncle," you have a delicious sauce.

I would serve this poured over 1 pound of boiled pasta (spaghetti, linguine, angel hair, or whatever) cooked al dente and sprinkled with the remaining chopped parsley. Another way to finish the dish is to add the pasta directly into the oil and clams, stir, and serve straight from the pot.

I am going to mention a couple of things you can do to this original, pure sauce (I should present these all as separate recipes and have the column space filled in no time). You may add ¼ cup of dry white wine when you begin the steaming, or you may add a Tbsp. or two of butter, or a pinch of crushed red pepper.

Many Italians say you don't need or possibly shouldn't have grated cheese with seafood. This irritates me because I like some good grated Parmigiano Reggiano with my clams and pasta. You have my permission to do the same.

I am giving you next a very similar recipe from *The Compleat Clammer* by Christopher R. Reaske.

WHITE CLAM SAUCE

"Open and shuck several-dozen hard-shelled clams. Save the liquid and chop the clams. Sauté two or three cloves of chopped garlic in pure olive oil (approximately ¼ to ½ cup). Do not brown the garlic as it will become bitter. Add clam liquid, chopped parsley, and black pepper (red if desired) and simmer approximately 10 minutes. Add the chopped clams – the more the better – and cook for only 2 to 3 minutes. If you cook it too long, the clams get a bit tough. Pour over hot spaghetti or linguine. The exact proportions of spices will vary to taste."

This is a magnificent dish. I recommend it unequivocally! It's rare that I don't find something to quibble about – just ask my dear wife. (The "dear" was put in for self preservation.)

These recipes are all similar, and you will soon develop your own, but if you at first follow these instructions before setting out on your own, you will benefit. Think of it as hiring a guide to fish in new waters – always a good idea.

Mark Bittman, "New York Times" food writer and hero of mine, provides this recipe, which he humbly claims to be "Wonderful and Authentic." I admire chutzpah.

SAUTÉED CLAMS WITH PASTA (for 2)

1 dozen littlenecks or other hard clams
1/3 cup olive oil
2 cloves garlic, peeled and crushed
1 dried hot red pepper
½ cup dry white wine
½ cup minced parsley (flat-leaf is best)
1 tsp. minced garlic
Salt and freshly ground black pepper to taste
2/3 lb. linguine or other long pasta

Bring a large pot of water to a boil. Wash and scrub the clams well, then dry them. Heat the oil in a 10-inch skillet over medium-high heat. Add the crushed garlic and hot pepper and cook, stirring occasionally, until garlic is lightly browned. Add the clams, one or two at a time, stir briefly, and cover. Put the pasta in the hot water and cook as directed on the package.

Check the clams every minute or two; when the first one pops open (it will take just a few minutes), remove the cover and add the wine. Continue to cook over medium-high heat, shaking the pan occasionally. When most of the clams are open, add the parsley, minced garlic, and salt and pepper. Drain the pasta when it is done, put it in a warm bowl and top with the clams and sauce. Serve with the clams on the side of each plate. If any remain closed, open them with a knife.

If you follow Bittman's advice about unopened clams, open them away from the main dish, for they may be dead or "mudders," either of which would ruin your grand production. Also be careful, for a good unopened clam will be full of hot steam.

The next recipe was improvised when I found myself with 6 extra guests for dinner (making 12 in all), so to extend I added mushrooms to the sauce because as Edmund Hillary would say, "They were there."

WHITE CLAM SAUCE WITH MUSHROOMS (for 12)

1 gallon hard clams (quahogs)
2 cups dry white wine
1 large onion sliced
1 stalk celery roughly chopped
1 carrot roughly chopped
½ cup olive oil
¼ cup butter
6 cloves garlic
¾ cup chopped parsley
¼ cup chopped fresh basil or ½ tsp. dried
Freshly ground black pepper
Hot sauce (Frank's, Tabasco, etc.)
1 lb. mushrooms, chopped
4 Tbsp. flour (optional)

Put the wine, onion, celery, carrot, some peppercorns, a sprig of parsley, and a squashed clove of garlic in a covered kettle that is big enough to hold all the clams. Bring the wine and vegetables to a boil, reduce the heat to a simmer and cook gently for 10 minutes. Put the clams into the pot with the simmering sauce, cover, increase the heat, and boil until the clams open. Drain the clams, saving the broth, and allow them to cool. I used a food processor to chop the parsley, mushrooms, and clams.

Melt the butter in the olive oil in a pot big enough to hold all the sauce ingredients. Lightly brown the garlic in the oil and butter. Now, add the chopped clams, parsley, and basil and stir for about a minute. At this point, I stir in the flour and cook it, stirring for two minutes before adding the reserved clam broth to the pan. This makes a thicker sauce, which I like. The flour is optional. Now, add 3 cups of broth and stir. Add pepper and hot sauce; you probably will not need salt. This will sauce 3 pounds of pasta, enough for 12 normal eaters.

That is enough about clam sauce for now. I have a mess of quahogs in my fridge right now; I guess I will get at them and try not to eat too many. ◀━

Just add clams.

Chapter Three:
MARCH

M y grandson Cooper would say that there is nothing better than "that first taste of clam chowder," but white clam sauce in its elegant simplicity would not be far behind. March is a time for shellfish, available fresh all winter, for soups and chowders, and maybe even some "tinned" fish, as they say in Britain. It's a time for anything warm and comforting, as "Farch's" depressing dismalness continues.

Toward the end of March, the crocus begin to bloom, dandelions begin to brighten up the lawn, the tautog begin to bite after spending the winter in warmer offshore waters, and we begin to feel stirrings of the miracle of spring. I think I will make some marinara sauce and some salmon croquettes, or better yet, a spicy squid stew.

Squid Stew

Dear Pops,

We caught some cod the other day, and the crew filleted them for us. It was delicious, right up to the point when I noticed the worms in it. What are these worms? Are they dangerous? Is there anything we can do to avoid this? We threw the fish out, which broke my heart, but I felt like I was on an episode of "Fear Factor." I cannot find any information about this at all.

Pamela Kearney

These worms may be found anywhere the cod are found and are on the increase locally because of the ever-growing number of seals, an intermediate host in this parasite's *(Phocanema decipiens)* life history.

One case of human illness from this source has been reported from Great Britain. Considering the amount of cod consumed, this shows the worm to be minimally dangerous.

If you cook the cod correctly, the worms will be killed; freezing also kills the worms. If you are merely disgusted by the thought of eating worms, you can usually remove them easily. If you candle (hold in front of a bright light) the fillets, you can spot the worms that are not on the surface. You will find most of the worms in the belly flaps of the fillet.

I usually remove the most obvious worms and hope my guests don't find any. These worms are often found in swordfish, so if you are really worried, stay on your toes. We who eat many fish all eat worms.

Dave,

Friends often give us mackerel. Here's a question: Is there a way to cook it that will eliminate the strong fishy flavor?

Ed Schroeder

The way to change "the strong fishy flavor" of mackerel lies not with the cooking but with your friends. You must urge them to ice the mackerel the moment they take them off the hook, to fillet or gut them as soon as possible, and to keep them chilled until delivery. Strong smells or flavors in any fish result from poor handling or old age, but I do not expect fish to smell like peaches, either.

Hi Pops,

I was wondering if you could help me out with something. I'm a surf-fisherman, and I don't always have my weighing scale with me. Since most of my fishing is catch and release, I was wondering if there is a way for me to figure out the weight of a fish without using a scale. I seem to recall reading an article in one of my fishing magazines that included a formula for finding a fish's weight without using a scale. Are you familiar with this formula? If so, will you please share it with me? I'm fairly good at guessing how much a fish weighs, but it would be nice to do it more "scientifically."

Thank you.

R. Milliken

There are many formulas around for estimating fish weights, even by species. The one general formula that I like is fairly simple and fairly accurate for most species: Girth (in inches) x Girth x Length/800 = weight in pounds; thus a fish 15 inches in girth and 29 inches long will weigh 8.16 lbs. (15x15x29/800=8.16 lbs.).

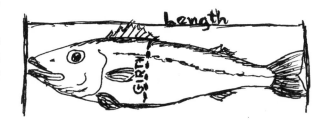

Cod, the Salt of the Sea, the World is His Oyster.

By March, spring will be in sight, one of our few remaining herring will be in one of the runs, the redwings will begin to call, and the remaining black-back flounder will be stirring in the mud with visions of sea worms in their peabrains, just as I will be having visions of bass in mine. But for now, most of us must stick to winter store-bought fish although I may manage a few shellfish myself. It has been so warm, so far, that there is no ice on the estuaries, so warm in fact, that I heard a spring peeper on January 17. I think it was a peeper – the temperature was over 50 degrees F.

Fish was once poor man's food, especially salt fish, but salt cod now costs as much or more than fresh cod. I do enjoy salt cod in winter, especially in fish cakes, though it is also nice blanched and served in chunks in a green salad with a garlic, lemon juice, and olive-oil dressing. Codfish balls made from salt cod make a fine "exotic hors d'oeuvre." These used to be Saturday night peasant food served with baked beans in Boston.

I have recently found salted pollock in supermarkets at about one-third the cost of salt cod. Salted pollock can substitute for salted cod in any recipe. Salt cod is often 10 dollars a pound, and as the cod population drops, it will become a more costly delicacy; it is already far more expensive than salmon. Wow! I say get some now, give it a try, and decide for yourself if the demise of the cod population is a disaster.

FISH CAKES

½ lb. (1 cup) soaked salt cod
1 lb. (2 cups) potatoes
1 egg
1 tsp. butter
1/8 tsp. pepper
A few drops onion juice
Salt pork fat or lard or peanut oil

Boil soaked cod and potato together until potatoes are soft, drain, and return to pot. Add egg, butter, pepper, and onion juice. With wet hands, shape in flat cakes and sauté in fat or oil until nicely browned on both sides. Drain on brown paper or kitchen towels and serve with tartar sauce and ketchup.

This recipe from "The Boston Fish Pier Seafood Recipe Cookbook", published in 1913, almost a hundred years ago, is good, but mine is better, so I wrote a bigger recipe.

IMPROVED SALTFISH CAKES

Ingredients from first recipe plus ¼ cup chopped onion, 1/8 cup chopped celery, 1 tablespoon minced parsley and a dash of hot sauce.

Wet your hands, form cakes, and dip in a combination of white flour, corn flour and cornmeal. Fry over medium heat until browned on both sides. Serve with lemon, hot sauce, ketchup and tartar sauce.

With either of these recipes, you may make small balls, roll in flour or cornmeal, and deep-fry, brown, put on a tooth pick, and serve as a hot canapé, and your guests will think you are a magician.

3rd
Fish cake

My son-in-law Scott, super shellfish server and cook, came up with a superior treatment for oysters that caused me to resent his assault on my position as senior seafood savant and cook in the family. I can keep ahead of him in alliteration, but I am losing ground in new recipes. He topped raw oysters with chipotle peppers and other stuff, broiled them, and turned them into seafood ambrosia.

BRITTON'S OYSTERS "CASINO" *for 50+ oysters*
(Serve four per person as an appetizer, as many oysters as you need on the half shell.)
For the topping:

4 red peppers
2/3 bunch fresh cilantro
1 clove garlic
2 Tbsp. pine nuts
4 Tbsp. virgin olive oil
2 or 3 Tbsp. breadcrumbs
Salt and pepper

Roast the peppers by placing right in the flame of a gas burner and leave until totally charred on one side; turn with tongs until blackened all over. Put peppers in a paper bag for about 15 minutes, remove peppers, and scrape off all black material; cut in half and discard seeds and pulp.

Now put all ingredients in a Cuisinart or blender, omitting olive oil. Blend until combined, and gradually pour in oil until you have a fairly smooth paste. Taste for seasoning. Put 1 teaspoon on each oyster; flatten topping. Put the works under a preheated broiler until first signs of blackening show, remove, and devour. This is splendid dining – world class – and my son-in-law came up with it, alas.

You should have leftover topping. It will keep a week or more in the fridge. Try spreading some on a fillet of fish and bake it in a 415 degrees F oven. I have not done it yet, but I will, and it will be delicious! What am I going to do with this guy? Someone said, "Man's virtue is in striving," so I will keep at it.

SUPER DELUXE PORTUGUESE CODFISH CAKES

2 cups desalted salt cod
3 cups mashed, boiled potatoes
1/3 cup minced linguica or chourico
¼ cup chopped celery
¼ cup chopped green or sweet red pepper
1/3 cup minced onion
1 clove minced garlic
½ tsp. ground pepper
Cayenne pepper (optional)
½ cup corn flour
½ cup baking flour
¼ cornmeal
¼ cup chopped green onion top, scallion tops
¼ cup parsley
1 large egg
Tabasco or other hot sauce, to taste
2 Tbsp. olive oil

Put the oil in a skillet over medium heat; sauté sausage and vegetables very gently until barely cooked. Stir them into mashed potatoes and salt cod along with the egg and add seasonings. Mix ½ cup corn flour, ½ cup baking flour, and ¼ cup cornmeal. With wet hands, form the mixture into cakes, coat them with the cornmeal flour blend, and fry gently until prettily browned on both sides. Drain excess oil and keep the cakes warm in a 175 degrees F oven until all are finished. Serve with additional hot sauce, lemon, tartar sauce, or whatever you wish. These are great! You will be applauded.

You can use this recipe with leftover fresh fish as well – if you use fresh fish, you will have to add salt.

Boston baked beans, fish cakes, and creamy coleslaw make a classic New England Saturday night dinner, and a damned good one!

Is it Chowder Yet?

I enjoy eating a good chowder on a cold winter day about as much as anything I ever do, or remember doing, outside of art, gardening, fishing, cooking or any other sort of procreative activity, the details of which I shall not go into. The splendid chowder I had for lunch at the Daily Brew, a coffee shop and lunch restaurant in Cataumet, deserves going into in some detail; this rich, ambrosial chowder is worth traveling for. I have only had three fish chowders in public restaurants that are worth mentioning in my adult memory, all with Cape Cod connections. One, no longer available, made by Falmouth chef Dave Mutti, the second in a restaurant in Maine owned by Howie Shaw of Cataumet, and now the ambrosial fluid made by Glenn Corriveau, also of Cataumet. I live in Cataumet myself and am not ashamed of the fish chowder I concoct. The locals may be largely unaware, but Cataumet seems to be the inspirational source for several fine chowder cooks – another mystery.

Corriveau's fish chowder deserves closer examination; it contains twice as much fish as potato, no evaporated milk, plenty of cream, onions, celery, good bacon, and a bit of commercially made lobster bouillon. I spoke, at some length with Glenn, who was generous and enthusiastic about his chowder and chowder in general. His generosity of spirit is shown in his ratio of fish to potato. A "generous Yankee" (possibly an oxymoron) might use as much fish as potato, though probably not. I have known Yankee chefs to go as low as one part clam meats to four parts potato and heard rumors of some even less generous. Corriveau, on the other hand, goes overboard in the other direction. He told me how he makes a four-gallon batch of his ambrosia, which I will try to bring down to a home-sized recipe.

GLENN'S FAMOUS FISH CHOWDER (for 4)

1 ½ lbs. fish (your choice, but not salmon)
1 lb. potato, cubed
1 small yellow onion, chopped
1 Tbsp. chopped celery
2 slices of bacon, sliced thick and cubed
1 pint half-and-half
½ pint light cream
Salt and pepper
A pinch of thyme
1 Tbsp. lobster bouillon

Gently render the fat from the chopped bacon. When bacon is opaque but not crisp, add celery and onions to the pan and sauté gently until vegetables are soft.

Meanwhile, gently poach your fish in water in which you have dissolved the Tbsp. of lobster bouillon. Use enough water to barely immerse the fish. Stop simmering the moment the fish easily flakes.

While the fish is simmering, boil your potatoes until just tender and drain. Now, in a heavy-bottomed pan, combine the bacon, celery, and onions, the fish and the potatoes, handling the fish gently; we do not want to crumble it into tiny pieces. Pour in the half-and-half and the light cream. Heat gently; do not boil. Test for seasoning and add salt and pepper (optional: a dash of Tabasco).

Stir in a pinch of thyme just before serving. If the chowder seems too thick, add more cream or even milk, and there you have it – joy in a pot, smiles on your friends' faces, and a growing culinary reputation, just like Glenn Corriveau.

My own method of making fish chowder is roughly like Glenn's, but I am cheaper, using equal amounts of fish and potato, salt pork rather than bacon, and evaporated milk instead of cream. I boil my potatoes in fish stock or diluted clam juice and cook my fish in the same pot with the potatoes after the potatoes are soft. I then add a couple of cans of evaporated (not condensed, which is sweetened) milk, some black pepper, a shot or two of Tabasco, and a pinch of thyme. I almost forgot! The sautéed salt pork and onions go in with the fish and potatoes! I might even melt a dab of butter on top, and there you have it – Pop's fish chowder. These chowders are good things to make with some of last summer's fish, which are still lurking in the freezer.

I get into heated arguments about chowder, maintaining that chowder always contains either milk or cream, seafood, and some kind of fat, preferably salt pork. I have bent a little to include corn chowder and even chicken chowder (peculiar to Martha's Vineyard) but never New York clam chowder which contains tomatoes; they serve this ersatz soup as far east as Rhode Island and call it chowder. I will never dignify it so.

The Oxford English Dictionary, my usual authority on all things verbal, says, "a chowder is a thick soup or stew made of fish or clams." Again, I must question authority, what do "Brits" know about quahogs anyway? I had better stop. I am getting worked up and unreasonable and there is not even anyone here to argue with.

I read a fine article about Maine lobstermen, fishermen, and the condition of the cod and lobster fishery in Maine waters that implied the reduction of the stock of cod benefits the lobster fishery. "The Boston Globe" printed this story in early January of '07. One of the lobstermen, Dick Bridges, is famous for his lobster chowder; I will make this chowder in the very near future. I almost never present a recipe that I have not either prepared or sampled, but I am going to make an exception here, for I am certain that it will be delicious!

LOBSTER CHOWDER (*Adopted from Mr. Bridges*)

1 stick butter
1 medium onion roughly diced
6 cups lobster broth (or cold water)
½ tsp. sea salt
¼ tsp. black pepper
5 lbs. lobster (live weight) cooked
  and shucked, claws intact, tails
  cut in large chunks
3 cans evaporated milk
1 tsp. dried basil
1 cup cream or milk if needed
3 large russet potatoes, peeled and cubed

Lobster chowder

Sauté the onions gently in two Tbsp. of butter in a pot large enough to hold entire chowder (about 4 quarts) until soft. Add the potatoes, six cups water or lobster broth, salt and pepper and simmer for about 30 minutes. Meanwhile, melt 2 Tbsp. remaining butter in a skillet and sauté 1/3 of the lobster meat for about a minute and set aside. Do this two more times with remaining butter and lobster meat. Now, add the sautéed lobster meat to the potatoes and onions. Add the canned milk and basil to taste; adjust for salt and pepper. If too thick, add milk or cream. Mr. Bridges likes to add a handful or two of Maine shrimp to his chowder. With or without the shrimp, this is truly a chowder! Serve it with pride as I will.

A chowder, like pornography, is hard to define but easily recognizable when you see it, or in this case, taste it. Hurrah for true chowder! ◄

It May Be March, But You Gotta Eat

It is too early to garden, too late to ice-fish, too cold to enjoy shellfishing, and the ocean fishing seems very far away. This is my least favorite time here on Cape Cod. The days are generally drizzly and gray, and so is my humor. As dismal as this all seems, there is still joy to be found in the kitchen, even if it means tinned fish (as they say in England) or trips to the commercial seafood counter. The pleasures of the kitchen and dining table do not have to be dampened by the weather, so let's get to it.

We will start simply, with the humble potato, which is a noble companion to any fish.

FISH AND POTATOES *(for 4)*

Kosher salt (or other pickling salt)
2 lbs. of white fleshed fish, cut thickly if possible, 1 inch or so
2 or more potatoes
½ cup extra virgin olive oil
Black pepper
Chopped fresh parsley for garnish

Preheat oven to 400 degrees F. Meanwhile, sprinkle a 1/8-inch layer of salt on a platter or tray large enough to accommodate the fish. Place the fish on salt and cover with another 1/8-inch layer of salt and set aside. Some people call this process corning, particularly when left overnight.

Peel the potatoes and slice in ¼-inch (or thinner) segments. Put potatoes in a Pyrex or other ovenproof pan – a 12-inch skillet will do. Toss potatoes with 2 Tbsp. olive oil and liberal amounts of salt and pepper, arrange them evenly, and bake for about 30 minutes. Shake the pan a couple of times to keep them from sticking.

Rinse the fish and pat dry, then arrange on top of the cooked potatoes. Pepper the fillets liberally. Return dish to oven and bake for another 10 to 12 minutes. I forgot to mention drizzling 2 Tbsp. olive oil on the fish before baking.

Remove from oven, garnish with chopped parsley, and there you have it! This is good served with cooked spinach dressed with olive oil and vinegar or lemon juice. The brief salting provides the fish's unique flavor. Healthy, tasty, and easy – try it, you will not be sorry!

This is a good dish to try on fish species many of us neglect: cusk, pollock, hake, tilapia, monkfish, etc.

Here is another easy, simple, elegant and delicious idea for presenting white fish. Cook the fish in any manner you wish other than fried – although even that will work.

BRAISED MONKFISH ON MASHED POTATO *(for 4)*

2 lbs. monkfish (or any firm white fish)
2 lbs. mashed potatoes
Salt and pepper
1 small onion
½ stalk celery
2 sprigs parsley
1 clove garlic
1 Tbsp. vinegar or ¼ cup dry white wine
4 peppercorns

Put enough water to cover fish in a saucepan just large enough to hold it, then add vinegar and white wine or lemon juice. Before braising fish, gently simmer parsley, sliced celery, sliced onion, pepper and crushed garlic clove in water for five minutes. Add fish and simmer until fish is opaque all the way through. Remove fish from water with a slotted spoon and arrange atop individual servings of mashed potatoes. Garnish with chopped parsley and serve accompanied by a vegetable of your choice or a green salad. Simple and elegant. Your family may even be impressed.

MY MASHED POTATOES WITH SCALLIONS

2 lbs. potatoes (I like Yukon Gold)
2 Tbsp. butter
3 Tbsp. milk, half & half, or cream
4 scallions chopped fairly fine (white and green sections)
Salt and pepper

Melt butter in the milk in microwave.

Boil potatoes in salted water until soft, drain and mash. If you want lump-free potatoes, do not add butter and dairy until lumps are nearly gone. Add the chopped scallions, butter, and milk and mix or whip until smooth. Salt and pepper to taste, then serve. I love tiny frozen peas, just thawed, with this. Spinach is also a good choice. You can do whatever you want. I suppose I don't need to say that.

Another good variation is to add 1 tsp. thyme to the braising liquid and to garnish the dish with a sprig of fresh thyme or a few chopped leaves.

This is a simple, elegant way of presenting any variety of fish – salmon is great this way! Remember that any leftover fish and potatoes can easily be transformed to fish cakes, noble in themselves.

The fish for this dish does not have to be braised; you can sauté, bake, or grill the fish and then present it on the mashed potato.

If you do braise the fish, save the braising liquid for the foundation of a fish stew, soup, or chowder. You won't be sorry.

SAUTÉED SCALLOPS WITH LEMON-THYME BUTTER SAUCE *(for 4)*

1 ½ lb. scallops (bay scallops if you can get a loan, or use quartered sea scallops)
Olive oil
Juice of two lemons
¼ tsp. fresh lemon thyme or regular thyme
2 to 4 Tbsp. butter
Salt and pepper (some people say white pepper, I don't care which)

Heat a sauté pan that can accommodate the scallops in one layer, coat bottom with olive oil, dump in scallops and sauté. Shake the pan occasionally until scallops just begin to brown, not much more than one minute. Stir in lemon juice and chopped thyme. Turn off heat and swirl in the butter. That is it. Heaven!

Things should soon start brightening up, and we may even be able to get some shad roe next month. I will be ready for it and will probably include a recipe in April's column – if April ever comes.

From Tuna Casserole to Coquille St. Jacques

I have taught many people how to fish and find shellfish in my lifetime, skills that were taught to me in my first years on Cape Cod almost 50 years ago. I am eternally grateful to my mentors and very appreciative of the rewards I have been receiving from those mentored by me. I recently wrote about a gift of bay scallops, oysters and salmon sent to me by one of my boys from 25 years ago at the Penikese Island School, and I presented recipes on how I cooked these gifts; one more appears below.

I got a call from another former student at Penikese of whom I wrote somewhere, telling the story of how he caught a 6-pound bluefish using an 18-inch piece of lathe with a nail hammered through it. Anyway, he came upon this tale and called me to tell me he would get me two or three monkfish tails next week. He is now a commercial fisherman. He said even his father was proud of him. His life has followed a rocky path to where he is now happy on the North Atlantic in winter. He said he wants to thank me for helping him get happy and famous. The North Atlantic in winter is no joke.

Yet another young man, not a delinquent, gave me a couple dozen oysters yesterday. I am a wealthy and happy man; money has little to do with this. Even though this increased generosity from my former students may have something to do with my getting older and less able to gather those things myself, this is only partly so. I would give them all a run for their money on a clam bed, yet I would not want the idea that creeping decrepitude is affecting me to vanish because they might not pity me enough to make more donations to the "old boy."

I will never be too proud to refuse the gift of a brace of lobsters, a dozen oysters, a pint of scallops, or a peck of chowder clams from one younger and more fit than I. I would be a "damn fool" if I did. I am eager to get the monkfish!

I had a visitor, my wife's friend, Brigette, from France last week, so I decided to make her a modified version of a classical French dish, Coquille St. Jacques, with the bay scallops my former student sent me. Rather than cooking the sauce and scallops together and serving the finished product in a scallop shell, I cooked the sauce and scallops separately and served them over spaghetti. It was a grand success!

PASTA WITH COQUILLE ST. JACQUES

1 lb. bay scallops or quartered sea scallops
2 cups dry white wine (Portuguese Vinho Verde is good and inexpensive)
¼ lemon
1 bay leaf
¾ cup milk
¾ cup cream
¾ cup Swiss cheese (grated)
2 Tbsp. flour
1/3 stick butter
Parmesan cheese (optional)
Salt and pepper
1 lb. pasta

Heat the wine with the squeezed lemon quarter and the bay leaf; add the scallops and poach them gently until opaque all the way through. Remove the scallops and save liquid.

Melt the butter in a saucepan, add the flour, and, stirring constantly, cook the roux over medium heat for at least 2 minutes. Pour in the milk and cream slowly, still stirring constantly. Add ¼ cup of the cooking wine and stir it in. Still over medium heat, add the Swiss cheese, stirring until it melts and becomes smooth. If the sauce seems too thick, stir in more of the wine poaching liquid until the sauce reaches the consistency you wish for.

Return the scallops to the sauce, heat thoroughly, season with salt and pepper, and pour over 1 pound of the pasta of your choice. I use spaghetti.

Traditionally the sauced scallops are spooned onto sea scallop shells or dishes resembling scallop shells, sprinkled with parmesan, and lightly browned under a broiler. You can mimic this classic by putting a pound of cooked pasta – rotini, elbows, shells or ziti – in a 9-inch by 13-inch ovenproof pan, pouring the sauce over the pasta, sprinkling with parmesan and browning lightly under the broiler. This is a great dish.

I can suggest several variations which may only be "gilding the lily," but they are delicious.

You can add ½-pound of sautéed mushrooms to the sauce.

You can substitute shelled and deveined shrimp for the scallops, or you can combine the two.

You can substitute lobster or crabmeat for the scallops.

You can combine ¼ cup of chopped lobster with a pound of cooked, cubed monkfish and pretend it is all lobster.

You could double the recipe and combine with a sampling of all the seafood I mentioned and have a magnificent seafood casserole. If you should do this and serve your friends, you will be risking celebrity, or at least growing fame.

When making the original recipe, based on a recipe from Howard Mitcham's classical "Provincetown Seafood Cookbook," I melt butter in a sauté pan and caramelize the scallops top and bottom. I then deglaze this pan with wine and add the result to the cream sauce.

Another fine way of making a seafood casserole is to prepare the cheese and cream sauce, boil the pasta until almost done and combine this with any combination of seafood you desire. Cover the mixture with breadcrumbs and parmesan and bake in a 350 degrees F oven for about 45 minutes or until bubbling and beginning to brown on top.

I always add a dash of hot sauce to any casserole I prepare. I am once again wandering, so I better close it down by urging you to experiment and make some dish of your own. You will not be sorry.

I remember another kid at Penikese: A muscular 17-year-old from Santo Domingo, who asked one day in late January if there wasn't some holiday coming up soon.

"What's it called Pops? You know, the one where the dude sees his shadow and... Oh, yeah, I remember, it's Quahog Day!"

I think we should celebrate our holidays each in our own way. A quahog's shadow can be as ominous as a groundhog's shadow – at least to me.

"Croquettes, Anyone?"

I believe that these coldwater trout taste better than the ones caught from warmer waters, fresh from the hatchery in spring and summer. I always prepare my trout simply, merely coating them and sautéing (pan frying) them, and seasoning them with salt and pepper.

TROUT FOR TWO
Two 10" to 12" trout (heads removed to fit in normal pans)
Seasoned flour
3 Tbsp. butter for sautéing or 3 Tbsp. oil (I use peanut oil)

I shake the fish in a plastic bag holding flour, salt and pepper until well coated.

Should you desire a thicker, crispier crust, dip flour-coated fish in a beaten egg or some Egg Beaters (no-yolk egg product) and then in breadcrumbs, panko, or cornmeal.

Now, sauté the trout in melted butter or peanut oil over medium heat until nicely browned on both sides. Remove from heat and keep warm in a 175 degrees F oven until ready to serve.

If there is hot oil left in the pan, or enough oil while the fish is cooking, I like to take sprigs of parsley and fry them for garnishing the fish. Take the stem in your fingers and immerse the leafy part in the hot oil. There will be a sputtering commotion at first, but when it stops, remove the parsley and drain on a paper towel or brown bag. This makes a unique and delicious garnish for the fish. Try it!

Once again I tell you to serve this with buttery and tiny frozen peas with a little lemon to gild the lily.

In the dead of winter I sometimes turn to fish market tuna and farm-raised salmon despite some ecological concerns. I am guilty, but I love them, especially salmon steaks or tuna slabs coated with sesame and sautéed in a hot pan until the seeds are light brown and the fish piece centers are still raw. This is great stuff!

I always buy about twice the amount of fish that I need for my wife and myself so that I will have leftovers for making hash or fish cakes or croquettes (glorified fish cakes).

MARK BITTMAN'S SALMON CROQUETTES
1 to 2 cups leftover cooked salmon
1 to 2 cups leftover mashed potatoes
½ to 1 cup minced onion or scallions
Breadcrumbs
½ cup minced parsley
1 tsp. minced ginger or garlic (optional)
1 egg
1 tsp. mustard
Salt and pepper
Lemon wedges

Salmon

Mix first eight ingredients (I add ½ cup of minced celery to mine); add enough breadcrumbs to stiffen while the mixture remains moist.

Shape into small cakes, coat with breadcrumbs, and dry on a rack. Now, refrigerate for 15 to 30 minutes. Heat a skillet over medium heat for 2 to 3 minutes, add a thin layer of olive oil, and cook the breaded croquettes until browned all over, 6 to 8 minutes. Serve with lemon wedges.

I like to serve these with a white sauce or gravy.

GRAVY FOR CROQUETTES

1 cup milk
1 cup chicken broth
2 Tbsp. butter
2 ½ Tbsp. flour
Salt and pepper

Melt butter in heavy-bottomed pan, add flour to make a roux, and cook, stirring over medium heat for at least two minutes to cook flour. As roux is cooking, heat milk and broth mixture to near boiling.

Remove roux from heat, pour in hot stock and milk all at once, and stir or whisk vigorously until smooth; return to heat and stir until thickened and smooth. Taste for seasoning and serve. Delicious! I like cranberry sauce with my croquettes and gravy. I bet you will, too!

I was given a cookbook by a locally famous, in lower Manhattan, cook and restaurant owner, Kenny Shopsin, sometimes called the "Soup Nazi" because he would only serve people he liked, or at the least didn't offend him. His book, not surprisingly, is called "Eat Me, The Food and Philosophy of Kenny Shopsin." I think most of you would enjoy it. In it he presents a recipe for a simple, delicious, and versatile marinara sauce that led to a new dish for me that was very good and satisfying.

SHOPSIN'S MARINARA

¼ cup virgin olive oil
½ large yellow onion (why not a medium onion?)
1 tsp. minced garlic (I use at least a Tbsp.)
½ cup red wine
One 28 oz. can tomatoes (San Marzano is best), including juice
One 6 oz. can tomato paste
1 tsp. to 2 Tbsp. sugar (depending on sweetness of tomatoes and your taste)
A small handful of fresh basil leaves
Salt

Heat olive oil in large saucepan over medium-high heat; add chopped onion and minced garlic and sauté for about 5 minutes. If onions start to brown, turn down heat. Add the wine and boil 1 to 2 minutes to burn off alcohol, add tomatoes and sugar, break down tomatoes with a wooden spoon, leaving a couple fairly whole, and simmer for ½ hour; now, add tomato paste and basil and cook to desired thickness. Thin with water if necessary.

Last week I took cups of this sauce, brought it to a simmer, and added four cooked Italian sausages and a couple of handfuls of shelled small shrimp. When the shrimp were barely opaque, I added ½ lb. of boiled spaghetti, stirred up the whole works and had a fine main course for two. Try it!

I should have put this in the trout discussion: trout fried in bacon grease served along with the bacon is also a fine thing. I like it for breakfast. I've thought of more things to do with the marinara, but they will have to wait.

The Love of Leftovers

I love leftovers and the fine dishes they can be turned into. I also enjoy the mellowing and blending of flavors that comes with an overnight sojourn in the refrigerator. Clam chowder is always best kept overnight; meat stews, squid stew, chili, and homemade meat sauce also blossom with a bit of aging. I always hoped the blossoming would happen with a little aging for me, but if it did, I think I missed it and have passed beyond improvement, leaving only its alternative.

I had a fine dish for breakfast this morning: a fish, pasta, and olive frittata, baked in the oven, made entirely with leftovers from last night's dinner with a couple of eggs added. Last night's dinner was spaghetti with a marinara sauce containing sliced olives with baked crumbed codfish fillet on the side and a green salad. This morning I used what remained to make:

PASTA FRITTATA WITH COD

1 cup leftover sauce and pasta
4 oz. leftover cod (or whatever)
2 eggs
¼ cup of Parmigiano Reggiano
Salt and pepper
2 Tbsp. heavy cream (optional)

Anoint a small baking dish or two ramekins with olive oil. Put the pasta and fish in the dish or dishes, pour in the beaten eggs and cream, if you are using it, and cover the surface with the grated cheese. Bake this for 15 to 20 minutes in a preheated 375 degrees F oven or until top is browned and the eggs have set.

I don't understand why simply prepared, delicious dishes like this are not more common in North American cooking.

You can use this same recipe with leftover shrimp, lobster (if there has ever been any), clams, sausage, or whatever and prosper. Your life will be enhanced, and you may even be admired.

A couple of weeks ago, after a roast beef, mashed potato, and cauliflower-in-cheese-sauce dinner, I found myself with a bounty of leftovers. Some beef was sliced for sandwiches and a lot of it became hash. This left me with enough potatoes and cauliflower for a meal for two. I had what turned out to be a fine idea for using the vegetables. I had bought a lovely (I feel that way about fish sometimes) 1¼-pound hake fillet that afternoon with no definite cooking plan.

I decided to bake the fish on top of the potatoes and chopped cauliflower, imitating my favorite bluefish and potato recipe.

LEFTOVER MASHED, VEG, AND FRESH FISH *(for 2)*

1 lb. white-fleshed fish (maybe salmon?)
Enough leftover mashed potato to cover bottom of baking dish with cooked
  vegetables mixed in (the vegetable could be almost any: carrots,
  broccoli, cabbage, kale, etc.)
½ cup Parmigiano Reggiano
½ cup breadcrumbs
Salt and pepper
Parsley for presentation
2 Tbsp. butter or olive oil

Butter an ovenproof dish large enough to hold the veggies and fish. Spread the potato mixture in dish and put it in the cold oven, which you now turn to 415 degrees F.

Salt and pepper the fish and dress with oil. When the oven reaches temperature desired, remove dish from oven and put the fillet on top of the potatoes. Sprinkle fish and potato surfaces with breadcrumbs and grated cheese. Either drizzle with olive oil or dot with butter. Return to hot oven and bake for about 12 minutes until fish flakes and cheese are beginning to brown. Sprinkle with parsley and proudly serve!

I served mine with carrots flavored with butter and fresh dill; creamed spinach would be nice, as would tiny peas. It is still morning, and I am getting hungry for dinner. Did I say the dish was good? I should have; it was kind of like an upside-down shepherds pie.

I have made a squid stew using Howard Mitcham's recipe from the "Provincetown Seafood Cookbook" for many years and love its intensity, heat, and deep flavor. It is so good that I never tried anyone else's squid stew until a week or so ago, when I prepared a recipe pretty much following David Waltuck's recipe from "Staff Meals from Chanterelle." It was very interesting to find that his recipe was much more like a conventional meat stew and not intense, though delicious. Here it is. Don't be discouraged by a long list of ingredients.

WALTUCK SQUID STEW (for 4 to 6)

¼ cup extra virgin olive oil
2 medium onions coarsely chopped
4 large cloves garlic coarsely chopped
¼ tsp. saffron threads (optional, but good)
1 cup dry white wine
2 cups canned tomatoes, drained, seeded and chopped,
* about 1 cup*
2 cups fish stock (or clam juice)
½ tsp. dried thyme leaves
½ tsp. dried oregano leaves

½ tsp. hot red pepper flakes (to taste)
3 lbs. cleaned squid cut in ¼" rings
½ cup frozen peas
1 medium zucchini cut in half lengthwise and cut into
* ¼" thick pieces*
2 medium carrots
2 Tbsp. unsalted butter
Fresh lemon juice, to taste
(I added a large cubed potato;
what is stew without a potato?)

Heat the oil in a medium saucepan over medium heat. Add the onions and garlic and cook, stirring until translucent but not browned, about 5 minutes. Add the saffron and cook, stirring, for 3 minutes more. Add the wine, increase the heat to high, and bring to a boil. Cook uncovered until wine is reduced by half, about 5 minutes.

Add the tomatoes, fish stock, thyme, oregano, and pepper flakes and bring to a boil. Add the squid, reduce the heat to low, and simmer uncovered for 20 minutes (says Waltuck; I say 30 or more). The squid will release liquid, making the mixture nice and saucy. Add the peas, zucchini, carrots, and potato and simmer until squid and veggies are tender, about 10 minutes more (I say 15 minutes).

Remove pan from heat, stir in the butter and lemon juice and serve. I served the lemon on the side so each diner could season his own.

The night I made this, the stew was good but not great; I was slightly disappointed. I had some leftover stew for lunch the next day, and it was outstanding. I ate more the third day, and it was great, but, alas, we had eaten it all.

Like many leftovers, this stew improved greatly with age. I wish I could say the same about myself. ◀─

Squid Stew

Chapter Four:
APRIL

April usually signals the end of "Farch" with a few lovely days interspersed with gray, clammy, overcast remnants of winter. However, the trout are feeding in the newly stocked ponds, herring (what's left of them) are running, and squid are gathering inshore to breed. Rumors of migrating stripers spread, and by the end of the month some will be caught.

In the meantime, I will prepare some salt cod, once the most mundane of fish, and sea scallops, always elegant, as elegant as the daffodils.

Salt Fish

Ask Pops

Dear Pops,

We often talk about the wonderful and edible animals that the ocean has to offer, but no one ever talks about the edible plants that come from the sea. I know that many other cultures integrate seaweed into their diets, but no one seems to do it around here. I would like to find out what species of local seaweed are edible, and if any of them are particularly tasty. From clams to crabs to fish and squid, I love collecting culinary delights from our local waters. I would love to add some new vegetable dishes to my menu. Please let me know what, if any, forms of seaweed are worth looking for, and what should I do if I find some.

Thanks!

Jared Bevelaqua

P.S. Are there any toxic ones I should know about???

I don't know of any toxic ones, but some look pretty bad.

There are several local seaweeds that are eaten in large quantities in other parts of the world. Lauer *(Porphyra purpurea)* is eaten in Britain, and Irish moss *(Chondrus crispus)*, sometimes called carrageen, has been harvested commercially in Massachusetts for food and as a thickener for soft ice cream. You are eating seaweed when you have a milkshake at McDonald's. Dulse *(Palmaria palmata)* is also harvested commercially. This stuff was chewed like gum in Ireland. Euell Gibbons, in his book *"Stalking the Blue-eyed Scallop"*, said it was kind of like chewing a salted rubber band. He says it is better eaten dried or cooked like spinach. It can

also be dried and used as a seasoning on seafood dishes; small bits are cut off the dried weed and sprinkled on food.

Samphire glasswort *(Salicornia virginica)*, a fleshy herb, not a seaweed, grows widely around the high tide marks of marshy shores and can be used fresh in salads or made into tiny salty pickles. This one I like.

I have eaten these seaweeds and find them generally uninteresting and bland, but I urge you to try them. I can provide recipes upon request.

Dear Pops,

I have a simple question. Can I clean and fillet cod (legal size) in my boat while at sea or must cod be brought intact and whole like striped bass? I am cod fishing for the table, not commercial. This summer during a routine inspection by an EPO person, I was informed that cod should be kept whole and any future cod fillet would be considered illegal. I have called two DEP offices including the Boston office seeking clarification on this. The people I talked to were not sure. Is this one of those gray areas or what? Can you tell me what the actual law regarding this issue is?

Richard Millbury

I spoke to a sport-fishing man at Marine Fisheries who told me the law probably was meant to apply to several species of fish, but that as it is written it only specifies the striped bass, so you may fillet cod while at sea. The EPO officers should know this. At the moment, as the law is written, this is not a gray area.

Why Shouldn't Fish Taste Fishy?

I have just returned from the Florida Keys, where I did some "geezer" fishing with an old friend. We once spent nine-hour days in a flats boat pursuing tarpon, permit, and bonefish with legendary guide Steve Huff. He once got us each grand slams (tarpon, permit, and bonefish) in one day. He told us that more people had walked on the moon than had simultaneous grand slams from one boat. It sounds like I am blowing my own horn, but I probably would not have even seen any of the fish we caught that day without Steve Huff, a mischief maker highly deserving of the term "living legend". "Geezer" fishing is floating bait, shrimp, crabs, or pinfish in a chum click and taking what comes, a far less physically taxing pursuit than flats fishing. It is fascinating in that you do not know what you are going to catch next.

How does this relate to cooking? I caught fish I had not seen nor cooked before. I added fish to my life list of culinary victims. My friend Maynard Albert, a life-long piscatorial predator, hooked and landed a fine "smoker" of a king mackerel, over 3 feet long and 20 pounds, with fierce teeth and no desire to board a boat. Like bluefish, this king mackerel is avoided as food by many people because its raw flesh is gray, it is oily, and it has a flavor. Most Americans seem to want mild (flavorless), white-fleshed fish, nothing with character or a "fishy" taste. They miss many great dining experiences because of this. Almost every year I sneak in a recipe I call the world's greatest bluefish recipe. I was eager to try this with king mackerel. I did, and it was a grand success – a dish I would serve to anyone on earth, except perhaps Britain's royal family. The flesh turned pearly white when baked, and the oil from the fish changed the flavor of the potatoes from merely delicious to ambrosial.

A few king mackerel were caught in Buzzards Bay each of the last two summers. If you get one, eat it or give it to me, or even invite me to cook it for you. You will not be sorry.

I get impatient with people who do not want fish to be fishy (can you imagine beef being discarded for tasting beefy?) – give me a break. What people call a fishy taste or flavor is fish that has begun to spoil. These same people often fear bones. I say, let them eat bananas for as the Calypso song says, "they have no bones."

This grump sautéed some fine grouper simply and served it with brown butter, parsley, and caper sauce.

Grouper, potato, scallion, zucchini

SAUTÉED GROUPER FILLETS *(for 4)*

2 lbs. fillets no thicker than 1 inch
½ cup Wondra (superfine flour)
½ stick butter
2 Tbsp. olive oil
2 Tbsp. capers (slightly crushed)
½ cup minced parsley
1 Tbsp. vinegar, white or red
Salt and pepper

Melt butter mixed with olive oil in a sauté pan big enough for your fish. Make two batches if you do not have a large enough pan to sauté all the fish at once. Keep cooked fillets warm in a 180 degrees F oven.

Coat damp fillets lightly with flour, and salt and pepper. Saute these lightly coated fillets in butter and oil until lightly colored and barely cooked through; remove from pan and keep warm.

Melt remaining butter in same pan; when it begins to turn brown, stir in wine, capers, and ¼ cup parsley. Mix, pour over fish, and serve garnished with remaining parsley.

I served this with garlic and scallion mashed potatoes and microwave zucchini (an easy delicious dish).

GARLIC AND SCALLION MASHED POTATOES
2 lbs. potatoes, peeled or not
4 cloves garlic, roughly chopped
4 scallions, thinly sliced
2 Tbsp. melted butter or olive oil
¼ cup milk or fat-free half-and-half
Salt and pepper

Boil potatoes until cooked through in water containing the garlic and white parts of scallion. Heat butter or olive oil in microwave in a bowl until bubbly hot. Drain potatoes and mash thoroughly without removing garlic; when smooth enough, whip in milk and butter or oil along with scallion green parts, and keep warm until serving.

MICROWAVE ZUCCHINI
2 medium zucchini, sliced
Salt and pepper

Arrange squash, sliced ¼-inch thick, on a dinner plate or platter; salt and pepper lightly. Cook for 2 minutes at full power in microwave; if not done enough, cook in 1-minute increments until it reaches the degrees of doneness you require. The vegetable will be bright green and delicious.

You can serve grated cheese, lemon or lime, and toasted breadcrumbs or sesame seeds as condiments with these dishes. This is a simple and grand meal suitable even for royalty if you leave the garlic out of the potatoes.

It is April, and the local ponds will be studded with wading trout fishermen. Remember when Opening Day in Massachusetts was such a big thing and many of us stood in the cold rain trying to catch stupid stocked trout that had never seen natural food? These fish are not as good as wild trout but are better than no trout, and the holdovers become increasingly tasty.

SAUTÉED TROUT WITH BACON *(for 2)*
2 trout about ¾ lb. each, cleaned
4 slices good bacon
1 cup cornmeal (or a mixture of corn flour and cornmeal)
¼ cup milk
Parsley sprigs (or minced)

Moisten trout with milk, dredge it in cornmeal, and set aside. Cook bacon until quite crisp and set aside, leaving bacon fat in pan. Sauté fish in bacon fat until nicely browned on both sides; serve garnished with bacon and parsley. Adding a little bit of Egg Beaters egg substitute to milk will make for a heavier coating when you dredge the fish.

I like a fried egg done in the fish pan and some grits with trout prepared this way, along with toast, coffee and orange juice. What could be better on a dank, dreary April morning on Cape Cod, or anywhere else?

Coquilles St. Jacques

Any recipes based on scallops can be called Coquilles St. Jacques, which means the "seashells of St. James." However, in modern times Coquilles St. Jacques always includes a white sauce and is usually served in scallop shells. I have even heard dark rumors of cream of mushroom soup jacked up with a little wine being used by unprincipled cooks, hopefully for consenting adults in the privacy of their own homes.

The two following recipes are adapted from Howard Mitcham's great "Provincetown Seafood Cookbook."

COQUILLES ST. JACQUES I *(for 2)*

1 to 1½ lbs. bay or sea scallops
2 cups dry white wine (Portuguese vinho verde or pinot grigio are good here)
¼ lemon
1 bay leaf
¾ cup cream
¾ cup milk
¾ cup grated Swiss cheese
2 Tbsp. flour
1/3 stick butter
Grated Parmesan cheese
Salt and freshly ground black or white pepper

Quarter or slice sea scallops before cooking. Leave bay scallops whole.

Bring wine with the squeezed lemon quarter and bay leaf to a boil and reduce the heat to a simmer, add the scallops and poach gently until they are opaque and firm. Remove the scallops, saving the broth. Keep scallops warm – at 175 degrees F in the oven is good.

Melt the butter in a saucepan over low to medium heat until bubbling, whisk flour into butter to make a roux, and stir constantly for two minutes to cook flour; do not brown the roux. If roux begins to brown, lift pan from heat source and continue stirring until bubbling ceases before returning to heat to complete the two minutes. Now add milk and cream a little at a time, stirring constantly until smooth. Add ¼ cup of poaching wine and continue heating gently as you put in the grated Swiss cheese until it melts and becomes smooth. Add scallops, taste, season with salt and pepper.

Place sauced scallops on scallop shells, individual ramekins, or even puff pastry tart shells, sprinkle with Parmesan and broil lightly under flame until tops begin to brown and edges of sauce bubble. Beautiful! Eat!

Coquille St. Jacques

COQUILLES ST. JACQUES II

¼ stick butter
3 scallions with 2 inches of green
½ cup chopped parsley
1 Tbsp. chopped parsley
½ tsp. powdered mustard
¾ cup chopped fresh mushrooms
Pinch of dill weed
Salt and freshly ground pepper

Prepare scallops and sauce as in first recipe, omitting the cheese.

Melt the butter in a skillet and sauté the vegetables until they are soft and translucent; add the mushrooms, dill, and mustard. Mix well, season with salt and pepper, add this mixture to the white sauce, and add the scallops. Stir and heat well but do not boil. Place the mixture on pre-heated scallop shells or in heated ramekins, sprinkle with parsley, and serve hot.

I must say, these dishes are delicious and well worth making, but I am partial to raw scallops fresh from the shell eaten "feathers and all" right on the beach, one of the great culinary treats in God's creation.

Now I will give you, the faint of heart, a low-cal version of this extremely rich dish, but nonetheless delicious, keeping the scallops' delicate flavor in the foreground.

DIETER'S COQUILLES ST. JACQUES

1 cup dry white wine
5 Tbsp. unsalted butter or margarine
1 small onion, chopped
1 sprig parsley with stems
½ tsp. thyme
1 bay leaf
1 Tbsp. fresh lemon juice
1 or 1½ lbs. scallops
1 tsp. cornstarch dissolved in 3 Tbsp. cold water
1½ tsp. grated Parmesan

Bring wine, lemon juice, herbs, butter and onion to a boil, add the scallops (sea scallops, sliced or quartered), reduce heat and simmer gently for no more than five minutes. Remove the scallops from the broth and set aside. Boil the liquid for about five minutes, reduce to a simmer, add cornstarch and water mixture, and stir until sauce thickens. If you object to the bits of cooked onion in the sauce, you can strain the liquid before adding the cornstarch mixture.

Put the scallops and thickened sauce in scallop shells or an ovenproof dish, sprinkle with Parmesan, and run under the broiler until nicely browned, and there you have it! "Bob's your uncle" and many things are right with the world. ◄█══

Codfish

Spring may be here, but there are few fish to catch. We have somehow seemingly extirpated the winter flounder around Cape Cod, our herring runs are depleted, and the bass are not back in their summer numbers. I know that sea herring trawlers are decimating the inshore run of river herring, and I suspect the disappearance of the flounder can be credited to the resurgence of cormorants and ospreys, along with pollution, algal blooms, and overfishing. It is hard to pinpoint a single cause for the depletion of a population; it is like death by 1,000 small cuts, each one almost harmless but fatal as a whole.

So what does this have to do with cooking? Well, if we can't catch them, how can we cook them? The answer is to use preserved fish, ones that were once the mainstay of the diet of a large part of coastal populations. I received this letter from a reader of my columns:

Dear Pops,
I see salted cod and pollock at the supermarkets. I tried it and liked it, especially when I used your "Cod and Scraps" recipe – it was delicious!
I would like to salt my own fish, as it is pricey in the stores. Would you have any ideas on how to salt my own fish – what to use, etc.? Any help you can give me will be greatly appreciated.
Many thanks,
Pat Cervolo

The salt fish industry was once the basis of the Cape Cod economy, employing hundreds to tend the fish weirs (fixed trap-netting enclosures that encircled the inshore waters of much of the Cape) and to make the salt used to preserve the fish caught in these weirs. This salt was produced by evaporating seawater in the myriad salt works that lined the shores. The picturesque windmills seen on the Cape once drove the pumps that brought seawater to the salt pans for evaporation. From the colonial period until the advent of refrigeration in the early 20th century, the salt fish industry provided inexpensive salt for preserving fish for both domestic use and export. It is no longer inexpensive, but is still unique and delicious in flavor when handled properly.

The writer of the letter speaks highly of my recipe for "Cod and Scraps," found on page 174 of my book, "Cooking the Catch." There are many other ways to prepare salt fish, some of which I will include here. There are at least 100 ways to prepare salt cod. Where to begin…?

All salt fish should be soaked in cold water for at least four hours, or better yet, soaked overnight. Change the water three times. Desalted fish should be simmered, not boiled, when it is precooked for some recipes.

The following two recipes are based on creations, or versions, of classical Portuguese recipes from Howard Mitchum's great "Provincetown Seafood Cookbook."

SALT CODFISH HASH WITH EGGS (for 4)

1 ½ lbs. salt cod (desalted)
¼ lb. salt pork, diced small
4 cups mashed potatoes
1 medium onion, grated or chopped very finely
8 slices bacon
8 poached eggs
Freshly ground black pepper (lots)

Cut fish in pieces and simmer for 20 minutes. Remove skin and bones if there are any. Fry the salt pork until golden, remove from pan, and set aside. Discard salty fat from pan, according to Mitchum. (A "health freak?" I doubt it!) Fry bacon in the skillet until crisp, remove, and set aside. Mix flaked cod (or any salt fish), salt pork, potatoes, onion and black pepper. I like to add finely chopped green or red pepper, or even a chopped jalapeño. Make this mixture into a cake the size of your skillet, fry in the bacon fat until browned on the bottom, and then carefully turn over and brown other side. I put a plate over the skillet and invert the skillet, leaving the cake browned side-up on the plate, and slide the cake back into the pan. Brown the cake over medium heat so you do not burn the bottom before the cake heats through.

Serve this with poached or fried eggs, and you will have earned your bacon – and your seat in breakfast heaven. Do it!

Mitchum says the following dish is nearly the national dish of Portugal. It is certainly delicious. Howard claims that when eaten at 2:00 a.m., "It exerts a steadying influence after a night on the town, carousing." Gomez de Sa was not a man; it's the name of a cooking utensil, for which we can substitute a Dutch oven or a deep skillet.

CODFISH A LA GOMEZ DE SA (for 4)

1 ½ lbs. desalted dried salt codfish (or pollock)
1 cup olive oil
3 medium onions, sliced
1 green pepper, diced
3 medium potatoes, boiled, peeled, and sliced
2 cloves garlic, sliced
3 hard-boiled eggs, sliced
¼ cup chopped bitter black olives
½ cup chopped parsley
½ cup white wine
Fish stock or clam juice (fish bouillon ok)
Freshly ground black pepper
Parmesan cheese
Pimento strips
(optional Tabasco, cayenne, or any hot sauce)

Salt Fish

Cut soaked fish in 2-inch squares. Simmer these for 10 minutes and drain; set aside. Put olive oil in a deep oven-safe dish and heat until nearly smoking. Add the green pepper and onions and sauté until vegetables are soft, adding garlic for the final minute or so (it should not burn or brown). Stir in the olives, parsley and at least a teaspoon of black pepper. Lay the fish pieces on top of this "sofrito," lay sliced eggs on the fish, then lay on sliced potatoes. Pour in the wine and enough fish stock to almost cover it. Cook in a low 225 degrees F oven for 2 or 3 hours; make sure the works don't go dry.

Remove pan from oven. Turn oven up to 400 degrees F. Sprinkle a thin layer of Parmesan over the whole works. When the cheese is bubbly and golden, remove from oven, decorate with pimento strips and parsley, and "Bob's your uncle!" Serve right from the pan. This is a grand dish, especially when served with Portuguese corn flour crusty bread and a cold vinho verde.

Treating the Young with Respect Pays! Monkfish and Memories

I am pleased to report that I am receiving more rewards from my former students at the Penikese Island School. Last week one of them, the best and most dedicated fisherman among the thousand boys I dealt with during my tenure, called to tell me he had the monkfish he had promised to get for me. This formerly severely troubled kid is now a respectable young man and a successful commercial fisherman and tuna-fishing guide. He does offshore lobstering and tuna guiding in the summer and gillnetting in the winter.

It was a delight for my wife and I to meet his fiancé and two-month-old baby when we picked up our gift, a beautiful 5-pound monkfish tail. The baby was also lovely. It was a joy to see my former student happy and proud, healthy and strong after battling drugs, booze, and petty crime in his adolescent and young adult years.

He used to drive us nuts at the island by always having cigarettes and sometimes "funny cigarettes." We could never figure out how he smuggled them onto the island when he returned from his home visits until one day someone disconnected one of the surf rods he always carried home so he could fish on his weekend visit. The rod was loaded with contraband. You can get a lot of stuff in a 10-foot surf rod, funny or otherwise.

Because of this former smuggler's largesse, I now had 3 pounds of fine white monkfish loins and a 2-pound piece of backbone, enough for several meals.

Monkfish, unlike most fish, does not flake easily when cooked but retains a slightly chewy, pleasant consistency, very much like lobster in texture. I have been accused of passing it off as lobster in lobster salad. As an experiment I once made a mixture consisting of one-third lobster meat, two-thirds cubed monkfish, minced celery, parsley, and scallions and served it as a seafood salad that was very well received. My guests thought it was an especially fine and delicious lobster salad. Should I feel guilty for not disabusing my guests of this notion? I don't think so. In fact, I think you should try it yourself.

I gave one pound of this fine fish to my son-in-law Scott, who I knew would treat it with the respect it deserved. I used the remaining two pounds of meat in two meals for my wife and me. The first meal was based on a Cantonese recipe for lobster, the second was breaded cutlets of monkfish served with tartar sauce. Both were delicious.

MONKFISH IN MEAT SAUCE CANTONESE

½ cup ground pork
3 Tbsp. cooking oil
2 slices ginger root
2 cloves garlic – crushed
1 ½ Tbsp. fermented black beans, or bottled Black Bean Sauce
2 tsp. dry sherry

½ tsp. salt
1 ½ Tbsp. soy sauce
¼ tsp. MSG. (optional, but desirable)
¼ tsp. sugar
1 ½ Tbsp. cornstarch dissolved in 2 Tbsp. water
1 beaten egg

Don't ever be scared by a long list of ingredients, just get them all together before you begin and go for it. I sometimes arrange them in the order I will be using them, but usually I just flail around. Pour the oil into a large heavy skillet or wok over medium-high heat. Put in the black beans, pork, ginger root, and garlic and stir for 2 to 3 minutes. Add monkfish pieces (slightly smaller than walnut size) and sherry for a few stirrings, then add

¾cup water, salt, soy sauce, MSG., and sugar. Cover and bring to a boil. Turn down heat and simmer for five minutes until fish is opaque and cooked through. Stir in the cornstarch and water mixture, which will thicken the sauce. If the sauce is too thick, thin with a little water. Add the egg, stir, and serve over rice. You will be overjoyed. If you wish, you may substitute a 1½- to 2-pound lobster, cut in 12 pieces, for the monkfish. If you are afflicted with a form of vegetarianism and don't eat pork, you may use chopped mushrooms or even cubed tofu instead and still have a fine dish.

Monkfish fillets are often nearly cylindrical and lend themselves to being cut into round cutlets or "coins." You can prepare these rounds or rounds of zucchini in precisely the same manner as the monkfish for an unusual and delicious meal.

MONKFISH AND ZUCCHINI COINS (*Fried for Two*)

Canola or peanut oil for frying
A beaten egg
1 cup breadcrumbs
Salt and pepper
1 lb. zucchini
1 lb. monkfish

Cut the monkfish and zucchini into 3/8-inch rounds (no thicker than ½-inch). Dip each round first in egg and then in breadcrumbs, coating both sides, and set aside.

Heat a half-inch of oil in a large skillet over medium heat. When hot enough (oil will sizzle if you drop breadcrumbs in), sauté each coin for about two minutes or until nicely browned on each side. Drain on brown paper and keep warm in a 175 degrees F oven until ready to serve. Do not stack or they will get soggy. Sprinkle these rounds with sea salt and ground pepper and serve with tartar sauce and some quartered lemons, add some bread, some white wine, and a little salad and there you have it – pure pleasure.

QUICK TARTAR SAUCE

1 cup mayonnaise
3 Tbsp. chopped sweet pickle relish
3 Tbsp. white horseradish, measured after draining
½ tsp. sherry vinegar

Whisk all ingredients together until well-blended. This will keep for at least three days in the refrigerator. It is very good! You may garnish with chopped chives, parsley, or scallions – or all three. Why not?

I used the backbone to make a fish stock base for a seafood chowder, to which I added whatever monkfish I could salvage off the bones along with a dozen oysters and a half-pound of shelled shrimp, both of which were also given to me. It pays to be nice to kids, in more ways than one.

I will always provide recipes and gratitude to anyone who gives me seafood. I would be foolish not to. Thanks, kids!

Are "Blue Stockings" Scary?

My wife, Jeanne, is part of a women's reading group composed of alarmingly intelligent and outspoken women, an intimidating group indeed. They meet monthly for dinner and discussion along with discreet wine consumption. They discuss literature, politics, families, and others with enthusiasm. I am a little scared by them but enjoy hearing about their gatherings, and especially about their dinners, which reflect the culture of the book currently read.

They recently read a mystery set in Sweden that inspired the hostess of the month, Cheri Holdren, biologist and political activist, to come up with the simple and grand recipe I am presenting today.

Anyone who has read my book or followed my columns knows how much I laud the combination of fish and potatoes. I use cod in my presentation, but bass, haddock, cusk, or any white fish can be substituted. I think also that it would be delicious with salmon.

COD, MASHED POTATOES AND DILL *(for 4)*

2 lbs. cod fillets
4 Tbsp. butter
½ cup panko or breadcrumbs
1 lemon
¼ cup dry white wine
Salt and pepper
¼ cup minced fresh dill or 1 tsp. dried
4 cups mashed potatoes
½ cup grated Swiss or Scandinavian cheese

Make mashed potatoes in your favorite manner, using about 2 pounds of potatoes.

Heat a flameproof casserole or big skillet over medium heat. Salt and pepper the cod liberally on both sides and sear briefly in hot butter (about 1 minute per side). Carefully put cod aside.

Add 2 more tablespoons of butter, the juice of the lemon, the wine, and the dill to the juices released by the fish and boil for about one minute. Pour into a container and set aside.

While you are doing all this, preheat the oven to 415 degrees F.

Return partially cooked cod to the skillet or casserole, centering it so you can place the mashed potatoes on both sides, surrounding it. Sprinkle the panko or breadcrumbs on the cod. Now, pour the dill, wine, lemon, and butter sauce over the cod, moistening the crumbs. Sprinkle grated cheese on the potatoes, dot the potatoes with a little butter, and roast the whole works for 10 minutes until fish is done and the cheese is melted. If things are browning too rapidly (that means burning), turn down the oven temperature.

Remove this bubbly brown marvel from the oven, garnish with some chopped parsley and dill, and serve.

I would serve this with a plain boiled or steamed green vegetable, either peas, broccoli, green beans, or spinach, and sit back and bask in the praise of my guests after I had eaten my share.

That may have sounded complicated, but is actually very easy, and if you have any leftovers, you are already halfway to fish cakes for breakfast.

Last month I wrote about a grand pasta with marinara, Maine shrimp, and sea scallops. I am always saying how grand things are and what fine things I have cooked to the point of risking becoming sickening. Last week, Alex Friedman, a young friend of mine and former colleague in adventures at Penikese Island, brought me some fine, beautifully scrubbed oysters; they were wild ones from one of the South Shore ponds. I ate many raw, cooked a few, and had a few left. I decided to make the pasta and marinara dish again, and this time I decided to add a few oysters. Well, the oysters made no discernible improvement to the dish, and they were cooked to dullness, far from their glory on the half-shell. It made me feel bad that I had belittled the noble oyster to no avail.

However, here we go again with another grand and simple breakfast dish, fit enough for anyone on earth, and too good for many.

SOFT SCRAMBLED EGGS WITH OYSTERS *(for 2)*

3-4 eggs (beaten)
1 Tbsp. butter
8 to 12 shucked oysters
1 drop Tabasco (or other hot sauce)
Salt and pepper
Toast
1 tsp. chopped chives
½ scallion minced

This dish must be cooked in a double boiler, or some other device that keeps the cooking surface for the eggs away from direct heat.

Melt the butter in the double boiler, add the oysters and heat them until they begin to tighten up. Now, add your eggs and cook, stirring constantly to avoid the formation of large curds, until the eggs are wet, smoothly cooked, and still pour-able, and serve.

Garnish these with chopped chives or scallions and know that you are eating something as good as anyone on earth is eating, good enough for my wife's book group.

I came up with, inspired by my culinary show-off son-in-law Scott, a slight variation on a simple shrimp dish to serve as a starter for dinner.

The mildly flavored but sweet and delicately delicious Maine (or North Atlantic) shrimp have been available at a good price, and every shrimp lover should try them, particularly in this recipe.

MAINE SHRIMP VINAIGRETTE WITH PARSLEY AND DILL *(for 4)*

1 lb. Maine shrimp
Olive oil
Salt and pepper
Lemon juice or sherry vinegar
½ cup mixed dill and parsley

Shell the shrimp and briefly steam or boil them until they become opaque (no more than one minute). Mix 2 Tbsp. good olive oil with 1 Tbsp. lemon juice or sherry vinegar and pour over drained shrimp. Salt and pepper generously and mix in the dill and parsley.

I arrange the anointed shrimp on lettuce, mesclun or spinach leaves on individual plates for serving. You will be honored and possibly revered; I would even dare to serve this to Jeanne's book group, despite their talents at criticism, culinary and otherwise. ◀━

Keep It Simple, Dummy

As usual, I have been thinking about food and cooking and about how many people approach these all-important subjects.

I believe that cooking is a craft anyone can learn and is not an art. It can become an art after one has mastered the basic craft. Picasso went to art school for many years before taking off on his wildly creative career; a French chef spends the entire first year of his training chopping vegetables, I am told, before he even gets near a hot stove.

I have known many people who say they never use recipes or measure ingredients – they are people who usually cook a few dishes very well, or at least well enough, but have very limited repertoires repeated constantly, kind of like one-act movies. They often seem proud of their limitations, if they are even aware of them, and would benefit from a good bit of basic training or a good cookbook.

There are several things to know about fish and shellfish cooking. The first and most important rule is that they should not stink before or after you cook them. If you are at all suspicious of the freshness of the fish you are purchasing, ask to smell it. If the fishmonger objects, do not buy from him. Be particularly careful in supermarkets, where fish vary greatly in quality.

The second rule is, now that you have your sweet-smelling fish, do not overcook it and destroy its texture and usually delicate flavor.

We will start with sautéing fillets; the French call the results meuniére.

SAUTÉED FILLETS *(for 2)*
1 lb. thin fillets of white-fleshed fish
Flour, salt and pepper
1 Tbsp. butter
1 Tbsp. oil, olive, peanut, canola, etc.
Parsley and lemon for garnish

All you need

Coat the fillets with flour seasoned with salt and pepper. Heat oil and butter in a skillet – black iron or any nonstick – over medium heat. When oil and butter is hot enough, a pinch of flour will immediately sizzle when added.

Put fillets in hot pan, not crowding, and sauté until browned, about 2 minutes. Turn over and cook second side until lightly browned. Do not overcook – no more than 3 minutes per side. These fillets are now ready to serve.

I would now melt another Tbsp. of butter in the skillet and add a Tbsp. of minced parsley. Pour this over the fish and serve with lemon slices or quarters. You cannot go wrong with this recipe.

Pan frying is different from sautéing only in the fact that you use more oil and usually put a heavier coating on the fish.

PAN-FRIED FISH *(for 2)*
1 lb. white fish fillets
¼ cup milk
1 egg
1 cup breadcrumbs, crushed crackers, cereal or cornmeal, or a mixture

Put ¼ inch of butter, oil, or a combination of the two in a heavy skillet and heat over medium-high heat until a pinch of the coating will sizzle immediately when dropped in the oil.

Dip fillets in milk and egg, coat with chosen dry ingredients, and put in skillet without crowding. Cook until nicely browned on bottom, turn over and brown second side, and "Bob's your uncle," you have fried fish ready to serve with lemon and tartar sauce. Doing this will make you feel worthwhile, I promise.

Next comes the oven or the grill. The grill may be outside or in your oven.

Oven roasting or baking is perhaps the simplest and best way to prepare fish to experience its flavor in its purest form. It is a method I use frequently.

The general rule for the length of time to roast or bake fish is 10 minutes per inch of thickness at 415 degrees F in a preheated oven. This "10 minutes per inch of thickness" is a good general rule for all fish cooking, poaching, grilling, sautéing, steaming, or whatever. Deep frying, which I do not advise in the home kitchen, is an exception.

PLAIN BAKED FISH FILLET *(for 2)*

1 lb. fish
Salt and pepper
2 Tbsp. melted butter or 2 Tbsp. olive oil
Optional breadcrumbs

Fish Saute Pan

Preheat oven to 415 degrees F. Salt and pepper fish on both sides; anoint with oil or butter on both sides. If you use the breadcrumbs, sprinkle a light coating over the fillets and drizzle oil or melted butter.

Put fish in oven-proof dish and bake (roast) for 10 minutes per inch of thickness and – voila! – nearly perfect pristine fish.

I like to serve it with mashed potatoes and petit peas, garnished with parsley and lemon. This is a grand, simple meal.

Poached or steamed fish are easily prepared and good either hot or cold. The poaching fluid or steaming medium may be merely salted water or fish stock or bottled clam juice. You may make your own fish stock or buy cubes. Fish stock base is also available in small jars. These concoctions work fine!

POACHED FISH *(for 2)*

1 lb. white-fleshed fish, fillets or a steak

Immerse fish in simmering liquid and simmer – do not boil – for 10 minutes per inch of thickness at thickest point.

Fish poacher

STEAMED FISH *(for 2)*

1 lb. fish, whole, fillets or steaks
salt and pepper

Salt and pepper fish, put on plate, and cook over boiling water or stock in a steamer for 10 minutes per inch of thickness and "Bob's your uncle!"

These two recipes provide you with fish to sauce in any way you wish. These basic recipes form the foundation for most fish recipes, which merely fancy up the pristine glory found in simplicity. ◄►

Chapter Five:
MAY

The lights of summer are coming on, gardens are growing, and spring flowers adorn the rapidly greening landscape, beginning with trailing arbutus, the lovely, modest May flowers. Please try the "Fettuccini with Striped Bass" (or scallops, or shrimp, or bluefish, or a mixture). You will not be sorry!

Potential Sauce

Dave,

Do you have any recipes for cooking scup? Or, is there any method that you could recommend? Also, any tips on cleaning and/or deboning would be helpful.

Thanks, Ann Johnson

Scup are one of the sweetest, tastiest fishes available in our area. If you are worried about bones, fillet scup and remove the skin – not as hard as it sounds.

You can also scale them, remove the head and innards, and have a fine panfish. I remove the spiny bones on the back and the ventral bottom by making a shallow cut down each side and grasping the bones with pliers.

To cook the fillets or pan-dressed fish, dip them first in milk, then coat them with seasoned flour, dip in milk in which you have beaten an egg, and dredge with bread-crumbs or cornmeal (or a mixture of both), and fry in oil until nicely browned on each side – as good a fish as you will ever eat.

Pops,

I have two questions for you. With the bonito in full swing these days, even I have been fortunate enough to catch a few. Knowing your expertise as a chef (I still remember your wonderful mussel red sauce on board the Frenchman), my question is, what would be your technique for grilling bonito? I hope you are able to publish a cookbook. It would be sure to be a best seller.

My second question is, what is your method for bleeding fish? I cut the fish where the gills meet under the jaw and then place the fish either in a 5-gallon bucket filled with salt water or a fish box filled with salt water. Recently, I have been hearing that cutting open the belly is a better method, but I defer to you. I recently bled a

striper unintentionally and was very pleased with the results. Cooked that night, it had a much firmer texture. My kids now ask for "bled striper."

Nick Brigham

Bonito is so fine a fish that if bled immediately upon being caught, it needs very little enhancement to result in an excellent meal from the grill. I salt and pepper it liberally, anoint both sides with olive oil, and put it over a medium-hot fire. I want the surface to begin to brown while leaving the middle almost raw; serve plain with lemon or any fish sauce you enjoy, or a salsa, preferably homemade.

I bleed fish exactly like you do, right down to the bucket of salt water, but what you have heard about cutting open the belly is better if you remove all the viscera. I sometimes settle for merely bleeding a bonito when the fishing is fast.

A bled striper is somewhat better than an unbled striper, but a bled bluefish is vastly better than an unbled one.

Dear Pops,

I read your chowder recipe and have spent hours looking for "lobster bouillon." I presume cubes – where in the Sandwich, Cape Cod area can you buy lobster bouillon?

Thanks,

Jerry Kissell

The lobster bouillon I use comes in paste form in a glass jar labeled "Better Than Bouillon" which I bought at the Shaw's supermarket in Falmouth. I have also seen it at Trader Joe's in Hyannis. This is a good product.

Knorr makes bouillon cubes of fish, shrimp, and possibly lobster. I have found these products in Chinese supermarkets in Boston. Good luck!

You Caught It, You Clean It

I believe all fishermen should clean, fillet, scale, steak, and prepare for cooking all the fish they catch before giving it away, even to their wives. You come home with a 30-pound bass and throw it in the sink, all proud, and your wife thinks, "My God, what am I going to do with that?" So, I heartily endorse your wife quoting my subtitle.

This is a good month for catching large bass, but any month is good that provides large bass. I usually fish hard in May and catch my largest bass. So now you have caught a big one. Any bass over 20 pounds is big, any bass over 35 pounds is huge. What are you going to do with the beast?

You can fillet it and skin the fillets; from a 25-pound bass you should get two 4-pound fillets. Each one will feed eight people. If you go the fillet route – the easiest, especially if you skin the fillets – you will have a chunk of meat over two inches thick at the forward end, tapering down to nothing toward the tail. The thick end of the fillet should be sliced on the diagonal into ¾-inch-thick pieces until you reach the ¾-inch-thick section near the tail; now slice vertically. The final piece can be folded back on itself to attain the ¾-inch thickness. All these pieces will be ready for breading and frying, or baking in a sauce in the oven, or whatever your palate desires. You can discard the rack and skin or gut the fish and use it for making stock. If you choose to make stock, discard the gills.

I'll bet you will throw the rack out, or do what I do and bury it in the garden – the raccoons love it.

With a fish of 20 pounds or more, I will often make several steaks and a couple of smaller fillets than the previous method provided. I begin by scaling the beast using a butter knife or a tablespoon or the back of my fillet knife. The scales come off easily if the fish is wet.

Then, I eviscerate the fish by cutting from the cloaca to the base of the gills and severing the front of the gut and pulling out the whole works. I scrape away the blood around the backbone with a spoon or a butter knife and blast it all out with a hose.

I now cut off the head just behind the gill covers and proceed to cut four or five 1-inch steaks, moving toward the tail. I then fillet the tail piece. I now have several nice steaks and some manageable fillets and, except for the removal of the gills, a nice cleaned rack to use for making stock or the base for a fine fish chowder.

My hero, kitchen hero at least, Howard Mitcham, author of the "Provincetown Seafood Cookbook," says all you need to do to make fish stock is take head and bones from this fine fish, cover it with water, and bring to a simmer for a half-hour, and there you have it. Seems too easy to me.

FISH STOCK

Head and bones (rack) of big striper
1 stalk celery
1 medium onion
1 medium carrot
6 sprigs parsley
2 bay leaves
1 Tbsp. salt (to taste)
1 tsp. crushed black pepper
1 tsp. thyme
Water to cover

Wok   Bamboo Steamer

Put all ingredients in a large pot with water to barely cover, bring to a simmer, and cook gently for half an hour, no more. Strain, saving skeleton.

Taste the broth. If you want a stronger flavor of fish, boil it down until you are happy with its taste. If you are going to make fish chowder, remove all the meat you can from the cooled head and bones, and don't forget the cheeks.

STRIPED BASS IN CHOURICO SAUCE

The Sauce

1 medium onion
1 green or sweet red pepper
2 cloves garlic
1 stalk celery
½ cup chopped parsley
1 cup red wine
1 cup fish stock or water
½ cup olive oil
2 Tbsp. vinegar
1 Tbsp. sugar
½ tsp. cumin
¼ tsp. thyme, basil and crushed red pepper
Salt and pepper (to taste)
1 chourico, sliced ¼-inch thick
1 can Italian tomatoes, crushed up

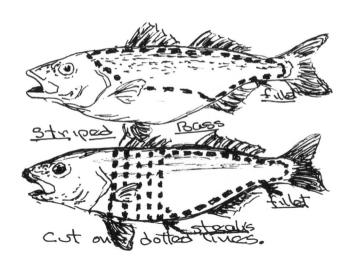

Sauté chourico, celery, onions, green pepper, and garlic in olive oil over medium heat until softened, add the tomatoes and everything else, and bring to a boil. Immediately lower heat to a bare simmer and cook for at least one hour; two is better. Stir occasionally to prevent scorching or sticking. Use little salt until final seasoning because of salt in clams that are yet to come.

The Dish

½ lb. striped bass per diner (can be steaks or fillets)
3 littlenecks per diner
4 mussels per diner
Enough fine cornmeal or flour to dust fish
3 Tbsp. olive oil

Coat the fish lightly with cornmeal or flour and sauté in a large ovenproof casserole until lightly browned; remove. If you are using a Pyrex or ceramic casserole, sauté fish in a frying pan and set aside.

Put your sauce into a shallow casserole, arrange the lightly browned fish pieces in the sauce, place the scrubbed shellfish around the fish, and put the whole works in a preheated 415 degrees F oven for about 10 or 12 minutes until shellfish are open; serve proudly. I would sprinkle parsley and maybe scallions on mine. I might even throw in a dozen shrimp for the last 5 minutes of cooking! This is so good!

Serve with white rice or boiled and mashed potatoes, or both, crusty bread, a green salad, hot sauce on the side, and a robust, unsubtle (cheap) red wine, and pride and renown will be yours, maybe even love. Go for it!

Florida Keys

I have just returned from a week in the Florida Keys, where I enjoyed some warm weather and tropical fishing with my old friend Maynard Albert, who introduced me to flats fishing for permit, bonefish, and tarpon many years ago. Some of the great experiences of my life on the water were made possible by this gift. Both Maynard and I have "aged out" of 10-hour days in a flats boat pursuing and fighting fierce fish, a sad but inevitable situation. We now anchor, put out a chum line, and accept whatever fish come our way. We drift shrimp, live pinfish under a float, or even a chunk of bait, and catch a great variety of fish: many kinds of snapper, Spanish mackerel, an occasional king mackerel, mahi-mahi, seatrout, blowfish, and many more. Great fun and always the possibility of something big; a cobia, a grouper, or who knows what? My wife, my friend Maynard, and I have been friends for five of the seven decades we have lived and still enjoy our time together both on and off the water.

We ate no meat during the week we spent in the Keys except for a couple of turkey sandwiches when we spent whole days on the boat, and I do not think we ate the same species of fish twice. We cooked them all simply baked, pan-fried, or in the case of fine wild shrimp, stir-fried. If we had any bait shrimp left at the end of the day, we stir-fried them, too.

STIR-FRIED APPETIZER SHRIMP (preferably wild)

½ to 1 lb. shrimp (tailed or whole)
2 slices ginger root
1 clove garlic (crushed)
Hot chili sauce to taste
Salt and pepper
2 Tbsp. peanut oil (or your choice)

Heat the oil to nearly smoking; put in the sliced ginger and crushed garlic. Remove the garlic when it begins to brown, or it will turn bitter. I add Chinese chili and garlic paste at this point or ½ tsp. Tabasco or other hot sauce; you can omit the hot stuff all together, but I would not. Put the shrimp in all at once and stir constantly until shrimp are all opaque and cooked through. Serve immediately with or without lemon or lime slices. I eat them "feathers and all" except for the tail flipper shells, the ones you pick them up with. A garnish of chopped scallions is nice on these delicious snacks. They cry out for cold beer or white wine.

I have read many opinions about the relative qualities of northern, coldwater fish, and southern, warmwater fish, with most people preferring the coldwater fish. I do not agree. I think they are of equal quality if both are handled properly. I cannot say that a haddock is better than a grouper or that scup is better than grunt or any of the small snappers. Coat any of them with seasoned flour, breadcrumbs or corn starch, and sauté until browned and just opaque, and I defy you to tell me which is better, or even to tell them apart in a blind test. I say, prepare whatever fish you have with care, no matter where they come from, and you will not be sorry. Here is a simple recipe for baked smelts without measurements. Any experienced cook will not need them here.

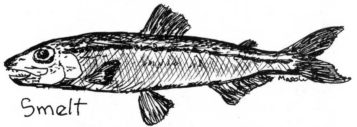

Smelt

SMELTS, BAKED
Smelts
Breadcrumbs
Parsley and scallions (or shallots)
Lemon
Optional anchovy paste
Butter

Trim away fins (I don't bother) from fish. Butter a baking dish, sprinkle with breadcrumbs, add a little salt and pepper, and sprinkle with finely chopped scallions and parsley. Arrange smelt on this bed until pan is full; sprinkle fish with breadcrumbs and a squeeze of lemon juice (you may mix the lemon juice with a little anchovy paste).

Bake in a 375 degrees F oven for 15 minutes, garnish with additional scallion and parsley with lemon quarters, and there you have it – pleasure in a pan and easy to do.

Here is another even simpler recipe.

SMELTS IN TOMATO SAUCE
24 (or so) smelts
Olive oil
Tomato sauce (homemade or store-bought)
Chopped parsley and lemon wedges

Brush smelts with oil and arrange in a baking dish. Cover with tomato sauce and bake for 15 minutes in a 400 degrees F oven. Garnish with parsley and lemon and serve.

This can be served hot or cold – with pasta, hot, or with crackers, cold. I prefer it cold or at room temperature.

Simple, Superb, Special Seascapes

I made and ate delicious scrambled eggs this morning. You may be thinking, "So what? This is a seafood preparation column," to which I will respond, "These eggs were scrambled with clams, bay scallops, quahogs, parsley and a little green onion, and they were delicious." Almost better than I deserve!

My lovely daughter Jennifer and her partner, Lisa, returned from a low-tide walk with three littleneck clams, four bay scallops, and a dead cockle. They were proud of their scavenging but had not gathered enough for a main dish for two. It was, however, enough to make memorable scrambled eggs. I shucked the clams and scallops and threw out the dead cockle – always a good idea. (Did you know that cockles are our only shellfish with pigmented, almost red, blood?)

SCRAMBLED EGGS WITH CLAMS AND SCALLOPS

3 eggs
2 littlenecks, shucked
4 scallops, shucked
½ Tbsp. chopped parsley
½ Tbsp. chopped scallion
1 Tbsp. butter
Salt and pepper

Beat the eggs. Melt butter in pan over medium heat, add chopped shellfish meat, parsley, and scallions. Sauté gently until clams firm up, add beaten eggs, and cook to desired doneness. Salt, pepper, and enjoy! I like mine soft and served on buttered toast.

Whenever you find yourself with small amounts of seafood, scrambling it with eggs is a grand way to go. Oysters are great this way, should you happen to have a couple. Mussels are good, too, and leftover fish or any seafood can be used. Try this – you will not regret it! I like to add a dash of hot sauce to my eggs before cooking. Life is good!

James Beard has always been my culinary hero and mentor. The "James Beard Cookbook" is my favorite basic cookbook and the first one I ever bought; I now own well over 200. I found a Beard book online called Beard of Pasta, which contains a couple of recipes that I particularly admire. In fact, there is not a bad recipe in the book. The first recipe for pasta with chicken gizzards and hearts is probably inappropriate for a seafood cooking column, delicious though it may be, but the recipe for pasta with striped bass is appropriate, easy, and delicious.

FETTUCCINE WITH STRIPED BASS (FOR 4)

4 Tbsp. butter
1 Tbsp. olive oil
½ lb., or as much as 2 lbs., striped bass
½ cup medium cream
Salt and pepper
1 lb. fettuccine (or pasta of your choice)
½ cup chopped dill or chives

Melt the butter and olive oil in a skillet. Liberally salt and pepper the bass fillets and cook in the butter and oil over medium heat, turning over until cooked through (it will flake), about five minutes. Flake the fish with a fork, add the cream, and cook down gently for a minute or two.

Meanwhile, have the pasta cooking. Drain the pasta. Pour the creamy fish over the pasta, sprinkle heavily with the chopped dill or chives, mix, and serve proudly! If chives are unavailable, scallions can be used in combination with parsley. Dill and chives can be mixed. All fresh, green herbs will work, but I like chives the most!

You may substitute any white-fleshed fish for the bass: flounder, cod, pollock, haddock, and even fresh bluefish (it turns white when cooked). This is a simple but great recipe to have in your repertoire.

SPAGHETTI WITH CLAM SAUCE

2 quarts littlenecks (the smaller the better)
White wine (dry, vinho verde is good)
4 or 5 large garlic cloves, crushed and minced
1 pound spaghetti
¾ cup chopped parsley
(I add freshly ground black pepper and either a pinch of cayenne or some
*   hot pepper flakes.)*

Potential Sauce

Scrub the clams very well to avoid grit in the sauce. Put the clams in a heavy saucepot with ½-inch of white wine or water and the garlic. Cover and steam until all the clams are open, from 5 to 10 minutes. Cook and drain the pasta, put in a warm bowl, and pour the clams and broth over it. Sprinkle with parsley (pepper if you choose) and serve. Salad, crusty bread, more wine, and joy will be yours.

You may also use mussels, oysters, or even slipper shells to make this dish. Beard says that you must scour mussels or oysters, rubbing any encrustations off the shells before you steam them, and he is right.

Next month, all of the summer fish except small tunas should be available to us fishermen, but until then, we are relegated to the shellfish beds and the fish market.

I am going to give you another Beard-based recipe for scallops. Jim recommends bay scallops, but I think less-expensive sea scallops cut in quarters do just as well.

SCALLOPS PROVENÇALE OVER SPAGHETTI

1 lb. sea scallops, quartered (bay scallops if you want to splurge)
2 Tbsp. flour
1 lb. spaghetti
2/3 cup good olive oil
4 cloves minced garlic
½ cup chopped parsley
Lots of freshly ground black pepper
Salt
2 Tbsp. cognac (optional, but grand)

Pasta should be nearly done when you begin cooking the scallops – it should be hot when you sauce it.

Put flour in a bag, dump scallops in bag and shake to lightly coat with flour. Heat the olive oil in a skillet. When hot, throw in the scallops and stir and toss vigorously for about 2 minutes. Turn off heat and stir in garlic, parsley and pepper for about a minute. Turn the heat back on and pour in cognac, cook for another minute, pour over the hot pasta and serve. I cannot properly convey how good this can be – so do it! Even greater renown will be unavoidable.

These recipes are simple and superb, so do not miss your chance to share them and revel in them yourself. Then invite some friends over and wow them with your talent!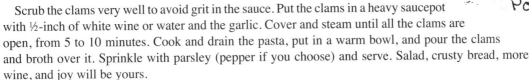

Great Dishes Under Duress

I was asked to participate in a large sport-fishing show in New Jersey last month. I was to present four fish-cooking demonstrations and answer general questions about handling and preparing seafood. The show ran from Friday afternoon through Sunday afternoon. I was to put on two demonstrations on both Saturday and Sunday.

I rode down to New Jersey with Neal Larsson, our distinguished general manager at "On The Water," who was towing down the trailer carrying the magazine's show booth. We were both delighted to learn that we shared a passion for Popeye's fried chicken and especially for their superlative red beans and rice. Neal, the navigator, knew of one on the Connecticut Thruway. Hot dog! We could eat seafood at home on the Cape, but not Popeye's spicy fried thighs.

On Friday morning I learned that I could not use cooking oil in my demonstrations because of fire laws, and that the oven I would have to use was 50 yards from my demonstration station. I would need help getting my pans from the cooking area to the oven and back. If I would have had to run back and forth to the oven, I probably would have had a heart attack at worst or lost my deserted audience at best. But the oven was my only means of cooking because I could not fry or sauté at the cook-top. The only thing that really worked at the cooking station was the overhead mirror.

Chris Megan, our illustrious publisher, took pity on me and assigned our newest young editor to be my runner. Rick Bach - young, smart, helpful, and kind - probably saved my life. So even though I could not sauté or fry anything at my station, I could prepare some dishes that Rick could shuttle to the kitchen for me. This would have to do, so I thought I was all set until I spoke to the manager of the entire event, who had hired me.

"Are you all set for tomorrow, Pops?"

"Yes, as soon as you bring in the fish I'll be ready to go."

"Oh my God, I forgot the fish!" he gasped.

"You forgot the fish? What am I supposed to do – cook hot dogs?"

"I am so sorry," he apologized, and went on apologizing and apologizing.

So instead of stripers and blues caught by New York and New Jersey fishermen, I had to go to the supermarket to buy cod, haddock, and salmon, all from New England.

I had chosen two of my very favorite baked fish recipes for the demonstrations: Portuguese Baked Fish in Tomato Sauce and the "World's Best Bluefish and Potato Recipe." I had hoped to use striper fillets for the first recipe and bluefish for the second, but now it would be cod or haddock for the first and salmon instead of bluefish for the second.

PORTUGUESE BAKED FISH IN TOMATO SAUCE (FOR 6)

2 lbs. fish fillets or steaks (striper, cod, haddock, swordfish)
2 cans diced tomatoes with zesty jalapeno (14 ½ oz. cans)
1 can stewed tomatoes (14 ½ oz. can)
¼ cup diced celery
¼ cup diced sweet red or green peppers
¼ cup diced onion
½ cup green or black or mixture of olives
½ cup diced linguica
2 tsp. powdered cumin
1 tsp. coriander
¼ cup white wine (red can be used)
¼ cup chopped parsley and scallions for garnishing
3 Tbsp. olive oil
¼ cup breadcrumbs
2 cloves minced garlic

Linguica, pepper, celery, garlic, onion, tomato and olives, fish needed.

Preheat oven to 415 degrees F. Oil a casserole or baking pan large enough to hold the fish and other ingredients without submerging the fish. Sauté the vegetables (not tomatoes) and sausage in olive oil, either directly in the baking pan or in a skillet. Add minced garlic to vegetables for the last minute of cooking. Mix sautéed vegetables with the canned tomatoes (crushing the stewed tomatoes with your hand), cumin, coriander, olives, and wine. Pour tomato mixture around fish in the roasting pan, sprinkle breadcrumbs on exposed fish, sprinkle with olive oil, and put in the preheated oven for 15 minutes. The sauce should be bubbling, and the fish should flake easily. If not, give it five more minutes and serve garnished with chopped parsley and lemon – Great!

Serve boiled rice, boiled or mashed potatoes and a salad with this along with some crusty bread, and love will be yours, at least for a while. This is a great, easy, and memorable dish!

The second dish I presented is based on a Marcella Hazan recipe. It actually calls for bluefish, but since I had no bluefish, I substituted salmon, an equally oily fish.

SALMON BAKED WITH POTATOES (FOR 6)
2 lb. fillet of salmon
1 ½ lbs. boiling potatoes
2/3 cups olive oil
2 Tbsp. minced garlic (I use more)
¼ cup chopped Italian parsley
Salt and pepper

Preheat oven to 425 degrees F. Slice potatoes thinly (3 times the thickness of a potato chip; do not worry if some are thicker or thinner). Put potatoes in a 9-inch by 13-inch baking pan (slightly larger pan is fine) along with half the minced parsley, chopped garlic, and olive oil. Salt and pepper liberally and mix until potatoes are coated with oil. Arrange potatoes like shingles, lining the pan with vertical slices on the sides. Put potatoes in the upper third of the preheated oven and bake for 15 minutes. While the potatoes are baking, use the remaining oil, garlic, and parsley to anoint the fish. Again, salt and pepper generously. Remove half-cooked potatoes from the oven and place fish in pan. Return to oven, and after ten minutes remove pan from oven and baste potatoes and fish with juice in pan. If fish flakes easily it is ready to serve; if it does not, return to oven for five more minutes. Remove, garnish with chopped parsley, and serve. This dish is guaranteed to please!

Be careful, fights have almost broken out at my table over the especially crisp potatoes that vertically lined the pan. These dishes are marvelous, – "slap your grandma good!" – and easy to prepare. So what is holding you back? Go for it!! ◄►

Roasting-pan lined with potatoes.

Fish, Family, and Frogs We Can't Kick

In my absence, my gourmet and fine cook son-in-law, either out of kindness or to gain ground — or even a lead — in our ongoing, unofficial cooking rivalry, lured my wife Jeanne over for a halibut-centered dinner. She said it was very delicious, and unfortunately I cannot doubt her judgment. I also cannot deny my regret over not getting to eat any and not being present to defend myself and make suggestions for improvement or snide comments about Scott "the gourmet" Britton to divert attention from his outstanding meal.

Here is the recipe as Scott gave it to me; I will take no credit for the result. I know I don't like it, but I know it will be very good if you follow his directions.

BRITTON'S HALIBUT WITH PRESERVED LEMON *(for 2)*

1 lb. of halibut (steak or fillet)
1 to 2 Tbsp. olive oil
1 medium shallot chopped fine
¾ cup canned tomatoes, roughly chopped
1 whole "Roland's Preserved Lemon" or 2 Tbsp. other preserved lemon
2 Tbsp. breadcrumbs (if needed)
1 to 2 Tbsp. chopped parsley

Preheat the oven to 375 degrees F. Salt and pepper the halibut on both sides. Sauté the shallots in olive oil for about two minutes or until softened, add tomatoes, and heat through. Add the preserved lemon and parsley and turn off the heat; stir so it is just warm. If there seems to be too much liquid, add some breadcrumbs to absorb excess moisture, but leave it very moist. Taste, and add salt and pepper to taste.

Place the halibut in an oiled baking dish and spoon an even layer of tomato-lemon mixture over the fish. Put in the preheated oven and bake for about 15 minutes, depending on thickness. Put on plates and pour any accumulated juices over fish and serve.

There it is, Scott's Recipe, and I do not think it can go wrong if you follow directions. I hate to say that, but it is so. I have too much respect for halibut to want to mess it up. I would serve this with asparagus and whipped potatoes. Maybe I can beat him at bocce this summer.

This halibut recipe will work with your first striper of the season, or any other one, but Scott says you must use preserved lemon and not fresh, and I am beginning to believe more and more that what Scott says, goes. Not liking it, but believing.

I still find my favorite way to eat most fish is breaded and pan- or deep-fried. This may not be considered gourmet food by some, but it is fine by me, though it may get monotonous. I recently came upon a recipe new to me that adds a delicious Asian touch to fish prepared in this way. The following recipe is for four lucky people.

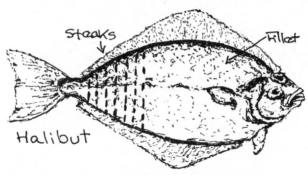

FRIED FISH WITH FRIED GINGER *(for 4)*

Two or three cups oil
½ lb. ginger
1-½ lbs. white fish fillets
1 cup flour
1 cup cornstarch
4 scallions
1 Tbsp. good soy sauce or fish sauce (Nam pla)
Cilantro leaves for garnish

Ginger Root

You can deep-fry or pan-fry this dish. To deep-fry, put 2 inches of oil in a skillet or pot large enough to accommodate the fish all at once. Heat to 350 degrees F.

To pan-fry, use only about 1/8-inch oil in pan. Peel the ginger and julienne it finely or slice it very thin with a potato peeler or mandolin.

When the oil is hot, fry the ginger until lightly browned, watching it carefully (which is the secret to all great cooking – paying attention). Meanwhile, salt and pepper the fish on both sides and combine flour and cornstarch in a bowl.

Remove browned ginger with a slotted spoon and set aside. Lightly dredge fish in flour and cornstarch mixture, shaking off the excess. Add fish to oil, watching the heat until browned on all sides and cooked through (less than 5 minutes). Turn fish once or twice. Remove fish to paper towels and keep warm.

Now, fry the scallions for 15 seconds and remove with slotted spoon. Refry the ginger for 30 seconds, remove, and drain.

Arrange fish on a warm platter and sprinkle with fried ginger and scallions, drizzle with soy sauce or fish sauce, top with cilantro, and serve.

This is special and spectacular, good enough for the worst snob who disdains fried fish. It sounds like a lot of trouble, but considering the results, it is actually not very difficult and works especially well with striped bass. It can be used with pollock, cod, haddock, you name it. It will be grand if you pay attention.

We can thank Mark Bittman, cook, columnist, author, and my current culinary hero.

I made a pilgrimage to my favorite Chinese Supermarket in Boston, Mings, newly tarted-up but still funky enough for my taste.

They carry a large inventory of fish of many unusual and exotic species. The fish are not always in the best condition but always worth checking out. This week they had bags of roe; I finally learned that the roe came from smallmouth buffalo fish (Ictiobus bubalus), *a freshwater sucker. It was very cheap, but I had no way to keep it cold until I returned home. Alas, I will get some next time. However, I did find frog legs frozen in 1-pound packages that were farm-raised in Vietnam. I used to gig them and catch them on hook and line when I was a boy in Michigan. My family found them to be delicious, probably the most exotic things we had ever eaten.*

I bought a couple of packages of frogs' legs and will invite my son-in-law Scott and his wife, my stepdaughter #1 Liz, over for dinner. I will prepare the legs in a classical French manner and maybe show him up just a little. Hey, I never said I wasn't small-minded.

Maybe I will casually serve them for lunch to show how cool I am.

Hush Puppy, Catfish Calls

I have just returned from a very fine visit to north-central Florida, my favorite part of the state, with its large cattle-and-horse farms and multitude of crystal clear springs welling up from a cavernous limestone substrate. We stayed in a house overlooking the lazy, lovely Suwannee River, not far from Cross Creek where Marjorie Kinnan Rawlings lived and wrote one of my favorite novels, "The Yearling". She also wrote a fine cookbook called "Cross Creek Cookery", so she is of value to food and natural history freaks like me.

This is a land of alligators, snakes, turtles, and the humorous armadillo. Boar, raccoon, turkey and deer hunting is of great interest to the locals, as are bass and catfishing. My wife ate more and better catfish than she had ever eaten before during our stay. She had one meal that featured eight small headless catfish, each about the size of large smelt, fried in a cornmeal mixture. They were delicious! You eat the meat off the backbone much like you eat corn on the cob. The fish was served with coleslaw and hush puppies, seasoned cornmeal-and-flour fritters supposedly made to toss to the dogs to keep them quiet as you ate your fish. These fried balls were made from the leftover catfish breading material. They are as common with fried fish in the South as grits are with breakfast or any other meal.

MARJORIE KINNAN RAWLINGS HUSH PUPPIES

1 cup cornmeal
2 tsp. baking powder
½ tsp. salt
1 medium onion, finely chopped
1 egg slightly beaten
1/3 cup milk
Oil for frying

Mix cornmeal, baking powder and salt. Add chopped onion and egg; mix well. Carefully drop mixture by the tablespoon into an inch-deep hot oil (375 degrees F) and fry for about two minutes a side or until nicely browned. Drain on brown paper or paper towels to keep warm in a 175- to 200 degrees F oven and serve with fried catfish.

TRADITIONAL SOUTHERN FRIED CATFISH *(for 4 to 6)*

Yellow or white cornmeal
Salt and pepper to taste
Catfish fillets
Frying oil (I like peanut)
Lemon wedges and tartar sauce

Combine dry ingredients. Rinse catfish and pat dry. Dredge the fish in dry ingredients and shake off excess. Heat ¼ inch or more of oil in a heavy skillet to 375 degrees F. Fry fish in hot oil 2 to 4 minutes on each side, depending on its thickness, until fish is golden brown. Drain on paper towels, brown paper, or newsprint and serve with lemon wedges and tartar sauce.

You can spice up this simple dish by adding 1 to 2 tsp. of cayenne pepper to 1 tsp. to a breading mixture of ¾ cups cornmeal and ¼ cup flour. The simple technique works well with the big striped bass fillets, trimmed to size, that you should be catching this month.

In Florida we attended a weekly seafood buffet in a totally unpretentious restaurant where they managed to ruin freshly caught Gulf of Mexico shrimp in more than six ways by overcooking them – a culinary disgrace; however, the fried catfish was good, as were the frog legs, and the crab cakes (more like fritters) were passable.

My respect for Florida seafood cooks increased greatly when I had an outstanding meal of broiled grouper prepared by my cousin, Dr. Ed Schroeder, retired veterinarian, master gardener, and worm rancher, among many other weird and remarkable things. Why do I dislike learning from my cousin – could it be testosterone poisoning?

Ed used a grilling basket that firmly grips the fillet so it cannot fall apart, as so often happens when fillets are placed directly on the grill. Many people do this because they want grill marks on their fish. Ed, being a Bolshevik, did not. He used a clever method to prevent said marks by laying the salted, peppered and oiled fillet on a layer of sliced onions in his grill basket, topping it with more onions, and closing the basket up.

ED'S GRILLED GROUPER (for 6)

3 to 3 ½ lb. grouper fillet, about 2" thick
Salt and pepper
2 Tbsp. olive oil
1 medium onion, thinly sliced

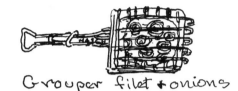

Grouper filet + onions

Follow directions preceding the ingredients list and grill for about 9 minutes per side or until onions are slightly charred and fish is white to the center. Terrific!

Ed's lovely wife, Carol, served her own tartar sauce with the fish. Carol cleverly added capers and a chopped boiled egg to a mundane tartar sauce, making it grand. Try it; you will not be sorry!

I recommend this technique for a big striped bass fillet. Go for it! ◄█

Phil's Provision Service and Surgery

White perch, to my taste, is one of the four or five best panfish on earth, whole or filleted. So you can imagine how happy I was when my personal protein provider, "Predator Phil", called me a couple of days ago to report that he and a friend had made a fine catch of white perch on Martha's Vineyard and, knowing me, he saved me a bunch of beautiful 4- to 5-ounce fillets. What a guy! I asked him where he caught them, and he replied, "I told you, on the Vineyard." Cagey, but generous. I have to give Phil credit, though; he had filleted these fish beautifully. The man is nearly an artiste with a fillet knife; he doesn't do badly with a steak knife, either!

I prepared them in one of the simplest manners there is and enjoyed a meal of fish as delicious as anyone else on earth had that evening, possibly even the best. If you can get some white perch fillets, or even whole fish, do not fail to try this recipe or your life will not be as full as it might have been.

PHIL'S ROAST WHITE PERCH A LA MASCH

Allow two 4-ounce fillets per person
Olive oil
Salt and pepper
Capers (1 tsp. per fillet)
Lemons
Parsley (minced)

Salt and pepper fillets liberally and coat with olive oil. Preheat oven to 450 degrees F. Also, preheat an oven-proof pan big enough to hold fish in a single layer. When oven and pan reach said temperature, carefully remove hot pan from oven. Now, arrange fish pieces side by side and return to oven to bake for about five minutes or until opaque and easily flaked. Serve garnished with minced parsley and lemon.

If you want to be a bit fancier, you can add ¼ cup of dry white wine to the juices, boil down a bit, and add the rinsed capers and 2 Tbsp. of butter or cream. Pour this over fish and serve garnished as above.

I had mine with creamy mashed potatoes and asparagus from my garden. We eat like royalty, possibly better in that the Queen of England won't allow garlic in her kitchen, but I think she would have loved these perch fillets.

Last night we had sesame-coated sautéed salmon steaks for dinner, this time with boiled potatoes and asparagus. There was enough left over to make a lightly cooked salmon, potatoes, and asparagus hash. Delicious with farm-fresh poached eggs and homemade bread toast with butter and jelly. The queen's kitchen could not have beaten this breakfast.

SALMON, POTATOES, AND ASPARAGUS GENTLE HASH

Leftover salmon
Leftover boiled potatoes (cubed)
4 or 5 spears leftover asparagus
Salt and pepper
1 scallion (chopped)
1 Tbsp. chopped parsley
Butter for sautéing

Sauté potatoes gently in butter until they are just beginning to brown. Add minced scallion, salmon and asparagus that you have cut into 1-inch segments. Heat and serve with a poached egg on top, garnished with parsley. There it is, beautiful and delicious.

You can do this with any leftover fish and end up with something better than just good.

Last week, to partially repay him for the perch, I invited Phil and his lovely lady friend Kelly (a good shot, sport, and fisherwoman) over for dinner. He said he would provide the fish, and I would do the cooking. He took me fishing with him on the morning of the dinner, for which we needed enough fish for six. A 12-pound bass would be perfect and should have been no problem to catch. Well, all we caught were two undersized bass and me. I managed to get a 7/0 siwash hook stuck through my left ear.

Phil, all heart, had to get some pictures before he used my multi-tool to set me free while killing himself laughing.

So back we went to Phil's house to search his fridge and freezer for main course ingredients. This was not at all a dismal prospect. We came up with 1½ pounds of striped bass caught the day before, a duck, and about 2 pounds of wild boar tenderloin. Not bad: we got a fine, unique dinner out of this mélange.

We had a fine meal of seared, marinated wild boar tenderloin, a roast duck, and braised striped bass Portuguese style along with an orange, avocado, and onion salad on fresh garden spinach and potatoes with a sherry-laced sauce. The sauce is just tarted-up gravy.

BRAISED STRIPER FILLETS PORTUGUESE (for 4)

2 lbs. striper fillets
1 green pepper (chopped)
1 medium onion (chopped)
3" celery stalk (chopped)
1 clove garlic (minced)
1 14.5 oz. can chopped tomatoes
1 tsp. cumin
3 Tbsp. olive oil
1/8 tsp. saffron (optional)
½ cup dry white wine
Salt and pepper
½ tsp. wine vinegar
1/3 cup minced parsley
¼ cup olives (black, green or some of each)

Preheat oven to 400 degrees F. Sauté peppers, onion, celery, and garlic in olive oil until onions become translucent. Add garlic when onions are nearly done. If you include garlic from the beginning, it may burn and make the sauce bitter; always add garlic last when including it in a recipe. Add the wine, optional saffron, cumin, olives, tomatoes, and ½ the parsley. Simmer (not boil) for 15 minutes.

Salt and pepper fillets, sprinkle with oil, and put them in an ovenproof pan. Bake in preheated oven for 15 minutes. Remove from oven, stir in the ½ tsp. vinegar, garnish with parsley, and serve with rice or potatoes. You will be happy, I promise.

With a friend like Predator Phil, one need never lack for protein, adventure, medical advice and treatment, good company, ridicule and laughter. If you go fishing with him and catch no fish (a rare event), you can always go to his larder for sustenance. This time it was duck, wild boar, and striped bass. If I get lucky, next time we will find a backstrap of elk in there, and who knows what else. I am a fortunate man.

Chapter Six:
JUNE

June is the month that "busts out all over." The summer fish are here, trout are still biting in the ponds, and the trees are fully green. Tulips shine in the flower garden, and lettuce and spinach abound in the kitchen garden. The garlic and onions are growing and life is good. Good enough to go fishing – the lawn can take care of itself for a few days. Hit the beach, rod or rake in hand, and bring home the goodies.

My son-in-law and competitor in the kitchen, Scott, has once again hit me where I live with his clams in black bean sauce recipe. It should become part of your repertoire. Drat!

Ask Pops

Hello, Dave,

I enjoy your columns very much, and I'm wondering if you can offer some help. . . .

My friend is vacationing on Cape Cod on the Vineyard this week, and he called me last night saying he had caught several nice-sized conch. Now this friend and I had caught and eaten several Caribbean conch on vacation before, but he didn't remember how I had cleaned them and was looking for advice. I told him to use a hatchet to break a small opening between the 2nd and 3rd ring on the cone, then insert a knife to cut the muscle and slide the critter out, before cutting away the guts and rubbery skin.

It occurred to me, though, that I had never ever heard of anyone catching or eating conch in New England, and I'm wondering if he caught something else and how edible that might be? Any thoughts would be appreciated.

Thanks & Best Wishes,

Sterling Shea

Your instructions for opening conchs are very good; however, the smaller northern "conchs" are somewhat more difficult for using your technique. The queen conch *(Strombus gigas)* is the delicacy eaten all over the Caribbean and considerably different from what we call conch on the New England coast: the channeled whelk *(Busycon canaliculatum)* and the knobbed whelk *(Busycon carica)*.

The whelks (conchs) are in demand by Italians and Asians. The Italians call them scungilli and usually serve them in a red

sauce over pasta; the Chinese stir-fry them after tenderizing. All the conchs are tougher than hell and must be tenderized. I boil conchs to remove them from their shells, rub off the viscera, grind the muscular foot, and make them into cakes or fritters, similar to crab cakes.

The market for conch has been so good for the past decade that many lobstermen in Southern New England trap them when lobstering is slow. This in turn is causing another problem. The best bait for conch is quartered horseshoe crabs; they are also the best bait for eels prized for bass fishing. This use for bait and the demand for horseshoe crab blood by the medical diagnostic community have caused the horseshoe crab population to plummet to such a low point that the scarcity of crab eggs is causing the population of some shorebirds to drop drastically. The world is complex and delicately balanced – we humans may be getting too heavy.

Dear Dave,

Is there a formula to make salt water by using kosher salt and fresh water? I'd like to be able to wash steamers or quahogs once I'm at home and not have to run to the beach for salt water!

Patrick Jenkins

My friend, Bill McBane, "the fishes' friend" at the Marine Biological Laboratory in Woods Hole, says 32 parts per thousand by weight is the formula; you can do the math. I say ½ cup salt per gallon of water is close enough for purging clams. If you are using tap water, it is a good idea to let the water sit for a couple of hours for the chlorine to clear before you add the clams.

Knobbed whelk

Channeled whelk

A 25-pound Bass Can Be A Pain In The...

This is the month when we on the south shore of Cape Cod are most likely to catch large striped bass, and by large I mean fish of 25 pounds or more, so many people will be faced with this big lump of maritime meat. So what do we do with it?

The first thing to do upon catching the fish is to keep it as moist and cool as possible in whatever situation you are in. Putting the beast on ice is best, but if this cannot be done, keeping the fish out of the sun and moist and cool is the way to go. If I catch a large fish while fishing from the beach, I often bury it in the sand; this keeps it moist and cool and protects it from rats, skunks, coyotes or other creatures that may be frequenting the beach. I keep burlap bags on my skiff, and they provide surprisingly good cooling – even on sunny days – if they are wet when the fish are put in them. This cooling is caused by evaporation.

The quality of the meat is preserved best by prompt gutting and bleeding of the carcass. Most of us are loath to do this before we weigh our trophy. This is not for bragging rights, but for truth in future descriptions of our catch. Some may believe this is true. I do, of course!

So now you have the big fish at home, and unless you have a huge oven or grill, you or your delighted fish-cleaning wife must break the carcass down to pieces suitable for cooking. Or you could look up my hero, Howard Mitcham, and follow his recipe for preparing a whole, stuffed 35-pound striped bass and have a helluva party, almost like a pig roast. I have never done this but would like to. I will not present the recipe here because I almost never include a recipe I have not tested myself. If someone on the Upper Cape should come up with such a fish, and might want to have a party featuring a whole, very large, striped bass, I would be happy to take part in cooking and eating the fish. This could be a whole lot of fun and might also be delicious.

If the fish is not to be used in this noble manner, it must be cut into steaks and fillets of a size useful to the normal family. I start by scaling the beast from the vent to the gill covers because I am going to turn this section into steaks.

I like the steaks to be at least one inch thick. I first cut off the head. An easy way to do this is to use a large chef's knife (or small machete) to cut down to the backbone, and then to strike the blade with a mallet or billet of wood to cut through the spine. Then, continue your cut through the other side and repeat this technique one inch at a time, lopping off steaks as you go until you reach the vent.

I did not scale the fish from the vent back because I am going to fillet this section and skin the fillets. This is easily done, just as you would fillet a whole fish, making an incision next to the backbone toward the tail and separating the meat from the rack (what fishermen call the exposed skeleton of a fish after it has been filleted). Now, skin the fillets, and there you have it, fish ready for the pot, the grill, the oven, or the frying pan. A 25-pound bass should yield about 10 pounds of steaks and fillets, plus the bonus of a bunch of bones and a head for preparing fish stock for future soups, seafood stews, or chowder.

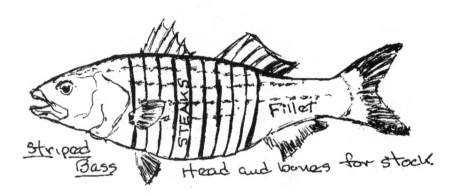

FISH STOCK

1 gallon water
5 lbs. of fish bones or the big fish head
  (gills removed)
1 medium onion, unpeeled
4 carrots cut in 2-inch pieces
3 stalks celery and leaves, cut in chunks
1 tomato, roughly chopped
10 black peppercorns
3 cloves unpeeled garlic

1 whole clove (optional)
2 bay leaves
1 tsp. dried thyme or 4 sprigs fresh
½ cup chopped parsley
1 cup dry white wine
Salt and pepper
2 Tbsp. olive oil (optional)

Don't be put off by the list of ingredients, they all just get thrown in a big pot, brought to a boil and then simmered for 45 minutes.

If a gallon of water does not cover all the bones, either add more water or, better for concentrating flavor, cover the pot for the simmering period. After simmering for 30 to 45 minutes, cool slightly and strain the whole works through a sieve or cheesecloth, correct the seasoning for salt, and there you have it, great fish stock for future meals or immediate use. This stock freezes beautifully. I try to always have some on hand.

You may want to make fish chowder from this stock at once. Save the meat from the head and rack, make your chowder base, add the meat, and there you have it: joy, satisfaction, and potential renown.

You may wish to grill your bass steaks; this is best done simply, merely oiling and salt and peppering the steaks on both sides and broiling them over a medium fire (cooler than you would use for beefsteak), being careful not to dry them out. I like to use a fish-grilling basket. I seem to have fewer disasters when using a basket than when putting fish directly on the grill. Serve these simply-prepared steaks with lemon butter, and pleasure, even joy, will be yours.

PORTUGUESE BAKED BASS FILLETS OR STEAKS (for 10)

5 inches linguica, chopped
¼ lb. salt pork, diced
1 large onion, roughly chopped
1 diced green pepper
1 stalk celery, diced
2 cloves garlic, minced
1 cup dry white wine
16 oz. can tomatoes
1 tsp. basil
½ tsp. rosemary
1 tsp. cumin
Salt and pepper
1 doz. olives (optional but delicious)
Parmesan cheese
5 lbs. bass steaks or fillets (almost forgot!)

Render the fat from the diced salt pork over medium heat; when pork begins to color, add chopped linguica, onions, peppers, celery, and garlic. Sauté gently until onions are transparent, add tomatoes (scrunched up with your hands), wine and seasonings, bring to a simmer, and cook about 5 minutes.

Preheat oven to 415 degrees F. Put a ladle full of sauce in a baking pan large enough to hold fish and sauce comfortably, lay fish on sauce, layer, and cover with remaining sauce. Put sauced fish in hot oven for 10 minutes, remove from oven and sprinkle grated Parmesan and return to oven; bake until cheese melts and begins to brown and fish is cooked through. Serve this with boiled potatoes, rice, or pasta and a salad along with beer, wine, and bread and you've got a party, a story to tell, and most of that "big" bass is gone. Congratulations! ◀━

Fish for Breakfast - Why Not?

It is finally summer. The flowers are blooming, the fish are back, and I am ready for the joy and abundance of summer! I even enjoy the arrival of the summer people, although I am also relieved to see them go in September. My skiff is in the water, and the local fish are in danger of my attention – as are the rabbits that frolic in my garden if left unattended. Distant relatives and old friends will soon be arriving to our community to enjoy the pleasures that we have all year, and while they are here, they must be fed. I enjoy surprising my guests with seafood for breakfast. I truly enjoy fish at breakfast, from smoked salmon or kippered herrings to fish cakes and fish hash made from the previous night's leftovers. I always try to prepare more for dinner than I need so that I'll have the basis for breakfast at hand. If I have shellfish, oysters or quahogs, I save a few to scramble with eggs. Last, but decidedly not least, is clam or fish chowder, piping hot with a pat of butter melting amidships. This is perhaps the most splendid eye-opener of all! I do not say this lightly: your life will be greatly improved by the occasional bowl of chowder in the morning. It leaves Prozac in the dust and perks up the entire day.

A while back, I did a book signing at a wine tasting and haddock dinner (four ways) at The Wine List, a wine shop in Hyannis. The haddock was prepared beautifully by David Kelley, the chef at The Naked Oyster, also in Hyannis. He used fish caught by day-boat fishermen out of Chatham; you can't find finer fish anywhere else. His preparations were excellent, and I will one day soon share some with you.

I was approached by several users of my cookbook, two of whom mentioned how much they enjoyed my basic fish hash recipe. For each of them, it was their first fish hash. I will present it here again along with some variations. As simple as this recipe is, it was praised by at least two people of outstanding good taste!

FISH HASH
1 cup cooked fish
1½ cups cubed, cooked potato
½ cup chopped onion
2 Tbsp. butter or oil
Pinch of nutmeg
1 Tbsp. minced parsley
Salt and pepper

Potential Hash

Melt the butter over medium heat. Add the other ingredients, mix thoroughly and sauté until a crust begins to form on the bottom. Turn the whole works over and gently brown the second side. That's it! What could be simpler?

I like a poached egg on this and some Heinz chili sauce laced with Tabasco on the side. Here are several variations of the recipe – same ingredients.

1. Substitute four strips of bacon or an equivalent amount of salt pork for the oil and butter. Sauté the bacon or salt pork until crisp and set aside. Crumble or chop the cracklings into pieces and stir into your hash.

2. Add ¼ cup of chopped celery and ¼ cup of chopped red or green sweet bell pepper to the mix before sautéing.

3. Add ¼ cup of chopped chorizo or linguica along with the celery and peppers for yet another taste.

4. Add a chopped (seeded) tomato and ½ tsp. of cumin to the above, and substitute cilantro for the parsley, and you are in Mexico! I like a fried egg in this case. Why? I don't know, but it seems more Mexican to me.

A clove or two of minced garlic may be added to any of the combinations with delectable results. Go for it! Maybe a little jalapeño, or cayenne pepper. It is your kitchen, so do what you want.

There are several other things you can do with these simple ingredients. For example, you could mix a cup of bread or cracker crumbs and an egg into any of the combinations, mix them thoroughly, form into patties, coat with cornmeal, and presto! Fish cakes. Great to serve with baked beans and coleslaw, even for breakfast. Your guests will talk about you for years, and probably favorably.

You can make a delicious frittata (a type of baked Italian omelet) by putting your mixture of potatoes, onions, fish and whatever else you have chosen in an ovenproof dish. Pour enough beaten eggs or egg substitute to just cover the mixture and bake the whole works in a 350 degrees F oven for about 15 minutes, or until puffed up and slightly browned on top. Allow to cool, and then cut it into serving-size pieces. This stuff is good warm and will still be good at room temperature – handy for picnics or lunches aboard the boat!

You can make this frittata even more exciting by stirring in grated cheese of your choice. I like to use Parmigiano-Reggiano or sharp cheddar. Try it: you will not be sorry!

Another one of my recipes that has been complimented extensively is for clam and corn fritters. This recipe is especially for those with turkey fryers. All that boiling oil scares me; it reminds me of what my Uncle Art said would happen to me if I was not a good boy.

CLAM AND CORN FRITTERS
2 cups ground or finely chopped clams or quahogs
1 small onion, minced
1 Tbsp. parsley, minced
2 Tbsp. chopped celery
2 beaten eggs
Milk (or creamed corn)
1 cup all-purpose flour
1 tsp. double-acting baking powder
½ tsp. Tabasco
1/3 tsp. salt
Black pepper to taste
1 cup fresh sweet corn, cut from the cob (or one cup frozen corn) – fresh is much better

Sift the flour and baking powder together. Add the beaten eggs and enough milk to make a stiff batter. Mix in all the other ingredients. Drop batter by the heaping Tbsp. into preheated 350 degrees to 375 degrees F oil and fry until golden brown. Drain on paper towels and serve. You may also sauté the batter in butter or olive oil rather than deep-fry it; just brown it on both sides. You will not be sorry, but your turkey might get neglected.

I once had a recipe for minnow pancakes, but I could not find it today. I tried them once and they were not much good, so you are lucky that you won't have to try them. Do give the other recipes a try, though. You can use oysters instead of clams in the fritter recipe and possibly become famous. ◄━

Why Bother, or Bother Me?

While reading the newspaper the other morning, I came upon a recipe accompanied by a photograph, for striped bass with fennel, turnips, picholine olives, and bergamot. For some reason this teed me off. ("Teed" was a polite choice of words for what I felt.) Why did this recipe irk me so? Perhaps it was because I did not know what either a picholine olive or bergamot was or because the combination of striped bass and turnip sounded dreadful to me, at least for the bass. Why would I want this stuff with my bass?

Fennel I can accept, but none of the other stuff will go with my first striped bass of the season, which I will catch in late May or early June. Late in September I may experiment with such exotic fare, but for now, I will treat my first noble bass with simplicity and great care, and I'll be damned if I will possibly foul it with exotic ingredients. Perhaps I am becoming, or have already become, a nasty, narrow-minded old curmudgeon, but I have earned, and will defend, my right to curmudgeonlyness. How's that for a word?

My first striped bass will be filleted. One fillet will be trimmed to individual serving-sized pieces for pan frying. The second fillet will probably be broiled whole either on a charcoal grill or in the oven. This sautéing and grilling will be done simply to allow the striped bass to display its natural, unadorned goodness.

After filleting the fish, I will boil up the head and rack (backbone and ribs) of the bass for stock, to be used as the base of a fish or mixed seafood chowder.

I have prepared and eaten fish in almost every way possible, certainly more kinds in more ways than most people, and enjoyed nearly all varieties and cooking methods, but my first thought when getting some particularly good fish is to either pan-fry (sauté) it, grill it, or braise it in the oven in a tomato-based sauce.

Pan-fried fish should be coated with something that will form a crunchy crust. These coatings can be made up of many different grains, nuts, or even vegetables, as you will see in one of this month's recipes. Flour, cornstarch, cornmeal, crushed walnuts, sesame seeds, crushed saltines, crushed Ritz crackers, or even crushed cornflakes are all acceptable, both alone or in various combinations. Don't hesitate to experiment when making coatings for pan-frying fish. I have tried and enjoyed every one that I have mentioned, and I neglected coconut.

Unfortunately, my young fish provider had a falling out with his skipper and left his berth on the boat, so I will soon be on my own in the search for fresh fish. I was saddened by his announcement but pleased to have some frozen fluke from the fish he gave me last month. I decided to pan fry these fillets using two coatings new to me, both of which I will now unequivocally recommend for pan frying fluke, haddock, cod, or striped bass.

WHITE-FLESHED FISH FILLETS
COATED WITH MASHED POTATO (for 2)

Oil for frying
1 lb. fish fillet, in two pieces
½ cup flour (optional)
1 beaten egg
1 cup (or more) instant mashed potatoes
Salt and pepper

There are two ways to go about preparing the fillets for frying. You can mix 1 tsp. of salt and ½ tsp. of pepper with the flour in a plastic bag, put the fillets in the bag, and shake to coat with flour. Shake off the excess flour and dip fillets in beaten egg (Egg Beaters or other egg substitutes are convenient to have for this purpose) and then add in instant mashed potato.

You can skip the flouring; salt and pepper the fillets, dip them in egg, and coat with instant mashed potato.

Heat a heavy-bottomed or cast iron skillet over medium-high heat. Put 2 Tbsp. oil in pan and allow to heat until a crumb dropped in bubbles immediately. Put your coated fish in the hot oil over medium heat and sauté until nicely browned on both sides. This should take no more than 3 minutes per side. The fish is ready when it just reaches the flaking point.

I will serve this with coleslaw and oven-fried potatoes or real mashed potatoes and tiny peas. My mouth waters as I write this. Give this a try; you will not be sorry.

No matter what coating you choose to use, the technique is the same. Coat fillets in seasoned flour, dip in beaten eggs and in final coating. This coating can be done ahead of time. If you should coat your fish in advance of dinner, store them in a single layer, not touching each other, until ready to sauté.

I like to add a little cayenne or other hot pepper to my seasoned flour. Experiment and make every recipe your own.

I mentioned two new coatings for pan-fried fish earlier. Here is the second: ham.

WHITE-FLESHED FISH FILLET WITH HAM (for 2)
1 lb. fish fillet, in two pieces
Oil for frying
Freshly ground pepper
Enough paper-thin sliced ham to wrap fish (prosciutto is best)

Wrap fillets completely in thinly sliced ham. Domestic prosciutto is much cheaper than imported and plenty good. Ordinary boiled or baked ham is good, but not nearly as good as prosciutto.

Heat 2 Tbsp. oil over medium-high heat in a heavy-bottomed or cast iron frying pan. Sauté the ham-coated fish for about three minutes per side. The ham will crisp up and adhere to the fish.

I think this would be great for breakfast with a fried egg and home fries and an English muffin. In fact I would bet on it.

Enough about pan-frying, no matter how dear to my heart. On to the grill or broiler, where my second bass fillet will be cooked.

GRILLED BASS FILLET WITH TOMATO JUICE
Large bass fillet, ½ lb. per person
1 medium onion, thinly sliced
1 lemon, thinly sliced
1 cup tomato juice
6 drops Tabasco (to taste)
Salt and pepper

Leave skin on fillet and preheat broiler or grill. Liberally salt and pepper fish, brush with Tabasco-laced tomato juice, cover with onion and lemon slices, baste again and broil until fish flakes, basting occasionally. Do not turn fish. On the grill, close the lid between bastings and cook until fish flakes. A dish of wilted dandelion greens or spinach with bacon and mashed potatoes would be great with this. Bluefish can also be prepared this way and is almost marvelous.

I will lighten up a little by autumn, when I am full of striper, and I'll look into bergamot and picholine olives when I am no longer angry, but I refuse to consider the turnip.

Simple Does Not Mean Simpleminded

I made a meal of poached codfish and vegetables last week that could hardly be simpler and used only one pot, an added bonus. But also, it was delicious, simply delicious. I am sure that this recipe will be just as good made with striped bass. This dish can be expanded to feed throngs if you need to. You will disappoint no one!

POACHED COD (OR STRIPED BASS) AND VEGETABLES (for 4)

6 cups water
¼ cup dry white wine
3 medium shallots or 1 large onion
3 medium boiling potatoes (red skin)
1 medium carrot
2 Tbsp. Kosher salt or 1 Tbsp. regular salt
2 bay leaves
1 Tbsp. black peppercorns
1½ to 2 lbs. fish fillets
½ lemon, sliced paper thin
6 parsley sprigs, coarsely chopped

Poached Cod Stuff

Combine wine, water, thinly sliced shallots or onions, halved and sliced potatoes, carrot thinly sliced on a bias, bay leaves and peppercorns in a pot large enough to hold the fish as well. Bring this to a boil, reduce heat, and cook until the vegetables are about half-done. Reduce heat to a slow simmer and add the fish in a single layer, making sure they are barely covered with liquid.

Poach gently until fish is opaque and flakes easily and vegetables are tender, about 7 minutes (fish is done when its internal temperature is 175 degrees F).

Some serve this as a soup, dividing the fish and vegetables evenly among four bowls and covering them with stock. I like to serve the fish and vegetables on plates with bowls of stock on the side for each diner. You can make your presentation grander by putting vegetables and fish on a platter, moistening them with stock, and garnishing with sliced lemon and minced parsley. Provide each guest with a plate and a bowl and let them serve themselves.

Whatever method you choose, be sure to garnish the plate with sliced lemon and parsley. I serve some Parmigiano reggiano on the side. A Portuguese vinho verde goes nicely with this exquisitely simple dish. I urge you to try this. It is quick, easy, and delicious.

This recipe will work for any white fish and also for salmon. Use dill sprigs instead of bay leaves if you choose salmon. Small whole fish could also be prepared in this way, or you could eliminate the salt and boil a few clams or mussels in the stock. The possibilities are simple and possibly endless. Go for it!

The next recipe will be, and in fact is, even simpler than the first. My wife says I should probably stick to the simple. I do not know if she says this out of concern for my readers or if she is implying something about the abilities of the writer. I do not intend to pursue this question, and I will present you with a very simple recipe for roasting fish fillets that will provide a fairly crisp exterior and a still-moist interior often absent in roasted fish.

ROAST FISH FILLET (BLUEFISH OR SALMON, MAYBE STRIPER) *(for 4)*

1 lb. of fish fillets of equal size (skin on)
1 Tbsp. olive oil
Salt and pepper

To get equal-sized fillets, cut a large fillet crosswise into four equal-sized pieces. For ease in cutting through skin, start cuts on flesh side of fillet. Pat fillets dry and rub with oil. Liberally season with salt and pepper and set aside.

Adjust oven rack to lowest position and preheat oven to 500 degrees F. Heat a baking sheet while oven is heating.

Carefully place oiled fillets on preheated tray, skin side down. Reduce oven temperature to 275 degrees F. Return baking sheet and fish to hot, but now cooling, oven, and roast until fish is barely translucent in center, about 10 minutes. Remove to plates or a platter and serve with a sauce or relish. Melted butter, parsley and lemon are adequate, but you might want to show off a bit with a fancy relish, maybe mango salsa. Marinara sauce is good, as is a simple tartar sauce or the following remoulade, a fancy tartar sauce. This is good with shellfish, fried fish, and even as a dressing for potato salad.

REMOULADE

2 large egg yolks
1 Tbsp. Dijon mustard
1 cup vegetable oil
1 tsp. Worcestershire sauce
1 Tbsp. freshly squeezed lemon juice
½ tsp. Kosher salt or ¼ tsp. regular salt
1 tsp. Tabasco or Frank's Red Hot
½ tsp. white pepper (or dark)
2 tsp. capers (or dill pickle)
2 tsp. shallots (or scallions)
1½ tsp. minced tarragon
1 tsp. minced parsley
2 tsp. minced bell pepper (red nicest)

Whisk egg yolks and mustard in a bowl until smoothly blended. Continue whisking as you slowly pour oil down side of bowl in a thin stream until everything is smoothly blended. Now, whisk in the Worcestershire, Tabasco, lemon juice, salt and pepper. Garnish with chopped red peppers and parsley and serve.

Now, sit back, and when people ask where you got that sauce, you say, "Oh, I made it – that's the only way to go. It is all fairly simple, you know." ◄

Great Scott! Not Again?

Yes, he did it again, my son-in-law Scott invited my wife and me to dinner and served us two classical seafood dishes, both beautifully and deliciously cooked. One dish was clams in black bean sauce, the other a Mediterranean fish stew, zuppa de pesca.

I thought he had a lot of gall, attacking me in my own cooking area. I thought the clam dish was especially risky for him because I consider myself the "King of the Quahogs" – "Queen of the Quahogs" sounds catchier, but doesn't describe me very well.

Most of us eat quahogs in one of three ways; raw, in chowder, or in clam sauce for spaghetti. Stuffed quahogs and fritters also appear. I have previously presented recipes for all of these dishes. These are classic recipes and I see my versions as pure.

Scott's serving of quahogs in black bean sauce led me to believe that I had a duty to try to add this to the classic quahog lexicon. I have cooked this dish for years but never published a recipe. I hate to admit it, but Scott's version was about as good as this dish gets. I do not have his recipe, but I do have a couple I have made that I considered successful and delicious.

SIMPLE CLAMS IN BLACK BEAN SAUCE

2 Tbsp. peanut oil
2 cloves garlic
¼ tsp. grated fresh ginger
1 qt. littlenecks in shells
1 Tbsp. fermented black beans or 1 Tbsp. canned black bean sauce
2 Tbsp. dry sherry

Gather your ingredients (you may have to go to an Asian market to get fermented black beans, but you can substitute canned black bean sauce which is available in many supermarkets). Put peanut oil in a hot wok or heavy bottomed kettle, add garlic and ginger and heat, stirring until fragrant. Add the clams and ¼ cup of water, stir and cover, allowing them to steam as you wash and mash the fermented beans. Add sherry to beans and add to steaming clams. Cover and steam until all the clams are open.

I like to garnish this with chopped scallion greens and serve on white rice. This will almost certainly become a favorite.

LESS-SIMPLE CLAMS WITH BLACK BEANS AND OYSTER SAUCE

2 Tbsp. fermented black beans or bottled paste
24 littleneck clams
2 ½ Tbsp. oyster sauce
1 tsp. soy sauce
1 tsp. sugar
1 Tbsp. dry sherry

2 Tbsp. peanut oil
2 tsp. sesame oil
1 tsp. minced ginger root
1 Tbsp. minced garlic
1 cup chicken stock
1 cup cornstarch mixed with ¼ cup water
¼ cup chopped scallions

Rinse black beans and mash them. Scrub the clamshells. In a small bowl combine the oyster sauce, sesame oil, soy sauce, sugar, and sherry.

In a hot wok or skillet combine the peanut oil, ginger root, garlic and black beans. When this begins to smell pungent, add the clams and chicken stock. Bring to a boil. Lower heat to simmer and cover. The clams should all open in about five minutes.

Add the oyster sauce mixture. Bring heat back to high. Stir for two minutes. Stir in the cornstarch mixture, garnish with chopped scallions, and "Bob's your uncle!" — you have an unforgettable dish, bound to become a classic. White rice and asparagus would please me as side dishes. This makes a great meal!

I am not going to present a classic fish soup recipe today, but rather a new-to-me and unpretentious soup that is a kind of pasta fagioli, one of my favorite soups, with seafood.

SEAFOOD MINESTRONE

2 Tbsp. olive oil

1 medium onion, chopped

1 each small zucchini and yellow squash, diced

2 leeks white and light green part, sliced 1/4" thick

3 cloves garlic, minced

1 can (14.5 ounces) diced tomatoes with juices

2 tsp. chopped fresh oregano (1 tsp. dried)

2 bay leaves

¼ tsp. crushed red pepper, or more

1 cup white wine

4 cups bottled or fresh clam broth

1 cup water or more

Salt and pepper to taste

½ cup pasta; elbow, ditalini, whatever

1/3 lb. peeled and halved shrimp

1 can (15 ounces) white cannellini beans

6 ounces fresh or canned crabmeat, monkfish, a few clams, whatever seafood you have around (about 1 ½ lbs. of seafood is adequate.)

Basil pesto for garnish (optional)

Aioli for garnish (optional)

Heat the oil in a soup pot over medium heat. Add the onions and sauté for about 6 minutes, stirring now and then; do not brown. Add the zucchini, squash, and leeks. Cook, stirring often, for 8 minutes more, add garlic and cook another minute. Stir in the tomatoes, bay leaves, oregano, red pepper, wine, clam broth, cup of water, salt and pepper. Be careful not to over salt. Bring to a boil, reduce heat, and simmer for 10 minutes.

Cook the pasta in a separate vessel until al dente (softly firm). Drain the beans and add to the simmering soup; now add whatever seafood you are using except the shrimp to the pot and heat through. Now, add the shrimp and simmer until opaque and pink; do not overcook. When shrimp are done, garnish with parsley. Serve pesto and aioli alongside the marvelous soup along with baguette slices you have toasted and rubbed with a little olive oil.

You will be famous, maybe even loved. Soup can be magical.

The cannellini beans in the last recipe reminded me of a quick, simple salad that can be the center of a lunch or served on garlic toast as a summer appetizer. This is almost sinfully simple and delicious.

CANNELLINI AND TUNA SALAD

1 can cannellini beans (15 oz.)

1 can tuna in oil (5 oz.)

2 Tbsp. chopped celery

2 Tbsp. chopped scallion

Salt and pepper

Italian salad dressing

Drain beans, mix with tuna and chopped veggies, moisten with salad dressing, and taste for seasoning.

This is good just as it is but can be tarted up if you should want to. Sliced boiled egg goes nicely with this salad. Even the "great Scott" could not improve much on this simple beauty. You could even replace the tuna with chopped clam meat.

Drum May Be Hard to Beat

Last week as I began thinking about my column, I visited the magazine's offices to see if there were any new questions for me, and to talk to our illustrious publisher, Chris Megan, about printing my cookbook. He was in a meeting, so I took my questions and left. Before I got out of the parking lot, Chris came running up, not to talk about my book, but to ask if I could make some video footage in my kitchen for the "On the Water" TV show. He had caught a 60-pound black drum the day before and hoped I could cook it that evening. I had never even seen a black drum, but figured it could not be much different from most other fish. Of course I could cook it, but whether it would be good remained to be seen.

I looked through many collections of fish cookbooks and found no black drum recipes. I then resorted to the Internet. I did find several recipes there, but only for using a 2- to 3-pound drum. In fact, one source said they were nearly inedible when over 8 pounds, and I had a 60-pound behemoth to deal with. I was pleased that the beast came already cleaned and cut into massive chunks.

Alan Davidson, in his "North Atlantic Seafood," says, "Its scales are remarkable. They are large and silvery and very firmly attached, so that a very heavy blade (or even an axe) is needed to get them off." Now that's a tough fish. I knew I would skin it.

I also found reference to a restaurant that served an all-you-can-eat entrée of barbecued drum ribs. I had never heard of fish ribs of any kind, barbecued or not. I was intrigued. When I found two sets of ribs with connective tissue attached in the package of mystery fish, I decided to improvise a recipe. I would flour the ribs and deep fry them and serve with a barbeque sauce, combining two Southern techniques.

DEEP-FRIED FISH RIBS WITH BBQ SAUCE

2 racks of drum ribs (if you can find any big enough in other fish, I am sure they would also work)
1 ½ cups all-purpose flour
½ cup cornmeal
2 tsp. salt
1 tsp. pepper
1 Tbsp. chili powder
¼ tsp. cayenne (optional)

Prepare oil for deep frying by heating to 350 to 375 degrees F. I used three quarts. Combine all the dry ingredients in a paper grocery bag. Put damp racks of ribs into bag and shake to coat evenly. Shake off excess and carefully add racks to the hot oil and fry until golden brown. Remove and degrease on towels or brown paper. Serve these with your favorite barbeque sauce that you have warmed. A little coleslaw and potato salad, and you have it – a unique meal!

I was impressed with how much these ribs had the taste and texture of pork ribs. My TV co-host Andy Nabreski thought it was more like veal or chicken. The ribs were really good! I was pleasantly surprised.

I have since learned that these ribs are prized by many on the Delmarva Peninsula during the drum's annual spring breeding run.

So now I was left with many pounds of drum fillets. I found a recipe for Creole black drum.

CREOLE BLACK DRUM

1 lb. drum fillets
¼ cup flour
½ tsp. salt
¼ tsp. black pepper

½ cup boiling water
2 Tbsp. melted butter
¼ tsp. paprika (I would use hot)
2 Tbsp. minced onions

Preheat oven to 350 degrees F. Sprinkle the drum pieces all over with salt, pepper, paprika, and flour until nicely coated.

Combine remaining ingredients and pour over the seasoned fish and bake, basting once or twice for 20 minutes. Turn the fish over and cook 8 minutes longer. Serve with boiled rice and green salad, and you have a quick, easy meal.

You could cook striped bass this way, but I would cut the cooking time in half. The above recipe worked with supposedly inedible meat from a big drum. It was good, like chicken breast or veal in texture.

I think that if you were a little dishonest, as I have been known to be, you could add an equal amount of cubed cooked drum to whatever lobster meat you have for a salad and have no one the wiser. I have been accused of doing this with monkfish. This charge has not yet been proven. I now know even large drum are not only edible, but good! I know that small drum fillets would be grand if blackened because they are close relatives of red drum. I think you could make a fine drum and noodle casserole or a fine salad using drum instead of chicken. I think it would be good in fish cakes.

DRUM CAKES (for 4)

1 ½ lbs. drum fillets
1 cup breadcrumbs
1 beaten egg
2 Tbsp. pickle relish
1 tsp. light soy sauce
3 Tbsp. butter

Poach fish in simmering water for 10 minutes, drain and mix with other ingredients. Form mixture into patties (keeping your hands wet helps in this process).

Melt butter until foaming subsides and gently sauté the patties until browned on both sides and heated through. Serve with tartar sauce and lemon quarters.

You can use this simple recipe with good results with any cooked fish.

The boss said he would show up for some of the taping and eating, but because he was so busy, he did not. I think he was either afraid of the drum or worried about my wanting to talk to him.

Floundering Around with the Boss

A couple of weeks ago my protein provider, Predator Phil, gave me a 17-pound striped bass. Phil also provides me with venison, wild boar, and ducks in season. I used this fine gift in many ways; first I made some fish prints, then I filleted and skinned the fish for eating, saving the skin and rack to make fish stock for chowder.

I gave my son-in-law and cooking rival, Scott, 4 pounds of fillets and kept nearly as much for myself. I proceeded to make a fine stock with the rack.

STRIPED BASS FISH STOCK

1 striper rack from 12 to 20 lb. fish, gills removed
2 cups white wine
1 medium onion sliced
1 carrot sliced
2 stalks of celery with leaves

6 sprigs parsley
8 peppercorns
1 tsp. thyme
¼ tsp. hot sauce (Frank's or Tabasco) optional
Salt to taste

Combine all ingredients in a large pot with water to cover, bring to a boil, turn down burner, and simmer for 20 minutes. Drain stock through a colander, and when the meat is cool enough, salvage the meat from the rack to put in a fish chowder. I ended up with about 7 cups of delicious fish broth. This broth, because of the gelatin in the bones, sets up like Jell-O when chilled.

I was proud of this stock. I used 2½ cups in a small chowder for two people, so I had 5½ cups of primo fish stock left. I could have frozen it, though my freezer was pretty full. So, I decided to offer it to son-in-law Scott, half hoping he would turn me down so that I could write snide and snotty comments about his snobbishness in this column, but he said, "Great, how much have you got?" I said, "Five and a half cups." "Good, that's just what I need for the seafood gumbo I'm making!" Damn, he took the wind out of my sails and made fine gumbo, with Paul Prodhomme's gumbo recipe as a guide. I was left with a good meal and nothing to complain about, alas.

SEAFOOD GUMBO WITH SMOKED SAUSAGE

2 cups chopped onions
1 ½ cups chopped bell peppers
1 cup chopped celery
¾ cup vegetable oil
¾ cup all-purpose flour
1 Tbsp. + 2 tsp. Chef Paul Prudhomme's Blackened Redfish Magic
1 Tbsp. chopped garlic
5 ½ cups seafood stock
1 lb. Andouille sausage (or other smoked pork sausage) cut in ½" pieces
1 lb. peeled medium shrimp
1 dozen oysters and juice
¾ lb. crabmeat
2 ½ cups cooked white rice

Gumbo

Combine onions, bell peppers, and celery in a bowl and set aside. Make a roux by heating the oil in a large heavy skillet over high heat until it just begins to smoke. Begin gradually whisking in the flour, stirring constantly until the roux is dark red/brown, about 3 minutes. Immediately add half the vegetables and stir with wooden spoon for 1 minute, add remaining vegetables and stir 2 minutes longer. Stir in the Seafood Magic seasoning and stir for 2

---

minutes longer, add garlic, stir for 1 minute more and remove from the heat.

Bring the stock to a boil in a 5½-quart pot and bring to a boil. Over high heat add the roux a spoonful at a time to the boiling stock, stirring to dissolve between additions. When all the roux has been added, reduce heat to medium, add the sliced sausage, and boil, stirring occasionally for 15 minutes. Reduce heat to low and add the seafood and stir now and then until seafood is done; do not overcook.

For serving, put ¼ cup of rice in a bowl and serve 1 cup of gumbo over each mound of rice, making sure everyone gets some of everything. This will serve 10 as a main dish.

You can substitute fish for half or all of the other seafoods. Use clams instead of oysters or any combination you desire. Be brave; it is not difficult, and it can make you famous, even loved, and certainly admired. If Scott can do it, so can you. Just a little shot – I could not pass it up.

My big boss, Chris Megan, called one morning last week to say he had just caught a bunch of blackback flounder on a shoot for the "On The Water" TV show and asked if he could come to my house to film footage of me cooking them. I jumped at the chance for two reasons: he is the head honcho and I wanted to eat some fresh flounder, a win-win situation. I had not had winter flounder for several years.

Gumbo seems complex, but sautéed or simply baked flounder could not be simpler or more delicious.

BAKED FLOUNDER FILLETS *(for 2)*

2 ½ lbs. flounder fillets
2 or 3 Tbsp. melted butter
Salt and pepper
Lemon
Parsley minced for garnish

Winter Flounder

Heat oven to 415 degrees F. Salt and pepper fish on both sides. Dip in butter and bake until white throughout, about 8 minutes.

Remove from oven, pour on more melted butter, garnish with parsley, and serve with lemon. Great!

BAKED BREADED FLOUNDER

The same ingredients as previous recipe plus a beaten egg and breadcrumbs. After dipping fillets in beaten eggs followed by breadcrumbs, proceed as in previous recipe. Tartar sauce goes nicely with these baked fillets.

SAUTÉED FLOUNDER MEUNIÈRE

Follow first recipe's ingredients again, plus some flour. Dip salt and peppered fillets in flour and sauté in skillet until brown on both sides. Put on a warm platter, add a Tbsp. of butter to hot skillet and brown slightly. Pour this over fish and serve; again, garnish with minced parsley and lemon. This is a French classic.

You will have to try hard to go wrong with these simple recipes for a delicious fish. The boss was happy after trying these dishes and left me with more flounder than I could use, so I had to give some to Scott. These recipes are even simple enough for him.

Filet Saute

Chapter Seven:
JULY

Full summer at last. Most of us will have our grills going, especially for the 4th of July. The first of the local sweet corn will be available, and the clams are there for the digging. Clams and corn seem to be made for each other. You can serve them from the grill and serve them with snail butter. My wife says you can serve shoelaces with snail butter and receive compliments. Grill the corn along with the clams. When the clams open, serve with plain or snail butter. Marvelous! You also must try the clam and corn fritters!

Barbacoa

Ask Pops

Dave,

The inshore and offshore season is upon us, and I have resolved to expand my horizons on the seafood that I eat. I love mako steaks, but I also catch and release dogfish and blue shark. I am told that some sharks, like the latter, "sweat" their urine through their skin, making them unpleasant to eat. But then I read that in Europe most of the fish and chips dinners are spiny dogs! I recall but cannot find your previous comments on preparing dogfish for consumption. In light of the season now, could I beg you to repeat the information?

In addition to the urea dilemma, I understand that blue shark meat is full of nitrogen that expands when cooked and turns the meat into an "angel food cake like" consistency. Is removing the nitrogen possible, and is it reasonable to assume the average knucklehead like me can properly prepare blue shark for eating?

Is there anything that I should know about thresher steaks? Are there other species likely to be found off the coasts of Connecticut, Rhode Island and New York?

Regards, Kevin Kiss

I don't think sharks "sweat" urine through their skins; in fact, I don't think sharks sweat at all. It is true that the skin contains urea. Because of this urea, dogfish are always skinned when being filleted. These skinned fillets are the biggest selling and cheapest fish variety available in fish and chip shops in England.

Skin, fillet, and chill your dogfish as soon as you can after catching. Prepare as you would cod or haddock.

I don't know anything about nitrogen in blue shark, but I do know the meat is soft and, to me, unpalatable. I will make no comment on the abilities of the "average knucklehead," but I suggest you release the blue. Thresher shark steaks are edible and actually quite good.

There are many more species of shark present off the south coast of New England, both inshore and offshore, but none of much culinary interest. We may be of more culinary interest to them than they are to us.

Hello, Pops,

Your articles are the last ones I read when I get my issues in the mail. I like to save the best for last!

I've bought your cookbook and have tried several recipes. My cooking is, like my fishing, hit or miss. Hopefully your cookbook will increase my "catch ratio." Anyway, I noticed that there are not any recipes with beer. I've seen plenty with wine. Have you tried cooking with beer as an ingredient? It would be great to combine my love for seafood and beer into a gastronomical pleasure!

Thanks, Matiss Purins

After reading the first sentence I almost threw this question away, but fortunately I read on and relaxed.

Here is a recipe for braising a piece of fish in foil on the grill or in a hot oven. This will work with bluefish, bass, salmon or any fish.

FISH FILLET BRAISED IN BEER

1 ½ lbs. fish fillet, in one piece
2 tsp. garlic salt
3 Tbsp. brown sugar
4 Tbsp. butter, cut in ¼" pieces
1 small red onion (white will do)
1 bottle (can) beer

Make a tray of aluminum foil to hold fillet. Put in fillet, season with salt and sugar, spread butter bits over all. Place thinly sliced onions over the top and pour in the beer. Cover the tray with aluminum foil. Put package of fish and beer over medium-hot coals, close the lid if grilling, and cook for 8 minutes; if the fish flakes easily it is done, if not, cook two more minutes.

Hooray for the Red, White, and Bluefish!

A meal of salmon, new potatoes and fresh peas has been as traditional as fireworks on the Fourth of July for many, many years, but alas, wild salmon are no longer available from New England waters. Therefore, I propose bluefish as a suitable and delicious substitute that will provide you with "fireworks" if you catch your own. A freshly caught bluefish that has been properly bled is easily as tasty as a farm-raised salmon. Both bluefish and salmon are high in omega-3 fat (the good fat) but unfortunately the farm-raised salmon may contain residual antibiotics; the bluefish will not. It is sad that no fish available in our modern world is free of harmful chemicals of some kind. Bluefish contain trace amounts of mercury and PCBs. The declining state of our earthly life-support system is truly frightening. Remember what Pogo said: "We have met the enemy and he is us." Eating ocean (saltwater) fish even three times a week is probably safe and may even be good for you, but the same cannot be said about consuming freshwater fish. As I have said before, I intend to eat fish until you will be able to tell the temperature by looking into my eyes because of the amount of mercury in my system.

Enough of that. Let us get on with preparing a red, white, and bluefish that is both patriotic and delicious. I suggest littlenecks on the half shell for starters, followed by grilled or baked whole bluefish, served with new red potatoes dredged with butter and minced parsley, and buttered tiny peas, preferably fresh, ending with strawberry shortcake. It does not get much better than this!

GRILLED WHOLE BLUEFISH #1 *(4 to 6 people)*

4 to 6 lbs. whole bluefish (scaled)
Sea salt
Freshly ground pepper
1/3 cup olive oil

Shallowly gash fish from top to bottom at 1½" intervals, salt and pepper, cover both sides with olive oil and grill.

Preheat a gas grill or prepare a charcoal fire. You want the fish to grill slowly so keep it at least six inches above the heat. Slide a spatula under the fish occasionally to prevent sticking. Turn the fish once after about 10 minutes, using two spatulas to keep it whole (for presentation on a bed of parsley or lettuce). After another eight minutes or so peek to see if meat is white to the backbone. If so, remove from heat and serve by scooping pieces out between the gashes in the skin. This is good, but for something even better try using a marinade suggested by Mark Bittman in his fine book, "Fish, A Complete Guide to Buying and Cooking."

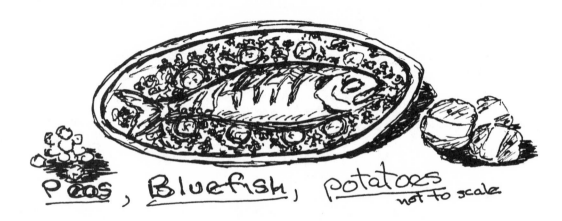

Peas, Bluefish, potatoes not to scale

MARINADE

1 cup soy sauce
½ cup dry red wine
A dash (1/2 tsp.) red or balsamic vinegar
1 inch piece fresh ginger, minced
2 Tbsp. ground cumin
4 cloves garlic, thoroughly crushed

I find it easiest to marinate a large fish by putting it in a double plastic bag, pouring in the ingredients of the marinade, and putting it in the fridge.

Mix the marinade, pour over bagged fish, and soak for at least one hour and up to 24 hours. Remove fish from marinade, pat dry, and paint both sides with olive oil, and grill as in previous recipe. You will not be sorry!

It is easier to bake the bluefish in a 415 degrees F oven for 10 minutes per inch of thickness than it is to grill it. The fish will not fall apart because you do not turn it over, you just slide a couple of spatulas under it and lift it from your roaster to your serving platter, and "Bob's your uncle"!

NEW POTATOES IN PARSLEY BUTTER

2 – 3 lbs. new red-skin potatoes (small)
½ stick butter
¼ cup minced parsley
Salt and pepper

I peel a circle around each potato, creating a kind of sexy bare midriff look. Boil or steam the potatoes until barely done, drain, pour on melted butter, add parsley and salt and pepper, and you are all set. Don't hesitate to make a lot of these; the leftovers make great home fries, to say nothing of contributing to the fish cakes you may want to make later.

TINY PEAS

1 lb. tiny peas
3 Tbsp. butter (or ¼ cup heavy cream)
Salt and pepper

Boil or steam peas until brightly colored and heated through. Mix drained peas with butter or cream in a bowl, salt and pepper to taste.

On a big platter, make a lush garland of greens around your whole fish, garnish with lemon, put the bright peas in a white bowl, and the potatoes in a heap of red, white and green and make a show of your patriotic hard work. Invite your guests to the table, pour a chilled dry white wine or crack open some beers, and celebrate the birthday of our great country and the official start of summer! You could substitute salmon for the bluefish, but I say, "Let's start a new tradition!" ◄━

Why Throw It On The Grill?

After landing a fine fish, a successful angler will often say, "I'll take this home and throw it on the grill and…" And then what? He will have either a culinary delight if done properly, or, more often, a dried out, overcooked piece of fish that falls apart as he tries to get it unstuck from the grill. Accompanied by enough beer, even this disrespected fish is edible, but for it to be good, some rules should be followed.

The fish should be cleaned as soon as possible and kept chilled until it reaches the grill. If fillets are to be grilled, they should be scaled and the skin should be left on to help hold the meat together when cooked. If the fish is large enough, steaks of individual serving size – about one-half pound – can be cut. These grill very nicely. Cooking any fish "on the bone" and with the skin left on is always more flavorful than if the fish is filleted.

Now the chef must decide if he or she wishes to marinate the fish, or merely salt and pepper it, coat it lightly with oil and "throw it on the grill." Men always say "throw it on the grill" – why not "place it" or "rest it?" I guess it sounds more masculine to "throw it." This is probably another result of the testosterone poisoning that all men must live with from time to time.

The term "barbecue" comes from the language of the Arawak tribe of Native Americans who inhabited the Caribbean Islands, the first folks Columbus mistreated in his travels. The Arawaks used wooden platforms made of saplings to cook, smoke, and dry fish and meat over an open fire. This process was done slowly, unlike our technique of quick cooking on our metal grills.

The first thing to do is prepare your fire and preheat your grill. You do not want the grill so hot that the outside of your fish is charred before the inside is cooked. A good way to test for the proper heat is to hold your hand just above the grill. If you can keep it there for 4 to 5 seconds you have the proper temperature for fish; for beefsteak, 2 seconds tolerance is about right.

When your grill is hot, clean the grates with a wire brush or steel wool and oil them lightly with vegetable oil. Soak a paper towel in a little oil and run it over the grill. I have been told that rubbing the cut surface of a raw potato on the grill will serve the same purpose. I have not tried it, but I will. This oil and potato rubbing is aimed at preventing the fish from sticking to the grill.

Now, we are ready to cook our fish. I find that a liberal sprinkling of salt (I like kosher or sea salt) and freshly ground or cracked pepper (I prepare mine with a mortar and pestle on site) and a light coating of olive oil on the fish to be an adequate treatment.

Many people like to marinate fish before grilling. If you wish to marinate your fish, keep the marinade simple and don't soak the fish for longer than half an hour. Commercial vinaigrettes or premixed salad dressings are good, or mix your own with olive oil, crushed garlic, salt and pepper, and lemon juice.

MARINADE #1 (for 2 lbs. fish)

1/3 cup soy sauce
2 Tbsp. olive oil
Mix together and soak your fish.

MARINADE #2

1/3 cup olive oil
2 Tbsp. lemon juice
1 crushed clove of garlic
½ tsp. ground pepper
1 tsp. salt
Mix well and add to fish.

Barbacoa

A plastic zipper-lock bag is a great vessel for marinating anything.

Now we have the fish oiled and seasoned, the grill is at the proper temperature, and we are ready to go.

Remember the general fish-cooking rule of about 10 minutes of cooking for every inch of thickness at 425 degrees F. I think 7 or 8 minutes total time on the grill is about right.

Put your fillets, skin-side down, or your steaks on the grill. Allow them to cook for at least two minutes before you succumb to sliding a spatula under them to see if they are sticking. After about 4 minutes for fillets and 5 minutes for steaks, turn them carefully. Use two spatulas for fillet flipping.

The fish is done when it is opaque all the way through. You can check by opening it at the thickest point using a knife point, or use an instant thermometer; 120 to 130 degrees F is desirable. The fish will cook slightly after you remove it from the grill.

This simple fish dressed with only lemon is delicious. I had not said, but I have been thinking about striped bass all along. Serve this on a bed of wilted spinach with garlic and olive oil, and your renown will widen. Add one or the other of the seasoned butters listed below after cooking the fish, and you may become insufferable.

ANCHOVY BUTTER
2 sticks unsalted butter, softened
2 Tbsp. lemon juice
1 can anchovies in oil (2-oz.)
25 mint leaves (optional, but great!)
Freshly ground pepper

You can mash the ingredients together by hand in a mortar with a pestle until smooth, or use a food processor. Put butter in processor, add lemon juice, pepper and, if you wish, mint leaves, and blend until smooth.

SNAIL BUTTER *(Garlic and Parsley Butter, normally used on escargot)*
1 stick butter (unsalted) or margarine
1 Tbsp. lemon juice
½ tsp. salt
Freshly ground pepper
3 cloves minced garlic
3 Tbsp. chopped parsley

Process butter until smooth, add lemon juice, seasonings and garlic and mix thoroughly – fold in the parsley or just throw it in and give it a pulse or two.

Shape these butters into logs, wrap with plastic and store in your fridge. Cut off a Tbsp. or so and let it melt over your grilled fish, and look out for happiness. Don't just "throw it" on the grill, treat it with a little care and present it nicely – works better than testosterone! ◀█

A Philosophy of Sausage?
How Good Can It Be?

I had previously written in my column about a seafood sausage I once had as an appetizer at Chanterelle, a world-class Manhattan restaurant. That sausage was one of the very best things I had eaten in my life. I would never have tasted this ambrosial sausage but for the generosity of my stepdaughter, Elisabeth Swan, and her husband, Scott Britton. They took my wife, Jeanne, and me on a weekend of cultural and culinary exploration in New York City as a birthday reward for our combined ages nearing 150 years.

Scott often appears in this column as a rival for the position of head cook in our family. I think I will grant him the title and settle for head bread baker. All that is beside the point, however. Scott, a culinary adventurer and explorer, enjoyed the sausage as much as I did, and we decided to try to duplicate the recipe or devise a reasonable facsimile. We rifled through our memory banks, Googled and searched the Web, and finally found the following recipe, allegedly the grail of seafood sausage itself. Last week Scott and I made the sausage. It was a grand success!

We made one fathom of sausage meant to serve as an appetizer course for eight. A single serving at Chanterelle costs $16, so we created $128 worth of sausage. Scott provided the kitchen, kitchen gear, sausage casings, booze, and pignoli nuts. I provided the seafood.

Our local fishmonger, Peter Fisher of Cataumet Fish, kindly sells my cookbook for me and owed me $75 from book sales (Peter pays me in seafood), so that amount plus $14 more bought the seafood. Our $128 worth of seafood cost us about $90 to make, along with four man-hours of work. This is valuable stuff.

GRILLED SEAFOOD SAUSAGE WITH BEURRE BLANC SAUCE

2 egg whites

½ tsp. salt

2 lbs. tilefish or black sea bass (we used cod), cut in ½-inch cubes

2 cups heavy cream

Note: The above ingredients should be very cold before proceeding.

1 lb. fresh shrimp, peeled, deveined and coarsely chopped

1 lb. sea scallops, coarsely chopped

2 lobsters (1½ lb. each), cooked, shelled and coarsely chopped

2 oz. pignoli nuts, toasted

Salt

Cayenne pepper

Port

Brandy

Pork casings, cleaned

Nutmeg, optional

Combine chilled egg whites, salt and fish in either a blender or a food processor. Puree, gradually adding the heavy cream. Pour mixture into a metal or glass mixing bowl. Add shrimp, scallops, lobster and toasted pignoli nuts. Mix well and season with salt (I would start with 1 tsp.), cayenne pepper (1/4 tsp.), port (1 ounce), brandy (1 ounce) – all of these are to taste. Stuff the mixture into casings (not too tightly). Tie off into 4- to 6-inch links.

Poach in water over a low fire until thoroughly heated and water has approached (but not passed) the simmering point. Submerge sausage. If the water boils, the sausage will burst. Remove from stove and cool in the poaching liquid. Chill. At serving time, heat oven to 350 degrees F. Slash the top of the sausage at intervals and brush with butter.

Broil until just slightly browned. Place in oven until warmed through.

Serve over beurre blanc sauce. I like the sausage served with melted butter and lemon, but the beurre blanc will impress the heck out of your guests.

BEURRE BLANC SAUCE

¼ cup finely chopped shallots
¼ cup red wine vinegar
½ bottle white wine
3 Tbsp. heavy cream
¾ lb. cold sweet (unsalted) butter cut into small cubes
Salt
Pepper
Tarragon (optional)

In a non-aluminum pot, reduce vinegar, white wine, and shallots until almost dry – the stuff should be syrupy. Add the cream and reduce by half. Put over low heat and gradually whisk in the butter. Season with salt. Add additional vinegar if needed.

It is likely that not many of you will try this, but if you do, I promise you will not be sorry! For me this was one of the best things I have ever taken part in preparing. You cannot go wrong when every ingredient you use is delicious all by itself. Just don't do anything to destroy it.

Now we get to my philosophical dilemma regarding this aristocrat of sausages. I see sausage as more of a working-class product made from the scraps, weird bits, extremities, and trimmings left after butchering a large animal. For example, we have haggis (essentially a big sausage), blood sausage, various liver sausages, hot dogs (whose contents may include things too fierce to mention), and bologna, another mystery meat. All of these sausages are greater than the sum of their parts, but I cannot say that about this glorious fish sausage. Each part is great to begin with, so its construction may be likened to gilding a bouquet of already lovely lilies – yet it is still sausage, an almost reverential sausage, the summit of sausage making!

I could go on musing about sausage existentialism, but I will not. I can hear a collective sigh of relief from my readers, but I still feel ambivalent about seafood sausage being grouped in the sausage lexicon.

Be that as it may, you will benefit from making this ethereal sausage at least once in your life. Follow the directions carefully, pour some beurre blanc on a plate, adorn it with this celestial sausage, serve it up to loved ones, enjoy your own, and bask in the accolades you will so rightfully have earned. Go for it – ambivalent or not!

Azzuro - Blue

Yesterday evening my dogs and I went to the Bell Road parking lot at the west end of the Cape Cod Canal to hobnob and check out the fishing. This is the last week of May, so the fish should be here and active. The "Canal Rats" were lining the rip-rap and the fish were breaking far out in the current. The tide was nearly slack, an ideal situation for surface plugs. The boys were hard at it and were taking fish, both bass and blues. The bass were as big as 25 pounds, and 6-pound blues were being thrown back.

For some reason, many fishermen have little respect for blues, though they fight much harder, pound-for-pound, than a bass does, and if bled immediately upon being landed, provide what many feel to be more flavorful meat than that of striped bass. I love them both. I have eaten bass several times already this spring, so I asked for one of the about-to-be-discarded bluefish and was given it. I bled it immediately and will have it for dinner this evening. I am not too proud to accept free fish. They taste just as good, and I do not lose gear catching them.

This was a very successful visit to the Canal for the dogs and myself. I got to tell lies with the two-legged "Canal Rats," and my terriers got to seek the many four-legged rats that live in the rip-rap.

I even sold a cookbook. The dogs found some aged menhaden to eat and roll on. So I went home with a 6-pound bluefish, a $20 bill, and two smelly and happy dogs – altogether an exciting and profitable excursion.

I will cook the bluefish using one of the following recipes. I am writing in late May, and you will read this in July, when the bass fishing will slow somewhat but the blues will be readily available, with the exception of brief periods when they mysteriously disappear — but that's another story. Let us deal with the fish we have in hand.

For years I have been extolling a recipe from Marcello Hazan, a great Italian cook, that I call the "World's Best Bluefish Recipe," made simply from potatoes, parsley, garlic, olive oil and bluefish. I will now present two more recipes for bluefish from the same source that may be as delicious. Marcella Hazan writes, "Azzuro – 'blue' – is what in Italy we call all such dark-fleshed fish as tuna, mackerel, sardines, and anchovies. These species, and several of their related varieties, are dense in the Italian seas, yet among them there is nothing to surpass a freshly caught Atlantic bluefish." This is praise indeed for the oft-maligned bluefish. Hazan goes on, "Freshly caught [and bled - my addition] is the necessary distinction, because the oils that make the flesh of this fish sweet and succulent begin to turn rancid and sharp within 36 to 48 hours after it is landed."

BLUEFISH WITH BAKED ONIONS, PEPPERS AND POTATOES

2 large red bell peppers
½ lb. new or boiling potatoes
¼ cup olive oil
3 medium onions, sliced thinly, about 3 cups
1 large clove garlic, sliced very thin
Salt and freshly ground black pepper
2 lbs. bluefish fillets with skin on
1 Tbsp. fine breadcrumbs

Bluefish Filets

Preheat oven to 415 degrees F. Split peppers lengthwise, remove seeds and pulp, and peel with a swivel peeler (not as hard as you may think). Now slice the peeled peppers in ½-inch wide strips. Peel the potatoes and slice very thin.

Choose an ovenproof casserole pan or Pyrex dish that can hold all the ingredients. Pour in 3 Tbsp. olive oil, add all other ingredients except fish and breadcrumbs, and mix thoroughly, salt lightly, and pepper generously. Bake this mélange in upper third of hot oven until veggies are tender, usually 30 to 45 minutes.

Turn vegetables after 15 minutes. Turn on broiler.

Push veggies to center of pan and lay bluefish on each side. Salt and pepper the fish, sprinkle with breadcrumbs and drizzle with oil, put under broiler at least 4 inches from flame. After 7 minutes, turn veggies over and broil about 7 minutes more, or until fish flakes. Spread some of the veggies over the fish, allow to settle for a couple of minutes and serve. Brilliant!!

You can bake the vegetables ahead of time and reheat them as you cook this fish at serving time. If you don't want to risk the broiling, merely bake the fish until its cooked. The only ways to go wrong are to burn the veggies or overcook the fish – now you wouldn't do that, would you?

BAKED BLUEFISH WITH LEEKS AND POTATOES

4 good-sized leeks
3 Tbsp. extra virgin olive oil
Salt and freshly ground black pepper
2 lbs. potatoes
3 Tbsp. butter
¼ cup freshly grated Parmigiano-Reggiano
2 Tbsp. breadcrumbs
2 lbs. bluefish fillets, skin on

Bluefish, peppers, and leeks.

Slice white parts of leeks into thin rounds, put in a s[...] cup water. Cover pan and simmer over low heat until leeks are reduced to a soft pulp. Remove from heat and add 2 Tbsp. of butter, stirring until melted.

Preheat oven to 450 degrees F. Choose a baking dish that will hold fillets without overlapping, butter the bottom, add sliced potatoes and leeks with juices and salt and pepper. Spread evenly over bottom of dish (you can stand some potatoes up on the sides for crispy wonder) and bake for 30 minutes – potatoes should be browning on edges. Combine Parmesan and breadcrumbs and sprinkle 2 or 3 Tbsp. over leeks and potatoes and bake 5 more minutes.

Lay fish fillets on potato-leek mixture, salt and pepper, cover with remaining cheese and breadcrumb mixture and dot with remaining butter. Return pan to oven and bake for 10 minutes or slightly longer, then run under the broiler for 2 or 3 minutes to form a light crust over fish. This broiling is a great touch, but optional – you already have a grand dish. Congratulations.

SIMPLE BAKED BLUEFISH (for 4 or 6)

2 lbs. bluefish fillets
½ cup milk
Salt and pepper
1 cup breadcrumbs
½ lb. butter (great, but ¼ LB. will do)
2 Tbsp. lemon juice
½ cup seafood seasoning (Old Bay, Zatarian's - I think ¼ cup is enough, suit yourself)

Preheat oven to 415 degrees F. Salt and pepper fish, dip in milk and then in breadcrumbs. Put in baking dish, sprinkle with seasoning and lemon juice, dot with butter and bake for 10 to 12 minutes until fish just flakes. Simple and delicious.

I would serve with potato salad and coleslaw or mashed potatoes and tiny peas. You cannot go wrong, at least with these recipes. Bravo! Bluefish!

Does Size Always Count?
What is Clampacho?

I am worried about the striped bass stock in general and schoolie stripers in particular. Where are they? The big bass are getting scarcer, also. We are more than two weeks into the commercial striper season here in Massachusetts and only about one quarter of the quota has been taken. In recent past years the quota has often been filled in less than a month. I spoke to my friend "Predator" Phil Stanton, and he agrees that, though he has taken bass from 12 inches to 40-plus inches this year, the bass population is down in Vineyard Sound and Buzzards Bay. Maybe the time has come to consider all possibilities to preserve this resource and fishing tradition; maybe "catch and release" is the way to go. Maybe a fisherman could buy a certain number of tags each season to allow taking trophy fish.

Hey, this is supposed to be a cooking column, so I will try to get back on track. I can connect my sentiments to cooking by again pushing my "one fish a day, any size" idea so that I can keep a 4- or 5-pound striped bass, which contains fewer toxins than a big, old cow, and I'd use it for baking and stuffing. If I had one, I would stuff it with clams, onions, breadcrumbs, etc., but since this would be illegal, I will not present the recipe.

A guy called me last week looking to buy a cookbook or two and to offer me a bunch of tiny quahogs, ¼ inches to ¾ inches in size, slightly larger than most seed. He had bought these to seed a grant that he thought he had, but was then denied. He felt he could not just strew them anywhere, so he decided to see if I wanted to cook some of the little beauties. I said yes, I would like some and would use them to see if tiny clams would taste different in a white clam sauce for spaghetti.

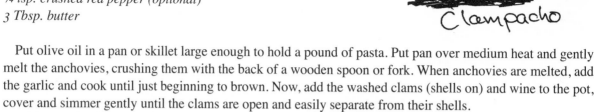

Clampacho

TINY OR SMALL CLAM AND ANCHOVY PASTA SAUCE *(for 4)*
1 lb. spaghetti or linguine
4 dozen of the smallest hard clams you can find (within reason)
1 can anchovy fillets (about 8 fillets)
4 Tbsp. olive oil
¼ cup white wine (dry)
1 tsp. freshly ground black pepper
2 or 3 cloves garlic, coarsely chopped
½ cup packed chopped flat-leaved Italian parsley
¼ tsp. crushed red pepper (optional)
3 Tbsp. butter

Put olive oil in a pan or skillet large enough to hold a pound of pasta. Put pan over medium heat and gently melt the anchovies, crushing them with the back of a wooden spoon or fork. When anchovies are melted, add the garlic and cook until just beginning to brown. Now, add the washed clams (shells on) and wine to the pot, cover and simmer gently until the clams are open and easily separate from their shells.

While all this is going on you should be boiling your pasta until al dente, about a minute less than recommended on the package. Drain the pasta, saving a cup of pasta water.

Now, stir butter and parsley, black pepper and optional red pepper into the clams, wine and oil. Add cooked pasta to the clam pan and stir until thoroughly mixed. It is now ready to serve.

If pasta seems dry, add either pasta water or more butter. Purists do not eat cheese on clam-sauced spaghetti, but I do and love it.

You can make this same recipe with mussels without regret, or you can mix clams and mussels. Go for it! If you use mussels, triple the amount of wine, for they produce less liquid.

CLAM PASTA FRITTATA (sounds nice)

2 cups (or more) pasta and sauce
2 eggs per person

Put pasta and egg mixture in a skillet or ovenproof pan and bake in a 350 degrees F oven until the whole works puffs up and browns a bit and the eggs are no longer liquid in the center. Serve hot, lukewarm, or at room temperature.

This is very good. I make mine with Egg Beaters, which work very well. You cannot go wrong except by overcooking. Do it!

My daughter Amanda brought me a mess of quahogs last week, which I chilled in the refrigerator. They will keep up to two weeks; never store them covered with water when they are alive, for they will suffocate.

I was making gazpacho, a Spanish tomato-based soup served cold in summer, and decided I would make one of tomatoes, raw peppers, onions and clams, using clam juice instead of water while being careful not to make it too salty. It was a rousing success.

CLAM GAZPACHO A LA "POPS" – CLAMPACHO!

3 lbs. ripe tomatoes, peeled, seeded and chopped
1 sweet red pepper, chopped
1 cucumber, chopped
2 scallions whole, chopped
¼ cup chopped cilantro (optional, but desirable)
1 large clove garlic, chopped
¼ cup wine vinegar
½ cup virgin olive oil
2 cups clam juice (from steaming clams open)
1 cup tomato juice
12 or so littlenecks or cherrystones
Tabasco to taste

Steam quahogs open, saving juice. Finely mince or process until fine but not pureed. Set aside.

Set aside a cup of chopped tomato, cucumber, scallion and pepper for garnishing. Put the rest of the ingredients in a food processor and puree. Now stir in the chopped clams, add garnish and stir. If the soup is too thick and not too salty, add more clam juice.

At this point I add black pepper and Tabasco. Now put the whole works in the fridge, preferably overnight, so the flavors can blend. Taste for salt and vinegar before serving. This can be ambrosial. I like to garnish mine with freshly chopped scallion and cilantro. A great soup for summers, or any other time.

By the way, the spaghetti made with seed clams was no better than one made with large ones, and a pain in the butt to eat – so I (legally?) seeded the several-hundred extras. Try the Clampacho! ◀━

Chapter Eight:
AUGUST

The month of bluefish. The world's best bluefish recipe is here, once again. It will appear in my column once a year for as long as I last. Remember to bleed these blues as soon as you catch them! Ice them down or damp–bag them and gut them as soon as you can.

Bluefish, handled properly, are among the world's best fish, despite what many piscatorial philistines may claim.

Dear Pops,

My questions concern sushi, of which I am particularly fond. I lived on the West Coast for a while and know there are parasites in some Pacific fish that parasitize California sea lions and can also infect humans should one eat raw fish that carry these parasites.

Do saltwater fish off our coast contain these or similar parasites that can infect humans? Although we don't have sea lions, we do have harbor seals. Not knowing has kept me from turning the local fish I catch into sushi.

I have made some delicious sushi rolls from some large brook and brown trout fillets taken from Cape Cod ponds and have received rave reviews from all who have tried them. I thought they would be safe, but later I thought maybe otter carry these same parasites in fresh water. Are there otter in Cape ponds? Do they carry parasites that can infect humans? Are some species safer than others?

Charlie Woods

Saltwater fish off our coast do contain the same and similar parasites to those on the West Coast. We have harbor seals here and a rapidly growing population of gray, or horse-head, seals. Even though some of these parasites can be harmful, they can be avoided by carefully examining the fish you are going to consume. You may wish to "candle" them. To candle, you hold the fillets in front of a bright light to show silhouettes of any parasites that may be lurking within.

Freshwater fish carry more parasites that are potentially more dangerous to humans than those in salt water – tapeworms, for one. In fact, many people, including experts, say that freshwater fish should never be eaten raw.

Otters do carry parasites and are intermediate hosts in the life cycle of parasites that appear in fish, and yes, there are otters in Cape Cod ponds.

Local saltwater fish may be eaten raw in sushi if examined carefully; freshwater fish should not be eaten raw. Trout sashimi is not a good idea, though you could probably eat it for years without serious consequences.

Hey, Pops!

A friend gave me an assignment the other day that I couldn't refuse. He asked me to eat a dogfish to confirm or deny the rumors that we hear about it being used as fish in the fish n' chips they serve in England.

I caught a smooth dogfish soon thereafter, bled it, and battered the fillet chunks and fried them. It was delicious!

The success I had has emboldened me, and I want to try to confirm or deny another rumor. I have heard for years about how skate are used as a replacement for scallops. It was fairly easy to fillet the dogfish, but I wouldn't know where to start on the skate or what parts to try to eat. Do you have any advice?

Jay Baver

I fail to see how the fact that you did or did not enjoy eating dogfish has any bearing upon the "rumor" that dogfish are eaten in fish-and-chips shops in England. However, they are eaten, and they are relished. At one time they were euphemistically referred to as rock salmon, but now they are called dogfish or shark and are usually the least costly fish on the menu. I like them!

My friend Dick Backus, retired head fish-man from the Woods Hole Oceanographic Institute, tells me that unscrupulous fishmongers have used plugs taken from skates' wings and sold them as scallops. I trust him, but think these "scallops" must have been sold to landlubbers. I don't think you could fool me with a skate scallop, but I suppose… No, you couldn't fool me.

Skate are delicious but a pain to prepare for the table. The wings are cut away from the body and then skinned, leaving a nice slab of meat. The skate's skin is full of tiny sharp scales that will rub you raw after a while if you don't wear gloves as you handle them.

All "Blues" Are Not Sad

High summer is here and so are all the fish that come with it, so let us catch some and cook them properly.

It is difficult to write column after column without getting both repetitive and boring for the reader, to say nothing of boring for me, but why should you care about my boredom?

Well, I know one creature that is never boring, either to catch or to eat, and that's the much-maligned bluefish. Respected by all as a magnificent fighter, it's a dangerous fish to handle, and when properly dealt with, delicious to eat. The bluefish is disliked by many for being oily, "fishy-tasting," and even repellent when cooked. These negative reactions are always about fish that were poorly handled when caught. Fishermen often catch blues quickly and in large numbers when the beasts are surface feeding, and in the excitement of the moment, the fish are thrown to the deck or put in boxes and forgotten until the commotion of the blitz is over, the tangled lines are straightened out, and the gear is overhauled. Then the fishermen must talk over the action before finally getting to the now dead fish cooking in the boxes or festering in the sun. Some people ignore this fish until they reach the dock, where they unload the spoiled fish to generously give it to their friends and neighbors, who soon learn to dislike the noble fish.

Every summer I write to exhort my readers to bleed each bluefish as it comes aboard. This is simply, though dangerously, accomplished by making an incision just behind the point where the gill covers come together on the underside of the fish. Do this carefully, for the sharp teeth and strong jaws and pugnacity of a bluefish will make short work of the flesh on a finger or thumb! I speak from experience. Large blues over 6 pounds should be dispatched with a "priest" or club of some sort applied vigorously to the top of the head before you make the bleeding incision. (The name "priest" for the chosen bludgeon is apt, for it applies the "last rites" to the fish.) I keep a bucket half-filled with water into which I put the fish after cutting its throat, to keep most of the blood off of the boat. As soon as the fish is bled out, I put it on ice or in a wet burlap sack, if ice is not available. Evaporation from the wet sack will keep the fish cool for as long as the sack remains damp. I then gut the fish as soon as possible, usually while still at sea.

If you follow my instructions, you will have a fine, generous gift for friends and neighbors who will no longer hide when they see you coming with "fresh" fish. In fact, they will greet you with open arms and thank you profusely, especially if you convince them to prepare the bounty you have provided in the following manner, using what I call the world's best bluefish recipe.

This recipe is not my own but came from Marcella Hazan's "More Classic Italian Cooking," published by Knopf in 1978. I have written of the recipe almost annually for the past eight years because I think it is important for the reputation of the bluefish as a culinary joy and for you and your reputation as a culinary treasure to your friends and family. It is also easily prepared. What more could you ask for in a recipe?

Olive Oil, Parsley, Garlic, Bluefish

BAKED BLUEFISH WITH POTATOES, GENOESE-STYLE ("THE WORLD'S BEST BLUEFISH RECIPE") (for 6)

2 bluefish fillets (skin on, about 1 lb. each)
1½ lbs. boiling potatoes
2/3 cup olive oil
1 Tbsp. chopped garlic
¼ cup chopped parsley
Salt and pepper

Preheat the oven to 450 degrees F.

Peel and slice the potatoes thinly (about 1/8 inch thick). Mix the potatoes with half the garlic, half the parsley, half the olive oil and a liberal amount of salt and pepper in a 16x10-inch casserole dish, preferably enameled cast iron. Arrange the potatoes evenly over the bottom and sides of the dish, place it in the upper third of the preheated oven, and bake for 15 minutes.

Remove the dish and place the fillets, skin side down, on the potatoes. Mix the remaining olive oil, garlic and parsley and pour over the fillets. Salt and pepper liberally and return the casserole to the oven for 10 minutes. Remove the dish from the oven and, using a spoon, baste the fish and exposed potatoes with some of the oil in dish. Loosen the browned potatoes from the sides of the dish and replace with unbrowned potatoes from the dish bottom. Bake 5 minutes more.

Serve piping hot directly from the casserole dish, scraping up browned potatoes stuck to the pan. Marcella says, "These are the most delectable bits, so save them for yourself or for someone you like nearly as well."

I sometimes use two baking dishes and twice as many potatoes with the same amount of fish to provide more of these "delectable bits." My family has almost come to blows over these browned potatoes. Does it matter which is tastier, the potatoes or the fish? Who cares? Go for it! Fame and glory or even appreciation comes seldom enough for the home cook.

This simple recipe is not only outstanding, but versatile; you can cook any firm-fleshed fish in this way. It's great with swordfish (if you don't dry it out), salmon, mackerel, and very good with striped bass; you almost cannot go wrong. The only dangers are not precooking the potatoes long enough or that most serious of culinary transgressions, overcooking the seafood. Try it with shrimp, scallops or both; or with squid, precooked octopus or a mélange of the whole works. You will not be sorry, and your renown will grow. I promise!

"Come Fry with Me...."

I love fried fish; deep fried, pan fried, or oven fried! I can sense the health food crowd groaning as they read this, but if they read and absorb a few simple rules they need not absorb large amounts of fat. I believe frying is the most common method of cooking fish in Western civilization; e.g. the ubiquitous fish and chip shops in Great Britain, the clam shacks and seafood emporiums of North America, and all the fast-food joints everywhere. The two basic rules to reduce fat in the final product are to have your frying medium (fat) at the proper temperature and to drain and soak up all remaining fat from your finished product. Fish should be fried in oil or other fat at 350-375 degrees F temperature and then drained on brown paper bags or paper towels before serving. The fish should have a delicious, crisp crust, a fine golden color and a succulent interior. This fine product can be prepared quickly and easily, especially if you have a nonstick skillet.

I believe that pan-frying and oven-frying should be used in home cooking and that deep-frying should be left to the professionals with professional gear. Heating large quantities of oil in the home kitchen is both awkward and dangerous, to say nothing of expensive and messy.

However, if you are one who deep-fries turkeys, you have the gear and the grease to deep-fry at home, outdoors I hope. It is great fun at a cookout to have a "fry master" turning out platters of mixed seafood: clams, oysters, shrimp, various fish, squid and (if you are rich) softshelled crabs. This "master" can also throw in a few batter-dipped vegetables: green or red peppers, zucchini, eggplant, sweet potato, and cauliflower. Have tartar sauce, cocktail sauce, ketchup, hot sauce, and lemons ready on a communal table, and you have a festival – a little cold, cheap wine and cold beer won't hurt a bit. Provide damp towels, and you won't even need silverware.

BIG BATCH BEER BATTER

3 cups all-purpose flour
½ cup cornstarch
1 Tbsp. salt
1 ½ tsp. paprika
Dash nutmeg (optional)
3 cups of beer
3 Tbsp. cooking oil

Mix all the dry ingredients, add the liquids, and stir until smooth. Let this stand about an hour before using. Enough for five or six pounds of seafood.

You can double, triple, or whatever to get the amount of batter you need.

The fry cook should cut his fish so that it all cooks and is done at the same time. Fish fillets should be no more than 1/2-inch thick; at this thickness the fish will be done as soon as the color is right if the oil temperature is no lower than 350 degrees F and no higher than 375 degrees F. At this temperature, squid, scallops or shrimp will not over-cook before turning golden brown.

The fry cook should dredge the seafood in a mixture of flour and cornstarch (I like to add cayenne pepper) before dipping in batter.

If you can find a charcoal grill "master," you might serve marvelous Italian-grilled vegetables dressed with olive oil and lemon juice. You will not be sorry, I promise! This "master" can also satisfy those Philistines who won't eat seafood with a burger or a "dog."

ITALIAN CHARCOAL-BROILED VEGETABLES *(for 8)*

4 ripe tomatoes
2 medium eggplants
2 large flat sweet onions
4 medium zucchini
½ lb. mushrooms
Olive oil
Salt and pepper
Lemon juice

Grill vegetables
Fry animals

Peel the onions and split horizontally, cut tomatoes in half horizontally. Split eggplants lengthwise, make crossed incisions in flesh, salt liberally, and let stand on end for 15 minutes to drain. Cut the zucchini in lengthwise 3/8-inch slices.

Light charcoal. When flames subside a bit, put onions on grill, cut-side down. Put the peppers on the grill to char the skin thoroughly. When onions are charred black, don't worry, turn them over and move them to sides of the grill, and anoint each slice with a Tbsp. of olive oil and 1/2 tsp. of salt.

Meanwhile, keep turning the peppers until charred all over. While they are charring, put tomatoes on grill, cut-side down.

Remove peppers from grill and remove charred skin as soon as you can handle them (assign this job to a hanger-on), cut lengthwise into 1-inch strips, and put in a bowl.

When tomatoes char slightly, turn them over and salt them. Cook them until they shrink a bit and add to peppers in the bowl.

Now scrape some of charred surface off onions, cut in quarters, and add to bowl.

Put 1 Tbsp. olive oil on each eggplant surface and grill until browned but not charred, turn over, oil again and cook until soft. Meanwhile put zucchini on the grill and brown on one side. Pour mushrooms on grill; they will cook in two minutes. Add the whole works to tomatoes and onions and peppers, salt and pepper liberally, add about ¼ cup of lemon juice and 1/3 cup of olive oil to the veggies, and have at it! You will not regret a minute of it, and your "masters" will be famous, as will you, even if you farmed out the cooking and supervised – a good idea! Right?

The vegetable grilling may sound complicated, but it is not difficult once you get into it, especially if you get someone else to peel the charred peppers. Even out of season, supermarket tomatoes develop a fine flavor when cooked this way, especially if you put some chopped parsley, garlic, and a bit of breadcrumbs on them during their final cooking.

Take advantage of this grand season and have a magnificent outdoor fish and vegetable feast. You could even cook the last of your seafood on the grill, and since it isn't breaded, make it into a mixed seafood salad – hey, another column.

Try this and enrich your own and your friends lives! ◄►

Again, and Again, and Again...

I have been accused of repeating myself on many occasions, but I do not think repetition is such a bad thing, especially if you're onto something good. I can think of one thing in particular that fits this category, but we cannot go into the details of that in a family magazine. Remember, most cooking involves variations on a theme, and when you have a good one, go with it! I am going to do that now in this column, using dishes I have written about before and for which I have recently prepared new variations that were outstanding, at least in my not-so-humble opinion!

The first will be for baked white-fleshed fish with tomatoes, in a Portuguese manner, a dish that can be prepared for twelve almost as easily as for two. It presents beautifully and can be served with various carriers with equal success, including plain boiled potatoes, mashed potatoes, pasta, or rice. It should be part of every cook's repertoire, as the creative cook can vary this dish in an infinite number of ways. It can accommodate fillets, steaks, or whole fish. I suggest that you start with my recipe and then go on to construct your own. I am going to use striped bass in my version because I usually have it on hand in summer, but you can substitute haddock, cod, pollack, hake, or even swordfish with delicious results. So, here goes.

STRIPED BASS WITH TOMATO AND CILANTRO

1 lb. striped bass fillet
1 can tomatoes with green chiles (14½-oz.)
1 tsp. powdered cumin
8 black or calamata olives, pitted and cut in half
8 green olives, halved
Salt and pepper
Hot sauce to taste
1 packet Goya Sazon seasoning with azafran (saffron) or achiote (annatto) — optional, but very good
1 Tbsp. olive oil
1/4 cup breadcrumbs
1/2 cup chopped cilantro (or parsley)

Preheat oven to 415 degrees F. Lightly oil a combination baking and serving dish that's just big enough to hold the fish and sauce while still leaving the fish's top surface exposed. Put fish in dish, surround with tomato, cumin, and olives. Add salt, pepper, and hot sauce to taste and the contents of a Goya seasoning packet, if desired. Sprinkle breadcrumbs on the fish and drizzle with olive oil. Put in the oven for 15 to 20 minutes, and there you have it, a fine main course! Garnish the dish with chopped cilantro and a few slices of lemon and you will have a dish both beautiful and delicious, I promise. Accompany this with a green salad or tiny peas and mashed potatoes and you will be lauded, perhaps loved.

I sometimes add a few shrimp, arranged around the fish, during the last 5 to 10 minutes of cooking. I also sometimes add a half-glass (4 oz.) of white wine before baking. You can sauté some chopped linguica or chourico in oil in the pan before adding the tomatoes. The possibilities are endless; scallops, mussels and/or clams can be added. (If you add clams, also add a little salt.)

You can start with diced tomatoes with Italian seasoning, add some tomato paste, 1 tsp. of sugar, 1 tsp. of oregano and/or basil, some chopped flat-leaf parsley, and there you have baked fish to go with pasta. You cannot go wrong except by using too much red pepper, over salting or overcooking the fish, but it is hard to dry the fish out with this method. Remember, the fish is done when it flakes all the way through.

I cannot urge you strongly enough to try this method and make your fish-cooking life easier. I guarantee an increase in fame, but you are on your own with love and fortune.

I will also guarantee success with the following recipe, which is based on the one I keep repeating for the good of everyone. "The World's Best Bluefish Recipe" can be made using farm-raised salmon, which is always available when we do not have a catch of our own. Let's not kid ourselves, for most of us this is the normal situation, so we should be prepared to "catch" something at the market and prepare it well.

SALMON BAKED WITH TARRAGON (for 4)

1½ to 2 lbs. boiling potatoes
2/3 cup olive oil
1/4 cup (or more) chopped parsley
1 Tbsp. (or more) chopped garlic
Salt and pepper
1½ lb. to 2 lb. salmon fillet or steak
1/4 cup chopped fresh tarragon

Preheat oven to 450 degrees F. Slice potatoes thinly and line the sides and bottom of a 16x10-inch bake-and-serve dish, preferably enameled cast iron. Put half the oil, parsley, garlic and salt and pepper in the pan and mix thoroughly (I use my hands). Arrange the potatoes like tiles or shingles on the sides and bottom of pan. Bake for 15 minutes, remove from oven, and place fish on partly cooked potatoes. Top the fish with remaining parsley, tarragon, oil, salt and pepper and return to oven for another 12 to 15 minutes. After 10 minutes, baste fish with pan juices and check for doneness. The salmon should not flake all the way through, but should be reddish-pink in the center. Garnish with lemon slices and serve to applause if they have any sense at all, and cheers after they have eaten. Go for it; you will not go wrong.

I cannot kill my own salmon, but I can catch scup, which can be cooked simply and elegantly in the following manner.

SCUP BRAISED SOUP-STYLE (for 2)

2 one-pound scup, whole or beheaded
1/3 cup minced onion
1 tsp. chopped garlic
2 Tbsp. chopped parsley
1/4 cup white wine
1/2 cup chopped plum tomatoes and juice
Salt and pepper

Braised Scup

Heat a saucepan large enough to hold both fish over medium heat. Saute onion until translucent and add garlic and sauté to a light golden color. Add parsley and white wine, followed by chopped tomatoes, and simmer gently for 5 minutes. Now add fish to pan, cover and simmer over medium-low heat for 5 minutes. Uncover, turn over fish, add salt and pepper, simmer 5 more minutes, and there you have it.

I would serve this right out of the pan with crusty bread, a glass of wine, and a green salad. I would be proud to serve this to anyone on earth, even (what's her name?) Martha Stewart. ◀━

We Got Them! Now What?

It is late summer (actually, it is mid-summer – here on Cape Cod, we think summer ends on Labor Day), and we bottom fishermen are bringing in a mixed bag of delicious fish: fluke, scup, black sea bass, and if you fish north of Cape Cod, the occasional cod or haddock. All great fish. The bigger game boys will be catching stripers, blues, and even small bluefin tuna, so let's get to cooking our catch.

By this time of summer, I get a little bored with bass and blues, but bored or not, any fish is better than no fish – with the possible exception of hagfish. I am going to provide several simple recipes that can be used with any of the aforementioned fish, and one new (at least to me) cooking technique for fillets that I found in a copy of James Beard's "Revised Fish Cookbook" when I was staying in a remote house on the Elizabeth Islands. This technique can be used with small whole fish as well.

FISH FILLETS BAKED IN THE SPENCER METHOD

(I have no idea who Spencer is, but I appreciate his technique)
For four people, use 4 fillets of about ½ lb. each
Milk
Breadcrumbs
Salt
Cayenne pepper (optional)
Parsley and lemon for garnishing

Salt a shallow dish of milk by adding 1 tsp. table salt or 2 tsp. Kosher salt to ½ cup milk. Spread breadcrumbs (with cayenne if desired) on a plate. Dip fillets in milk, coat both sides with breadcrumbs and set aside. While you are preparing the fillets, preheat your oven to 550 degrees F (yes, that is very hot). Butter or oil an oven casserole or baking sheet, arrange breaded fish pieces on it, and anoint each piece with 2 Tbsp. of bacon fat or melted butter. Place in the upper third of your preheated oven and bake for 10 minutes, checking at 8 minutes for burning breadcrumbs. Turn off the oven and leave fish in cooling oven. If burning is happening, 5 minutes will do it. This technique simulates deep-frying without the mess and hazards that go with it.

You can use whole scup in this recipe as well, with the head either on or off, and make a splendid presentation by laying them side by side on a large platter and surrounding them with a garland of parsley and lemon slices. You can certainly present breaded fillets the same way, but the whole fish look splendid. Your guests will be blown away (as will your competitive cooking friends) and the fish will be delicious.

In the summer, I suggest serving this with tomato and basil salad and potato salad. In winter, I would serve it with mashed potatoes and tiny frozen peas. You could also serve this recipe (as well as the next one) on a bed of mesclun or baby spinach, dressed with vinaigrette. I promise you'll receive rave reviews, so be proud, celebrate!

RED-FRIED FISH

Corn, grapeseed or peanut oil for frying

1 tsp. ground ginger

½ tsp. cayenne, or to taste

1 tsp. mild paprika

Salt and pepper

½ cup flour

1 egg

2 Tbsp. lime juice

1 lb. fairly thin, ½-inch fillets of white fish, flounder or fluke (though any fish will do) cut into 4-inch by 1-inch strips, like fish fingers

1 lime cut into wedges

Put ½-inch of oil in a cast iron skillet and heat over medium-high heat to 350 degrees F. (A drop of batter will sizzle actively but not violently at this temperature.) Meanwhile, combine ginger, cayenne, paprika, salt, pepper, and flour in a bowl. In a separate bowl, beat the egg with lime juice and ¼ cup water. Stir into spice mixture and stir in as much water as needed to reach the consistency of thin pancake batter. Stir in fish.

When oil is heated, gently (for safety) slide a few pieces of fish into it – do not crowd. Fry, turning once, until fish is crisp and golden-brown all over, 4 to 5 minutes. Repeat with remaining fish. After draining on a paper towel or brown paper bag, keep fish warm in a 175 degrees F oven.

Serve immediately with lime wedges. You will be delighted with your efforts, as will your guests. Better than at Long John Silvers – I guarantee!

A SIMPLE FISH CHOWDER

4 oz. fatback or salt pork cut into ¼-inch cubes

1 onion, thinly sliced

4 white potatoes, skin off or on

1 lb. fish cut into large chunks

½ cup crushed crackers or saltines

½ tsp. salt

1/8 tsp. black pepper

1 12-ounce can evaporated milk

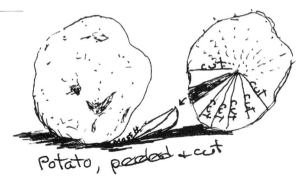

Potato, peeled + cut

Heat a heavy-bottomed saucepan over medium heat and "fry out" salt pork or fatback gently until nearly crisp. Add onions, stir and reduce heat to low. Cut potatoes into narrow wedges, like tiny pieces of pie, and arrange over onions. (You want the wedges to have a thick extremity that will remain intact as the thin extremity melts into the broth.)

Add fish chunks to pot in a single layer, then top with crumbled crackers. Do not stir. Sprinkle with salt and pepper. Add cold water to almost cover (clam juice or fish broth might be better, but don't worry, it will be delicious with water).

Cover pan after bringing to a simmer and cook for 15 minutes or until potatoes are tender. Remove lid, add evaporated milk and bring to simmer. Stir and serve. Additional crackers might be nice. I like to boost mine with a little Tabasco and, man-oh-man, ambrosia. Let this cool to room temperature and refrigerate overnight, and it will be good enough for dessert. It will beat the hell out of Jell-O, I promise!

"Do We Dare?"

I have previously mentioned the high mercury content of blues and bass, especially big ones. PCBs and mercury are either not metabolized at all or so slowly that they accumulate in the tissue of the fish over time, so the biggest and oldest are the most poisonous. They also accumulate lead, another poison, throughout their lives. This problem has been getting worse for years.

I remember calling the state health department in the mid-1980s when we were taking many huge bluefish – I called them "gorilla blues," and they weighed between 15 and 20 pounds – to ask how safe they were to eat, having heard hints about accumulated poisons. The "wise guy" state official said, "Well, you know, they glow in the dark." I did not find this very reassuring but ate them anyway, and I am still here.

I wonder if I, a big old guy, have built up unsafe levels of PCBs, mercury, and lead enough to discourage cannibalism should I fall into the wrong hands?

I suppose it is possible that if the bass and blues become truly toxic, fishing pressure will decline, and the possibly threatened species will prosper, unlike most fish species in the world's oceans.

Mark Bittman, "New York Times" food columnist and cookbook author (he wrote "Fish, the Complete Guide to Buying and Cooking," published by Wiley and winner of the Julia Child Cookbook Award), has recently written that he now rarely eats fish and only as a treat for several reasons. One is health, another is the depleted condition of most fish in the world's oceans. He says the only fish caught in the North Atlantic he eats without feeling guilty are mackerel, herring, squid and lobster, all of which seem to be harvested at a sustainable rate, though I worry about the herring. I respect Bittman's opinions and take them seriously.

So what can we eat? What should we eat? What should we avoid? I can't answer these questions for anyone but myself. I will continue to eat bass and bluefish, but less frequently than in the past, no more than 30 times a year total.

I will eat mackerel – if I can catch or buy it in edible condition – squid, herring (almost never available fresh), lobster, farm-raised clams and oysters, scup, black sea bass, haddock, and fluke. I will eat these all without guilt or fear.

I will, with some guilt, but little fear, eat shrimp, sea scallops, swordfish, tuna, salmon, and cod. I could probably list some more that I will selfishly consume, yet I am still alarmed.

My thoughts are that we should eat more smaller, younger fish, like snapper blues and barely legal-sized scup and black sea bass rather than trophy-sized veterans. I would like a "one bass, any-size" rule established for stripers, so I can eat small and less poisonous fish. We can also eat fast-growing fish like mahi more safely than slower growers.

Here are some simple recipes for fish I consider safe enough even for the young and potentially, if not actually, pregnant.

SIMPLE PAN-FRIED SNAPPER BLUES OR TINKER MACKEREL

Snapper blues (as many as you need, all no longer than 12 inches), beheaded and gutted
Seasoned flour (flour with salt and pepper added and hot paprika if you like, and/or other seasonings of your choice; you can even use a store-bought coating)
Enough oil to reach 1/8" depth in your sauté pan

Rinse fish. While they are still damp shake them up in a bag containing your seasoned flour, shake off excess flour, and arrange on a plate. Preheat the oil until a pinch of flour sizzles immediately when dropped in, add as many fish as you can without crowding until nicely browned on one side, about 2½ to 3 minutes, and turn to brown the second side. Adjust the heat to ensure cooking the fish through without burning the coating. When the meat easily comes away from the backbone when tested with a fork, remove the fish from the pan and drain on brown paper, paper towels, or a wire rack.

Serve these beauties with lemon and tartar sauce and some sliced, ripe summer tomatoes, and you have a dish fit for a king, a queen, or anyone on earth. I love these for breakfast!

When you prepare the former dish, always prepare more than you need so that you can use the extras in the following recipe. It's great for summer lunches or picnics!

TINKER OR SNAPPER ESCABECHE

Whatever leftover sautéed fish you have
Vinaigrette salad dressing (enough to moisten fish — I admit, I use a commercially available Italian dressing)
Thinly sliced red or sweet onion
Thinly sliced sweet red pepper (optional, but looks and tastes good)

Moisten your fish, onions, and optional pepper with the salad dressing and chill over night. The flesh will firm up and taste delicious.

I would like to see a one fish per day, any size, limit put on striped bass so that I could safely make fish fingers from a young bass that would be far less toxic than the large ones we are forced to take now if we want any bass at all. If I could take a small bass, I would cut it into fingers and prepare them using the previous recipe. I promise satisfaction and joy, but not eternal good health.

I have eaten so much striped bass and bluefish in my 45 years on Cape Cod that there is probably enough mercury in my system that you could get a temperature reading looking into my eyes. I probably contain a PCB level higher than the plumbing systems of the trophy houses that increasingly pollute our shoreline, and the heaviness in my legs may be not only the result of 72 years of use but also of lead accumulation. I have enjoyed the whole process, but I feel I must warn all you youngsters about the dangers brought to you by my generation. I probably should feel more responsibility and guilt than I do. Bon appétit! ◄►

The Clam Clan and a Moral Quandary

I recently, once again, had to admit to myself that my son-in-law, Scott, had made a particular dish not only as good as but better than any I have ever made. First, two years ago he outdid my fish cakes (he added scallops – was that fair?) and now he has made the best stuffed quahog I have ever eaten. He said that he made them the way the famous New Orleans chef Paul Prudhomme might have made them and hit the jackpot. Does it sound like I am jealous?

I tried to reproduce his recipe at home with very good results, but not as good as his. I baked mine in a casserole dish rather than in shells. I later used my leftovers to stuff a roast chicken with grand results; you too should try this.

SCOTT'S CREOLE STUFFED QUAHOGS (for 12 stuffed clams)

24 chowder clams, steamed open and chopped (save the broth)

4 oz. pancetta (or bacon)

3 Tbsp. butter

1 cup chopped onion

½ cup chopped sweet peppers (mix red and green)

1 clove garlic (minced)

¼ cup minced celery

1 tsp. oregano

½ tsp. black pepper

½ tsp. white pepper

¼ tsp. cayenne pepper

1 tsp. Old Bay seasoning

1 cup crushed Ritz crackers

1 cup breadcrumbs

A dash of Tabasco or Frank's hot sauce (optional)

stuffed Quohawg

Render pancetta or bacon over medium heat; do this in the butter. When the meat begins to color, remove and save. Add all the chopped vegetables except the garlic to the pan and sauté gently until translucent; add garlic for the last minute of cooking. Remove the whole works to a bowl and add the clams and seasonings and mix thoroughly. Now add a mixture of breadcrumbs and crushed crackers of equal volume to the clam and vegetable mixture and mix. Now add reserved clam broth to get the consistency you want; I like mine a bit moist. Stuff your shells or fill a casserole dish, heat and "Bob's your uncle" – you have Creole Stuffed Clams or casserole. From now on you can modify this and make it your own, but, dammit, Scott's is hard to beat!

My daughter Amanda has been keeping Scott and me knee-deep in clams this summer. She loves to gather them but does not eat them. This is great for us, a bit strange for her. Far be it from me to discourage her. Having so many clams gives me room to experiment. I found this recipe in the "New York Times," and because I think white clam pizza is delicious, I decided to try it. It was good; in fact, very good.

The recipe comes from Florence Fabricant. These delicious treats can be made on a grill or seared on a griddle or under the broiler.

WHITE CLAM QUESADILLAS (for 4)

2 oz. smoked bacon
4 garlic cloves, slivered
1 large jalapeno, cored, seeded and slivered
2 scallions, chopped finely
1 tsp. cumin powder
12 cherrystone clams, opened, drained, and coarsely chopped (you may steam them open, but raw is better)
4 large flour tortillas
4 oz. Asiago cheese (you may substitute longhorn, cheddar, mozzarella, or young provolone)
2 Tbsp. chopped cilantro
2 Tbsp. olive oil

Light your grill, preferably a charcoal one. While the grill is heating, sauté bacon on medium heat until lightly colored. Add garlic, jalapeno, and scallions and sauté until garlic turns golden. Transfer to a bowl and stir in cumin and clams.

Spread the clam mixture to within an inch of the edges of the tortillas, then scatter the cheese, which you have shaved with a vegetable peeler, and the cilantro. Fold the tortillas over and press down. Brush each side with olive oil.

When the coals are moderately hot, place the quesadillas on the grill and press down with a spatula. Watch closely to avoid burning; you may have to move them around a bit, depending on the heat. Grill 2 to 3 minutes on each side until browned and the cheese is melted. Transfer to a cutting board and cut each into 3 or 4 wedges. Arrange on a platter and serve.

I would serve these with salsa and cold beer. A little guacamole would go well with this, as well.

You could spread the clam mixture on pizza dough and serve it as a pizza after baking it about 15 minutes in a 500 degrees F oven. Serve with crushed red pepper or hot sauce or both.

TUNA TARTARE (for 6)

2 Tbsp. thinly sliced scallions
1 ½ Tbsp. minced fresh ginger
1 ½ Tbsp. chopped fresh dill
1 ½ Tbsp. chopped chives
¼ cup virgin olive oil
2 Tbsp. sherry vinegar
1 Tbsp. Worcestershire sauce
1 Tbsp. squeezed lime juice
Fine sea salt and freshly ground pepper
Toasted bread
2 lb. tuna cut into ¼" cubes

Put the scallions, ginger, dill, chives, olive oil, sherry vinegar, Worcestershire sauce, and lime juice in a bowl. Stir together and season with salt and pepper. Mix in the cubed tuna and chill.

Serve with toast on cold platters. This stuff is unforgettable!

Chapter Nine:
SEPTEMBER

Welcome to one of my favorite months of the year. It is the month of my birth, the month when the tourists go home (I enjoy seeing them come and also enjoy seeing them go), and the weather is usually some of the best of the year. This is a great month for big family gatherings around the grill or the turkey fryer. Have a mixed grill or fry, some cold beer, clams and roasted sweet corn, a sliced ripe garden tomato and basil salad, and celebrate life. Winter is coming, but not very soon.

Grill vegetables
Fry animals

Pops,

I recently started lobstering with a recreational permit for 10 pots. I've been having a great time, even though it's hard work and trashes the boat a bit. My question: every now and then I get a lobster with tail meat that's light brown before it's cooked, not the usual white color. What causes this? Is it OK to eat?

Thanks,
Alison

I have a question: how do you know the tail meat is light brown before you cook it?

Shell disease, which is common south of Cape Cod, will sometimes discolor lobster meat without affecting its edibility. Yes, I think it is fine to eat, though I am not sure what causes it.

Mr. Pops,

In the September issue you started talking about cooking sea robins but never finished. Quote: "We will get to recipes shortly." Then nothing. It sure would be nice if you could tell us readers how to clean them and then provide a couple of simple recipes. I have caught sea robins from shore and let them go because I didn't know how to prepare them properly. I have been told that some people eat them, but that's all they say. Thanks for any help.

Charlie

Sorry about leaving you hanging without a recipe or an answer. I will start with a quotation by Alan Davidson from his book *"Mediterranean Seafood"*: "These larger gurnards [the sea robin is a gurnard] have firm white flesh, easy to digest, of good flavor and comparatively free of troublesome bones, but tending to be rather dry.

They may be cooked whole, in fillets, or cut into sections. A large one, gutted and seasoned, may be baked in the oven with white wine, chopped mushrooms, and slices of lemon. Or, it may be simmered in water, left to cool, and dressed with mayonnaise (a method popular in Turkey). Epicharmas (of Sicily) recommended that gurnards be fried in oil, spiced, and served in vinegar, a procedure some authors believe to have survived in the *cuoccio marinato* or soused gurnard of Naples."

There, that should help. Gurnards are somewhat hard to scale because their scales are tiny and tight to the skin. Scale them, cut off the head, dredge in seasoned flour, and fry. I like to take them in hand and eat them like a chicken leg. If you have any floured and fried sea robin left over, dress them with bottled vinaigrette and keep them overnight in the fridge. The next day, you'll have a terrific lunch much like the *cuoccio marinato* of Naples, or the escabeche of Veracruz.

I go shellfishing often and find that my quahogs have mud in them. I clean them when shucking, but I have heard of a method that cleans them by putting them in water with cornmeal. Can you give me the details of this method? Do you use fresh or salt water? How much cornmeal? How long? Refrigerated? It would sure save me a lot of aggravation if I had a simple method to clean them before shucking.

Thanks, Jeff Howard

I have never found mud in quahogs, though bits of shell often get in when I open them, even if they are well washed. If you choose to purge them with cornmeal, submerge them in salt (not fresh, important) water with ¼ cup of fine cornmeal per gallon of water. Soak about two hours, and you will end up with clams full of soggy cornmeal. I like the cornmeal on my clams to be fried on the outside.

The simplest method to cleanse quahogs is to suspend them in a net bag under a dock or a boat for two hours, or as long as you would like. They will be clean as a whistle.

Other Fish to Fry? Sauté?

This column is going to be unabashed self-promotion and a tribute to Andy Nabreski, design manager of "On The Water" and an accomplished fisherman, along with some basic fish cooking advice.

It was Andy's idea that he and I should fish one day and that I should cook our catch ("Cooking the Catch" – right?) the next day. Andy wanted us to catch scup for food or bass bait, black sea bass, fluke, bluefish, and striped bass. He put us on the species we sought and we ended up catching a beautiful 4-pound black seabass, a 20-pound striped bass and our one legal fluke. We also had two legal scup in the livewell by late afternoon that Andy hoped to turn into stripers by drifting them as bait off Nobska Point.

Our first drift had barely begun when Andy's cell phone rang. It was a call from general manager Neal Larsson, checking up on us and hoping Andy had fueled up the boat. He had. Andy said suddenly, "Neal I've got to run. I've got a run – bye!" Line was steadily spooling off Andy's reel as a striper swam off with his scup in its mouth. Andy coolly let the bass hook itself and worked it back to the boat and into the landing net, a beautiful 20-pound striper. Andy had done what he both hoped and expected to do even before we left the dock hours earlier. He turned the scup into a striper. This is the mark of a fine fisherman. Two drifts later my scup was taken by a bass nearly identical to Andy's.

Andy had done his part; now, I had to hold up my end by cooking our catch along with some clams dug by Andy.

Andy, his charming wife Susan, and OTW graphic designer George Clondas were coming to my house to photograph the cooking process and final presentation of our catch. The three dishes I prepared can all be found in my first cookbook, "Cooking The Catch": Steamed Black Sea Bass with Scallions, Black Beans and Ginger; Braised Striped Bass in Tomato Sauce; and Portuguese Clams and Rice. All dishes came out beautifully, if I say so myself, in both appearance and flavor. The four of us nearly ate the whole thing, which made me extremely proud! I was both delighted with the company and stuffed with fish.

So, back to business. Today's business is pan-frying or sautéing fish, whole or more commonly filleted. Fish cooked in this manner are almost always coated with flour or breadcrumbs or some other coating that lends a crispiness and lovely golden brown color to the finished product. Most recipes start by instructing the cook to coat the fish with seasoned flour. This can be as simple as 1 tsp. salt and ¼ tsp. ground pepper to 1 cup of white flour, or for a crisper product try:

COATING FOR PAN-FRYING

½ cup all-purpose flour
¼ cup fine cornmeal
1 tsp. paprika
Salt
Freshly ground pepper and cayenne pepper — to taste

Preheat a frying pan; add no more than 1/8-inch coating of oil. I like peanut oil; butter or olive oil can be used. When oil is hot enough, a sprinkle of flour will bubble or a drop of water will sputter the moment it hits the oil. Lay your whole fish or floured fillets gently into the hot oil and sauté until done, turning once. How long should this take?

This fish is done when it will flake with a fork and is opaque or white to the center. Drain cooked pieces on brown paper or paper towels and serve at once or keep warm in a 175 degrees F oven until all are cooked.

Many people like a thicker crisp coating on fried (sautéed) fish. This can be easily accomplished by dipping the flavored fish pieces in egg mixed with milk or water beaten together (I usually use Egg Beaters mixed with milk) and then rolled in one of the following: cornmeal, fine breadcrumbs, crushed cornflakes, biscuit or pancake mix, cracker crumbs, potato buds, or almond flour.

I like to rest the coated pieces in a single layer until they dry a bit. Follow the chart for cooking time, watching carefully so that the fish does not brown too rapidly or too much. Different coatings brown at different rates. Your fillets will absorb less oil if the oil is hot when you put in the fish. Test for doneness; drain on paper, and "Bob's your uncle" – delicious fried fish!

Most pros use nonstick skillets, which require less oil. Some of us geezers use our iron skillets, a little messier but somehow satisfying to our aged souls.

Go for it! With a modicum of care and attention, you cannot go wrong. This can be the "best!"

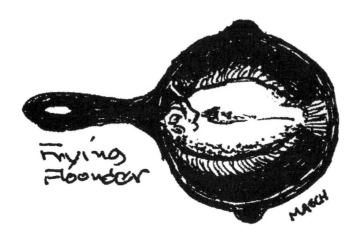

Frying
Flounder

MARCH

PAN-FRYING CHART

	1ˢᵗ Side	**2ⁿᵈ Side**
Whole Fish	3 to 5 minutes	2 to 5 minutes
Fillets: ¼" thick	2 to 3 minutes	1 to 2 minutes
½" thick	3 minutes	1 ½ to 3 minutes
¾" thick	5 minutes	1 ½ to 3 ½ minutes
1" thick	5 minutes	2 to 4 minutes

Yes, You Can Eat a Sea Robin

Children, fish, food, and cooking are central interests in my life, so fishing, cooking, and eating with children all give me great pleasure.

Do not buy kids cheap, poorly made gear, as it will only frustrate them. Simple, "old fashioned" hand lines are great for use from a skiff (useless from the beach) or a dock or pier. It is unlikely that you will shut them in a car door.

Scup are a great quarry for children and can be found in shallow water almost anywhere south of Cape Cod. Black sea bass have recently become abundant south of Cape Cod, and you may find an occasional fluke as well.

I suggest that you use squid for bait and that you cut plenty of nickel-sized pieces before you begin fishing, because if the fish are biting, you will be busy enough unhooking fish, baiting hooks, and untangling lines without having to cut bait as well.

Yes, sea robins are available, edible, and good; they have solid white flesh. They should be scaled, beheaded, dusted with flour or dipped in batter, then fried. You will not be sorry! You eat them – or at least I eat them – like chicken legs.

One can never absolutely guarantee success in fishing with hook and line, but there are other methods that are nearly foolproof and mostly legal. One technique that I, and all children, thoroughly enjoy is fishing with a seine while wading in the shallows. In the autumn, silversides can often be caught by the quart (spearing to some, Menidia menidia to others) when they gather on sandy beaches, along with many other creatures that are fascinating to adults and children alike. The tiny, pencil-thick, 2- to 4-inch silversides are delicious floured and fried and are a great seasonal specialty in the restaurants of fine hotels in London. There, they are presented wrapped in white linen or even damask napkins. You and your kids can do this at home and serve them any way you please and I guarantee that you will not be sorry.

FRIED NEW ENGLAND WHITEBAIT

(a meal for two, a snack for eight)
1 lb. silversides, rinsed
1 cup all-purpose flour
1 tsp. salt
½ tsp. freshly ground black pepper
¼ tsp. cayenne (optional)
Oil for frying
Lemon wedges
Parsley garnish

Rinse and drain whitebait. Mix salt, pepper (and cayenne pepper if you wish) and flour; dredge fish in the seasoned flour. Shake excess flour off fish (I use a wire strainer or colander to do so).

Heat oil until very hot but not smoking in a heavy skillet or saucepan, 375 degrees to 400 degrees F if you have a thermometer. If you have no thermometer, test oil by dropping in a fish. It should sizzle vigorously, sink, and rise almost immediately.

Gently put half the floured fish in the hot oil, separate, and fry to golden brown, about 2 to 3 minutes. Drain on paper towels or a brown paper bag and put on a platter. Keep warm in a 175 degrees F oven while you fry the remaining fish. Drain these also and serve at once. Garnish with lemon wedges and chopped parsley or keep warm as you fry some parsley. Yes, fry some parsley by dropping sprigs into the oil; they will sizzle and crisp almost instantly into a delicious garnish. Go for it. You will not be sorry!

QUICK TARTAR SAUCE

1 cup mayonnaise

1 Tbsp. chopped onion (scallion is best)

2 Tbsp. sweet pickle relish

2 Tbsp. chopped parsley

1 Tbsp. lemon juice

Mix these all together, let sit for five minutes, and go for it.

This recipe will work with sand eels, small sea herring (called smigs), or bay anchovies.

If you get an 8-foot seine and a couple of kids, I guarantee you can spend a delightful afternoon seeing creatures you have never seen before, followed by a fine meal indeed.

If you insist on pin-fishing with hook and line, fillet and skin your fish if you can and coat them with any of the following mixtures. Seasoned flour, like we used for whitebait, will work fine. For a crispier coating, add cornmeal to the flour. Panko, a Japanese bread crumb product, makes perhaps the crispest crust of all. I like to dust fish with seasoned flour, then dip them in beaten egg (or Egg Beaters) and sesame seeds before frying– all these possibilities are delicious and children usually like them when they're tempted to try. They are far more likely to try fish that they have caught and helped to prepare.

These coatings work on whole and beheaded fish as well as on fillets. After kids learn to like fried boneless fish fillets, they can easily be taught to lift the meat off the top half of a whole fish, remove the backbone and expose the (now-boneless) bottom fillet – a very valuable life lesson, and one we owe our children as long as there are fish left to catch and eat. Keep your eye on the kids; they are both quick and tricky.

A Shellfish Grilling Dilemma and a Solution

For many years, I have pondered the problem of how to make classic grilled shellfish dishes like clams casino or oysters Rockefeller on a charcoal grill. These delicious treats require overhead heat, so I have always made them in an oven broiler with grand success, but I wish I could make them in a social setting where people are hanging around an outdoor grill, drinking beer and telling lies.

The truth is, I have not solved the problem. Maybe coals could be held in a grilling basket and held over the clams, but I don't think so. You could leave the muscle uncut on one valve of the shellfish and let it dangle from the shell as it broils, but you would lose all juice along with whatever topping you had applied, and you'd probably destroy the meat as well. So, what to do? These problems are the sort of thing I am contemplating when my wife sees me leaning back in my desk's chair and asks, "What are you doing?"

"I'm working on my column," I answer.

"Yeah!" she says sarcastically.

I have read of a traditional coastal southern method of cooking oysters outdoors. In the Carolinas, oyster mavens like me will make a large fire and amass enough hot coals to spread into a large square, upon which they place a sheet of steel. They cover the steel sheet with oysters in the shell and carefully remove them as they open from their own internally generated steam. These are then dipped in butter and devoured as soon as they are cool enough to eat. Few things are better.

I was certain this technique would work well with littlenecks and cherrystones, so what was I waiting for? First off, I don't have any sheets of steel, but I do have an outdoor grill and smoker. I found that putting oysters and quahogs directly on the grill works very nicely, though you must pay careful attention and remove each shellfish as soon as it gapes or all its juices will boil away.

After removing the clams or oysters from the grill, you must cut them away from the shell if you have not over-cooked and ruined them. Ask an assistant wielding a clam knife to make these wonderful hot morsels available for consumption to you and your guests. Once people have had one, the rest will disappear as fast as you can turn them out. You may need a second assistant to act as a referee, especially if you provide the following condiments or flavored butter sauces.

CONDIMENTS FOR BROILED CLAMS OR OYSTERS

Plain melted butter

Melted butter with garlic and parsley

Melted butter with tarragon

Melted butter with thyme

Melted butter with mixed fresh herbs

Tabasco

Lemon

Ground black pepper

I was asked to speak and give a cooking demonstration at the autumn meeting of the Boston Chapter of Trout Unlimited, and I served clams and oysters prepared in the above manner. They were consumed eagerly and with delight by all present. I promise you the same reactions from your guests. I also served small pieces, about 2 ounces each, of quickly grilled tuna, almost burnt on the outside and almost raw in the center. Another show-stopper!

I first marinated the tuna in a mix that can also be used as a dipping sauce for cooked lobster or shrimp.

MARINADE OR DIPPING SAUCE FOR GRILLED TUNA OR COLD COOKED SHRIMP

4 scallions, chopped

1 Tbsp. sherry (cheap, dry)

4 slices minced fresh ginger

¼ cup soy sauce

1 Tbsp. peanut oil

1 tsp. dark sesame oil

1 clove garlic (minced finely or pressed)

Make a double batch of this magical elixir, and use half of the sauce to marinate 2 pounds of tuna in a plastic zipper bag. Serve the other half as a dipping sauce for grilled tuna or whatever.

GRILLED TUNA PIECES (OR SWORDFISH ENDS)

2 lbs. tuna, cut into 16 pieces
Marinade

Marinate tuna for about one hour in the above marinade or in a simple mixture of 1/8 cup soy sauce and 2 tablespoons of peanut or olive oil. Grill these tidbits on a hot grill for no more than 2 minutes per side. Remember to let each piece broil for at least one minute before attempting to turn over, as this will help prevent sticking. Serve immediately with dipping sauce and flavored or plain melted butter.

The grillmaster will be busy, so I will not suggest that you also grill some shrimp, but they do make a grand addition. So instead I'll suggest that you buy some pre-cooked shrimp and serve them with cocktail sauce and an aioli that will be delicious with the tuna and shellfish, and also with sweet corn and boiled potatoes.

AIOLI (GARLIC MAYONNAISE)

1 large egg
Dash cayenne pepper
½ tsp. dry (or 1 tsp. prepared) mustard
Salt and pepper
1 Tbsp. good vinegar or lemon juice
1 cup olive oil (more or less)
4 cloves garlic (or less, at least 2)

Put all ingredients except oil in a blender or food processor, and with the machine running, add oil in a thin, steady stream. When you have poured in about half the oil, the mixture will thicken, and then you can start adding the oil a bit faster until you reach the desired consistency. Store in your refrigerator. The aioli may be thinned with warm water or sour cream or thickened with boiled potato.

I would serve this whole thing with sweet corn and little boiled new or red-skinned potatoes, all of which are great with aioli or any of the flavored butters. The corn will keep the guests busy while waiting for their grilled tuna and shellfish.

This column started with a simple dilemma, and now I'm planning on turning it into a grand seafood feast to end the summer. I am getting excited just writing about it.

Except for the shrimp, olive oil, and soy sauce, all the ingredients can be local. This will make "locavores" happy, and I bet they will still eat the shrimp!

You will need plenty of napkins, and perhaps more importantly, plenty of chilled white wine and cold beer for this potential autumn bacchanalia. I am going to do it, and so should you.

We could throw in a ripe tomato and basil salad drizzled with olive oil and vinegar. I can hardly wait!

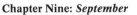

Quahogs AKA Hardshells, Chowder Clams, Round Clams, Cherrystones, and Littlenecks!

I have had quahogs (Venus mercenaria) on my mind for several days, and then quahogs appeared as a clue in "The New York Times" crossword puzzle this morning, so I guess I should write about them to get them off my mind. The answer to the clue, quahog, was "hard-shell clams," which is what they are called in New York and New Jersey. These non-New Englanders have other odd habits, like putting tomatoes in a clam chowder, even green peppers and God knows what-all, but we won't go into that now. At our boarding school for troubled boys on Penikese Island, a kid examining the first quahog he had ever seen asked me if the shell was his house.

"Yes, in a way," I said, "but he can never leave."

"So," says the kid, "There's kind of a little apartment in there? Weird."

The boy was right, in a way; a quahog is always at home. I hope clam beds are truly comfortable and that clams are happy. Perhaps they meditate.

Happy or not, they make me and thousands of others happy because they are delicious and easy to prepare and can be eaten raw, steamed, broiled, ground and stuffed, smoked, pickled, or in a soup or chowder. And, as an added bonus, their crushed shells make a fine driveway.

I consider myself to be one of the greater admirers of the quahog on Cape Cod, but I once met a cook who perhaps admired them more than I. (He even had one for a pet once; its name was Herman.) He became my culinary hero and inspired me to cook and to write about cooking. The "hero's" name is Howard Mitcham, once known as Cape Cod's Master Seafood Chef, and author of two great cookbooks: "Provincetown Seafood Cookbook" and "Clams, Mussels, Oysters, Scallops & Snails." These books contain fine, simply presented recipes and many fine reminiscences of forty years among the shellfish. Mitcham may be dead, but his stories and recipes are immortal. He inspired me to write a book, and I proudly borrow or steal from him; I must thank his spirit for influencing almost all of my recipes.

Mitcham and I agree that the best way to eat a littleneck or cherrystone is chilled and raw, though they are also grand opened and swooshed (Mitcham's word) down as you dig them. Here is what Mitcham has to say:

QUAHOG CLAMS ON THE HALF SHELL (for 1)
1 dozen littlenecks or one half-dozen cherrystones

Chill the clams. Place a layer of finely chopped ice on a serving platter. Open the clams and serve on the bed of ice with a wedge of lemon and Tabasco. Squeeze a little lemon juice on each clam and exactly one drop of Tabasco. Lift it up and swoosh it down right off the shell. I say you should chew it before it goes down.

Mitcham says there will always be "Philistines" — people who demand cocktail sauce. It can smother the clam's flavor. Here is something for them.

COCKTAIL SAUCE
1 bottle Heinz chili sauce
2 Tbsp. hot horseradish
1 Tbsp. lemon juice
¼ to ½ tsp. Tabasco
Ground black pepper

Mitcham says not to dip the clam in the sauce, but rather place a small dab on each clam before swooshing it down. This way, the clam's juice becomes part of the sauce.

So, on to simple, basic cooking.

STEAMED QUAHOGS DELUXE

1 10-quart bucket mixed cherrystones and littlenecks
1 large onion, coarsely chopped
3" piece linguica, thinly sliced
½ cup chopped parsley
½ tsp. black pepper
½ tsp. crushed red pepper
1 cup dry white wine
1 cup water
½ stick butter

Place everything but clams in a large pot. Wash clams and rinse well before adding to pot. Cover and steam for 10 to 15 minutes until all the shells are open. Serve with bowls of broth on the side. The liquid is the best part of the clam, says Mitcham, "an ambrosial nectar fit for the gods on Olympus." I agree - great to sop crusty bread in.

STEAMED CLAMS MARINIÈRE *(for 4)*

4 dozen littleneck quahogs in the shell
½ stick butter
½ cup shallots or two scallions with two inches of green leaves, sliced thinly
1 clove garlic, minced
½ cup chopped cilantro or flat-leaf parsley
½ cup dry white wine
½ cup water
¼ tsp. black pepper
Lemon wedges

Wash (scrub if necessary) quahogs and rinse. Melt butter in the bottom of a steaming pot, add the shallot (or scallions), the cilantro (or parsley), the garlic and black pepper. Cook over low heat for three minutes. Stir a few times. Add water and white wine, turn up heat, and steam for 10 minutes or until all the shells are open. Discard any that refuse to open. Serve in soup bowls with broth ladled over them.

I like crusty bread or crackers with this. Saltines or oyster crackers are fine. I also like a little hot sauce. Simple and delicious. The next recipe is just as delicious and possibly simpler.

GRILLED QUAHOGS

2 dozen littlenecks or cherrystones
1 stick butter
1 Tbsp. chopped cilantro or parsley
1/8 tsp. Tabasco
½ tsp. Worcestershire sauce
Black pepper to taste

Place washed clams on grill, 4 inches above hot coals. Melt butter and other ingredients together in a small saucepan. Mix well. When clams open, move them to a platter and remove top shell. Do this carefully, using gloves; they are very hot. Put a teaspoon full of butter sauce on each clam and devour them!

Is it a Salmon or the Grail?

I make an annual trip to the Matapedia River in Quebec in pursuit of the noble Atlantic salmon (Salmo salar), the most noble of fish, the fish of 1,000 casts, the leaper, and the object of the "Sport of Kings," fly-fishing for salmon. This trip is more of a pilgrimage than a fish-catching event. It is like the hajj is to Muslims for the fly fisherman. I have made ten trips and caught three salmon: two were grilse (fish that have spent one winter in the ocean) and one true salmon (a fish that has spent two or more winters in the sea). This year I made approximately 2,500 casts and had only one "pull" or strike from a salmon, and I missed it. I have more than 1,000 casts for each salmon I have caught, but I have no intention of abandoning the quest until I am physically unable to do so, which may not be very far in the future.

The camp that I stay in, La Chappel, is owned by spey-casting guru, Jim Rusher. It is a catch-and-release camp; the killing of salmon is not allowed or tolerated. There are no exceptions to this rule. Consequently, I have had no fresh wild salmon to cook and eat in the ten years I have chased them, until this year.

In the course of many years of fishing, I have become friends with a native Micmac fishing guide and river policeman, a remarkable man of great physical strength, knowledge, experience, and wisdom (he also ties a grand fly). This guy is impressive but not perfect. I will not mention his name because what comes next may not have been totally kosher.

I did not get to visit with him this summer, but while I was on the river he called and said that he had a present for me and would drive 100 miles round-trip to deliver it. That afternoon, while I was wading and fruitlessly casting, he appeared on the far shore of the river, which was running high and hard, too dangerous to wade across. It would have meant another 40-mile drive to get to where I was. He had a large garbage bag with him. We could shout to each other over the muted roar of the river. He told me he would hide my gift under some fir boughs until Jim Rusher returned and could canoe across to retrieve it. I yelled my thanks, and he vanished into the bush.

He knew I wanted to cook a fresh salmon. While on patrol the night before, he came upon a poacher's illegal net that held a beautiful, fresh from the sea, 13-pound salmon, and kept it to deliver to me, many miles away on the wrong side of the river. I have never been given a finer gift.

I dressed the fish reverentially, cutting it into eight steaks and two nice fillets from the tail section. I saved a couple of steaks in the freezer for my friend and prepared the rest for the guys in camp.

I would have liked to have been able to coat the steaks with sesame seeds and to serve them with dill and parsley butter, but these were not available in camp, so I had to improvise. I found some finely ground cornmeal and some dried tarragon and improvised a tartar sauce.

PAN-FRIED SALMON STEAKS

1 steak per person (1-inch thick)
Salt and pepper
Cornmeal and flour mixed in equal amounts
¼ cup butter
¼ cup vegetable oil
Lemon

Salmon steaks, filet

Heat a skillet big enough to hold your steaks. Add butter and oil and heat until butter starts foaming. Meanwhile, salt and pepper the steaks liberally and coat with the flour and cornmeal mixture. Brown steaks in hot butter and oil until nicely browned on one side, turn over and brown the other side. They should sauté for about 3 minutes per side and remain red and undercooked in the middle. I garnished mine with scallions; I would have used parsley at home and served them with a quick tartar sauce and lemon wedges.

They were absolutely delicious on their own, and doubly so for the generosity involved in our getting them. I would not say they were twice as good as farmed salmon, but they were uniquely delicious, and the two, farmed and wild, cannot truly be compared, wild being far superior.

QUICK TARTAR SAUCE

½ cup mayonnaise
¼ cup horseradish cream
2 Tbsp. sweet pickle relish
1 tsp. vinegar (the best you have)
2 Tbsp. minced scallion tops (optional)

Mix all the above together and serve. The sauce will improve with an hour in the refrigerator.

Here is another seasonal recipe that is hard to beat and may even be free if you are enterprising and lucky. We live at the northern extremity of the range of the blue crab (*Callinectes sapidus*). Sapidus means tasty, and there are few things better than blue crab, especially a fried soft-shelled crab in a sandwich made of white bread, dressed with mayonnaise, chopped lettuce, and a bit of red or sweet onion.

You can catch your own crabs in summer by wading with a bright light and a dip-net in our estuaries. The crabs come out to feed at night and roam all over. If you stay near the edges of weed beds, you may get lucky and find soft-shells. They stay near cover because they are more vulnerable when soft, and they are totally delicious.

If you should get some, clean them by cutting about ¼-inch behind their eyes with scissors; now remove the white gills. Turn the crab over, cut off the apron, and "Bob's your uncle!"

SOFT-SHELLED CRAB SANDWICH

¼ cup butter, olive oil, or a combination
4 soft-shelled crabs
Flour for dredging
1 large egg beaten with 1 Tbsp. water
Unseasoned breadcrumbs or cracker crumbs for dredging, seasoned with
  salt and pepper
Lemon wedges

Blue Crab Sandwich

Heat skillet over medium heat for 3 or 4 minutes. Melt butter in skillet; when foam subsides, raise heat to medium high. Dredge crabs in flour, dip in egg and water mixture, and dredge in crumbs. Now sauté for about 3 minutes per side in hot butter until nicely browned. Drain on paper towels and serve.

These make a splendid appetizer on toast points with a dollop of mayo. I like mine on homestyle white bread slathered with mayo, some chopped lettuce, a little sweet onion, and a whole crab. Magnificent! If you serve these as an appetizer, cut them in quarters. Serve with lemon on the side. I like my sandwich accompanied by a garden-fresh sliced tomato, lightly sugared, with a bit of mayonnaise on the side. My oh my! ◄

Autumn Clams

I am writing this in mid-September, feeling the onset of autumn and winter to follow, but the fishing is starting its fall eruptions, the waters are full of bait, and we are fattening up for winter.

Last week I entered my 70th year, which means I turned 69 years of age, the last year the Bible says I have coming; the rest will be a bonus. My memories are beginning to outstrip my plans, but as my memory weakens with age, my capacity for self-delusion increases – so plans and memories remain about equal.

Two weeks ago a peck of quahogs appeared on my doorstep with a note thanking me for teaching the donor how to find them 35 years ago. I was pleased and touched by this kindness. I decided to make a white clam sauce for spaghetti using the smallest quahogs and to turn the large ones into chowder, so I carefully washed the smaller clams and put them aside and steamed the big ones. Plain water is fine for steaming quahogs or clams, but when I want an especially tasty broth, I start with a glass of white wine, a cup of water, a sliced onion, a chopped carrot, a couple of sprigs of parsley, a crushed garlic clove, a few peppercorns, and maybe a hot pepper. I simmer these slowly until the veggies are soft, having released their flavor into the liquid, add the quahogs, turn up the heat, put on a lid, and cook until the clams are all agape. The pan will invariably boil over just as the clams open; once in a while I prevent this with vigilance, but not very often.

Now, put the pot aside for the clams to cool before removing the meats and to give the now ambrosial broth time to settle so you can carefully pour it off, leaving the sediment behind as you strain out the vegetable bits. This is great stuff for sauce flavoring, stuffing, moisturizing, cooking rice in, using as a chowder base or in miraculously delicious fish soups.

I like to keep a supply of the little wine bottles that come in four packs; four of these equal a normal bottle of wine. Each equals about a glass of wine, around the ideal amount to use in steaming clams, making court bouillon or tomato sauce. These things are hard to keep – a person who would like to have a drink of wine but does not want to open a whole bottle will take one of these – so I have taken to hiding them so that when I want a little in a dish I will have some.

Once my wife said as she savored a taste of red wine, "There ought to be a name for a person who loves red wine." "There is," answered my then 10-year-old son, "Wino!" End of discussion.

WHOLE LITTLENECK WHITE CLAM SAUCE *(for 4)*

32 (plus or minus) littlenecks in shells
3 Tbsp. olive oil
2 Tbsp. butter
4 or 5 cloves garlic (roughly chopped)
½ cup chopped parsley (preferably Italian)
¼ cup clam broth (or more)
¼ cup white wine
¼ cup chopped fresh basil leaves (optional)

Melt the butter in the olive oil using a sauté pan large enough to hold the clams and 1 pound of pasta (I like thin spaghetti or linguini for this dish) .

Add the chopped garlic and the parsley (basil leaves if you are using them) and sauté very gently until the garlic is soft; it may brown a little, but if it burns, start over. Now, add the reserved broth, additional white wine and the clams, turn up the heat, cover and steam until clams open.

While all this is going on, you should have water boiling for pasta. Boil the pasta until barely done – "al dente" – drain and add to sauté pan with the clam sauce, keep this over low heat until the pasta absorbs some of the liquid and serve, garnished with more chopped parsley.

I like to sprinkle mine with crushed red pepper and freshly ground black pepper. I also like grated Parmesan on mine (a crime to many, a joy to me). This is "slap-your-grandma" good. Remember the crusty bread and butter for sopping up the sauce. It makes me sigh just to think of it.

Last week I came home to find 4 pounds of softshelled clams and steamers in a bowl in my refrigerator. They were from the same kind soul who brought me quahogs the week before. Later that day, my daughter, Amanda, called to ask what we were having for dinner and said, "Damn, I'm about to drop some steamers at your house."

"Hey," I said, "you cannot have too many steamers!"

She dropped off 6 pounds, so I now had 10 pounds. So, I invited my stepdaughter Liz and her husband Scott over for steamed clams and sweet corn from the garden. I steamed the clams with the same ingredients I used for the quahogs the week before last. I threw in a few sprigs of fresh thyme as well.

Liz and Scott brought our grandson Sam with them, and the five of us, my wife Jeanne being the fifth, ate all of the steamers. I found it hard to believe. The clams were gone, but I had more great clam broth to add to my quahog broth. I now had enough to freeze a quart and have a quart and a half on hand for the next feast, which would be:

CLAMS, SHRIMP AND RICE A LA "POPS" *(for 6 to 8)*

2 ½ cups white rice
5 cups clam broth
1 medium onion chopped
6" celery stalk, chopped
½ sweet green or red pepper (chopped)
4 cloves garlic minced
½ cup cubed ham, linguica or chourico
3 Tbsp. olive oil
2 Tbsp. butter
2 packages Goya "Sazon Con Azafran"
½ cup chopped parsley or cilantro or both for garnishing plus 2 chopped scallions
18 littleneck clams
1 lb. shrimp, shelled or not

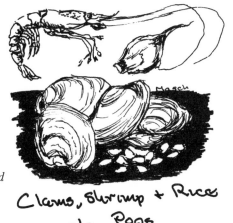

Clams, Shrimp + Rice ala Pops

Melt butter in olive oil in a heavy-bottomed pot that will hold the whole works. Sauté the ham, onion, celery, and pepper (I like to add a hot pepper here or some pepper flakes) gently until transparent. Add garlic last; you do not want it to burn. Now, add the rice and cook, stirring until it becomes opaque; add four cups of clam broth and one cup of water to rice and heat to boiling.

Place clams in rice as it is heating, cover and boil gently for 10 minutes. Now add shrimp to the pan, cover and cook another 5 minutes. If the rice seems too dry to steam shrimp, add more broth or water. Remove from heat, put a handful of parsley on top, and mix. Garnish with remaining greens and serve, to applause, from the pot or on a platter.

The shrimp were a gift from stepdaughter Jennifer in honor of my increasing age. She loved the rice. My clam donor and former clamming student "Leaping Liz" Prete, now honorary daughter, provided the clams. I am being amply rewarded for kid care done 40 years ago. Isn't that great?

Last week a brown paper grocery bag, partly covered by a bucket, appeared outside my front door. It held over 10 pounds of wild mushrooms, seemingly all of one species. There was no note. I think it was the kind generosity of a "friend," but the absence of identification caused me to have doubts. Maybe I was being repaid for something unappreciated 40 years ago. I have not yet eaten the mushrooms. ◀━

"What's Smokin'?"

You should not smoke cigarettes. You would not dare try smoking crack, and you should not smoke pot. So what should you smoke? The answer is simple: fish! You can and should smoke fish, especially bluefish!

My friend and benefactor Predator Phil (he gives me his extra fish and game) gave me several large bluefish that provided enough fillets (about 10 pounds) for me to run my smoker for an entire day. My wife and our neighbor both are put off by the smell. I cannot imagine why; it smelled good to me. I used dried corn and green applewood for the smoke source and produced some fine-tasting fish for this winter's consumption.

I hate being asked questions like, "What is the best way to smoke fish?" or "What is the best recipe for striped bass?" It is like being asked, "What is the best way to make love?" – a question that cannot be answered, though even the worst way is at least interesting. This is not so of the worst way of cooking fish.

I am not going to tell you how to go about making love or how to smoke fish, but I am going to tell how to use smoked fish to prepare dishes to please both yourself and your lover.

We will start with a couple dips or pátes, call them what you will. A dip is always thinner or lighter in texture than a páte, which must be spread.

SMOKED BLUEFISH PÁTE #1

½ cup crème fraiche or sour cream
1 Tbsp. rinsed and drained capers (or chopped dill pickles)
1 Tbsp. chopped chives or green onion tops
1 Tbsp. chopped fresh tarragon (or basil)
½ tsp. smoked paprika
Pinch of cayenne pepper
Freshly ground black pepper
8 to 10 ounces smoked bluefish
Juice of 1 lime

Mix all ingredients in a bowl, breaking the fish up with your fingers. You may chop the fish. Stir with a spoon until nicely blended and spreadable. Chill for at least an hour before serving on crackers or toasted bread rounds.

SMOKED BLUEFISH PÁTE #2

½ lb. smoked bluefish
4 ounces mascarpone cheese
2 Tbsp. lemon juice
1 Tbsp. prepared horseradish
1 tsp. Dijon mustard
Pinch of cayenne pepper
2 Tbsp. finely chopped red onion
Salt and pepper to taste

Mix all ingredients thoroughly until spreadable. Refrigerate for an hour for flavors to blend and have at it. I like it on Ritz crackers.

SMOKED BLUEFISH PÁTE #3

4 ounces cream cheese
4 ounces smoked fish
1 small chopped onion
1 ½ Tbsp. lemon juice

Mash together and "Bob's Your Uncle." What could be simpler? Go for it.

This is good enough as it is, but you can add whatever you want to it – chopped parsley, scallions, horseradish, herbs, spices – and make it your own.

These pates can be thinned out with milk, sour cream, half-and-half, or real cream to make into a dip. Try it, you will not be sorry. You can also mix a few chopped clams in your dip. Smoked mussels or oysters may be added or used instead of smoked fish. I will leave that for another day, probably in the dead of winter, when I often resort to canned (or "tinned", as the Brits say) fish.

My wife hates finnan haddie in any of its forms. This lightly smoked haddock is a treat for me, especially when creamed and served with boiled potatoes and hard-boiled eggs. My wife said she ate too much of it as a kid; her mom was from Nova Scotia, where finnan haddie was once an inexpensive staple. It is no longer inexpensive nor a staple. She, my wife, still doesn't like it, but she doesn't like Campbell's tomato soup, either. Weird, right?

CREAMED SMOKED FISH *(for 3 or 4)*

1 lb. smoked bluefish (or haddock)
3 Tbsp. butter
1 Tbsp. flour
½ tsp. mustard
1 cup milk, or cream
½ cup breadcrumbs
2 hard boiled eggs for garnish
Chopped parsley

Flake fish and put in a buttered shallow baking pan. In a saucepan melt 2 Tbsp. butter, stir in flour and mustard and cook, stirring for 2 minutes. Gradually add milk or cream, whisk to incorporate and cook gently until thickened, stirring frequently.

Pour sauce over fish and sprinkle with breadcrumbs mixed with remaining butter. Bake in a 350 degrees F oven for twenty minutes. Remove from oven, garnish with sliced egg and parsley. I like this with small boiled potatoes and buttered spinach.

Another great and economical way to serve smoked bluefish is as a substitute for lox (smoked Nova Scotia salmon) in the classic Jewish breakfast of bagels and lox. We can call it bagels and blues.

Spread some cream cheese on a toasted bagel, cover with smoked fish, garnish with chopped green onion or thinly sliced red onion and have at it.

This with some freshly squeezed orange juice and coffee is enough to set you up for a second one and a day of grand accomplishments.

Predator Phil is off in the north woods hunting wild boar in the evening and fishing for trout during the day. I love smoked trout, and I bet wild boar ribs could be delicious. Phil usually comes through, so I am hoping to offend my wife and neighbor with a bit more smoke in the near future.

Chapter Ten:
OCTOBER

Sometimes the grand weather of September carries right on through October, and the often fine fishing can be enjoyed comfortably.

This is the month to catch silversides in a seine and enjoy some whitebait, a true delicacy. Sometimes exotic southern species are caught in your seine or on hook and line to add to autumn's pleasures.

October also means that the bay scallops can be harvested. These scallops are among the very best bit of seafood on earth. Either gather your own or splurge on a pound or two. They are actually no more expensive in edible weight of meat than lobster. So, go for it. Winter is coming, so seize the day.

Fish, Scallop Cake

Ask Pops

Dear Pops,

I see salted cod and pollock at the supermarkets. I tried it and liked it, especially on your "cod and scraps" recipe – it is delicious! I would like to salt my own fish, as it is pricey in the stores. Would you have any ideas on how to salt my own fish – what to use, etc.? Any help you can give me will be greatly appreciated.

Many thanks,
Pat Cervolo
Framingham, MA

You can dry-salt any white-fleshed fish, including cod, haddock, cusk, or pollock. Oily fishes – mackerel and herring – are preserved in salt brine to keep oxygen from the fatty flesh. To preserve your own fish, fillet or split them, leave the skin on, and bury in pickling salt for about two weeks. Then remove fish from the salt and rinse and air-dry it until dry to the touch. I used to see split small cod hung from clotheslines in Provincetown, but that was almost 50 years ago.

Fish, treated this way, will keep for weeks at room temperature and indefinitely in the refrigerator. Remember that you must use pickling (kosher) salt for this process.

When I was a child and living in a small coal-mining town in Pennsylvania, we'd often travel to Delaware to catch crabs. My mother would make what were called 'deviled crabs' from the crab meat.

They were similar to the Chinese egg roll and deep fried. Could you help on how to prepare them?

Thanks,
Carl Kaskie,
West Haven, CT

Deviled crab is usually served baked in half a crab shell. I have never made it but will give you a recipe by my culinary mentor and hero, James Beard, which can easily be altered for deep-frying.

DEVILED CRAB

1 lb. crabmeat
1 ½ cups crushed cracker crumbs
¾ cup diced parsley
¾ cup diced onion
½ cup milk
1 tsp. dry mustard
½ tsp. salt
A pinch of cayenne pepper
2 Tbsp. chopped parsley
1 Tbsp. chopped green pepper
¼ cup melted butter

Mix all together and stuff into crab shells or a casserole and bake for about 1 hour at 350 degrees F.

To deep-fry this "deviled" crab, beat two eggs and mix them into the prepared mixture until it can be formed into cohesive balls for deep frying. If lighter fritters are wanted, add 1 tsp. of double-acting baking powder to the mélange.

Preheat deep-frying oil to 375 degrees F, drop heaping tablespoons of batter into hot oil, and fry until golden, drain and enjoy! Good luck!

Using the Blues, and Getting Soused

The engine on my boat has been acting up so, like Blanche Dubois in "A Streetcar Named Desire", I have to rely on the kindness of strangers when I want fish. I can usually count on "Predator Phil," a little strange but not a stranger. He came through with four pounds of bluefish fillets even though I had not asked for them, but now I had them and had to do something with them.

Bluefish should not sit around too long. Fillets will last three days at the outside if handled well and kept cold. I froze one fillet and cooked the other 2 pounds for breakfast and leftovers. I shook the fillet up in a bag containing flour seasoned with salt and pepper, dipped them in Egg Beaters diluted with water and soy sauce, then rolled them in panko (Japanese breadcrumbs) and a handful of sesame seeds I noticed in the spice cabinet. I sautéed the fillet for about three minutes on each side until it was nicely browned all over. It was delicious, and I had a pound and a half for leftovers. I could have made fish cakes, but I have made them several times recently, so escabeche was the answer – easy, delicious, good for a snack, a picnic, or as part of a fish hash.

Escabeche is a technique of soaking fried fish in a vinegar-based sauce for both preserving the fish and firming and flavoring it for serving later. The Spanish often do this, as do the French; the English use a similar technique in preparing soused fish or shrimp.

I intended to write about baking and roasting fish this month, but "Predator Phil's" generosity created a diversion that was delicious enough to pass on to you.

ESCABECHE FOR FOUR

3 cups white wine vinegar or white vinegar
1 ½ cups dry white wine
½ tsp. saffron threads or a small grated carrot
4 bay leaves
1 medium onion thinly sliced
4 cloves sliced garlic
Olive oil as needed
1 tsp. sugar
1 ½ Tbsp. paprika
1 tsp. salt
½ tsp. pepper
4 fish fillets weighing 6 to 8 ounces each or 1 ½ lbs. large shrimp or sea scallops
2 scallions chopped or shredded in 2" lengths or one shredded green, red or yellow sweet pepper
4 thin slices of lemon

Do not be daunted, ever, by a long list of ingredients; such a list does not make a recipe difficult. Refuse to be daunted.

Mix vinegar, wine, saffron (or shredded carrot) and bay leaves in a saucepan, bring to a boil, reduce heat to medium, and reduce to two cups.

As the liquids are reducing, sauté the onion and garlic in 3 Tbsp. of olive oil, add sugar and lightly brown onion. Add this to reducing liquid.

Mix salt, pepper, paprika and flour together in a bag or on a plate. Coat the fish or shellfish in this flour and brown evenly in oil. When the fish is a good golden color, remove from pan and put in a casserole that can hold fish and marinade (Pyrex is good). Add the scallions or/and peppers to simmering marinade. After a minute or two pour marinade over the seafood, put lemon slices on top and let stand for at least 10 minutes. Serve warm or at room temperature.

I prefer to cover this dish and refrigerate it overnight and serve it cold on a bed of greens the next day. If you want to serve it warm, reheat it in a 300 degrees F oven. This will keep for three days in the fridge. Recipe based on one found in Shirley King's fine book, "Fish: The Basics."

MY ESCABECHE
Whatever extra fried fish you have
1 sliced onion
Enough bottled Italian salad dressing and marinade (Wishbone is a good one) to wet the fish on both sides

Put sliced onion on your leftover fish in a casserole or bowl and wet thoroughly with salad dressing, chill overnight, and the next day "Bob's your uncle" – cold, delicious escabeche.

Please try this both ways, you will not be sorry. I bet you will try my recipe first. Do it!

My recipe is great made of snapper bluefish or tinker mackerel. I love these little guys served with fresh sliced garden tomatoes. I eat these fine fish and tomatoes with a hint of sadness because their availability means the end of summer is near.

SOUSED OR MARINATED FISH *(for 2)*
4 small fish, 4 to 6 ounces each (tinker, snapper) or 2 whole fish, about a
*   pound each*
Enough water and white vinegar, mixed in equal amounts, to just cover fish
1 small onion, thinly sliced
2 bay leaves
2 sprigs thyme or ¼ tsp. dried
1 Tbsp. salt
Freshly ground black pepper to taste

Soused Shrimp and fish

Heat oven to 400 degrees F and put the fish in a ceramic or Pyrex casserole just big enough to hold them. Put sliced onion on top of fish, add remaining ingredients, barely cover with vinegar and water mixture. Cover with foil and bake for 25 minutes; allow to cool to room temperature and then chill overnight. Eat with a salad. You will not be sorry.

You could substitute a Tbsp. of chopped tarragon for thyme and bay leaf; in fact, you can flavor this any way you damned please – go for it. Shrimp are good done this way, but cook only 15 minutes.

One morning last week I chopped up a small onion and some scraps of parsley, sautéed them briefly, added about 1 cup of chopped escabeche, some leftover boiled potatoes (cubed), salt and pepper, covered the whole works with Egg Beaters, baked it in a 400 degrees F oven until it was puffed up and done and had a quick and easy, impressive breakfast for four. Serve this with some hot sauce, toast and jelly, and the rest of the day will be a breeze.

While I am citing Shirley King's cookbook, I want to pass on her simple, quick marinade and glaze for filleted fish, shrimp, or scallops to be broiled.

GLAZE – MARINADE
¼ cup dry white wine
2 Tbsp. molasses
2 Tbsp. soy sauce
Black pepper to taste

Mix together, soak fish for five minutes, no more, and grill, basting with marinade. What could be easier? Not much could be better.

Sousing and marinating the bland freshwater shrimp we get from farms in Southeast Asia improves them greatly. My wife said I never improved when soused, but then I was never bland or Southeast Asian.

Threatened Yet Again

He has done it again, whether intentionally or not. My son-in-law, Scott Britton, has cast doubt on my claim to culinary supremacy in our family. Not only do I feel threatened, but I'm also shocked at the area of contention: fish cakes! This is an area in which I have always felt invulnerable. My fish cakes have been lauded far and wide, and have been a source of great pride for me, but I'm no longer confident they are always the best. Scott made some this past weekend that were "slap your grandma" good – as good or better than I have ever made or tasted! Granted, his were not spontaneously made from leftovers, but rather meticulously planned from start to delectable finish.

I was compelled to ask for more precise details about his preparation of these beauties. Although I had a pretty good idea of his technique, I needed further information before passing the recipe on to you. I was pleased when Scott said that my master recipe served as its foundation. At least I am still in the game, even if I'm no longer in the lead!

Scott made fish cakes for 12 people with the following recipe. He started by moistening 3 pounds of cod with olive oil and baking it at 415 degrees F until flaky (about 15 minutes). He also boiled 3 pounds of potatoes and mashed them. These two ingredients are the foundation for:

SCOTT'S SPLENDID FISH CAKES WITH SCALLOPS

3 lbs. cod fillets (or striped bass) cooked
3 lbs. potatoes (boiled and mashed)
1 medium onion, minced
1 large shallot, minced
2 cloves garlic (boiled, peeled, and minced)
½ cup minced parsley
2 eggs
1 lb. scallops, cubed (secret ingredient)
Salt and pepper
Breadcrumbs (for thickening and coating)

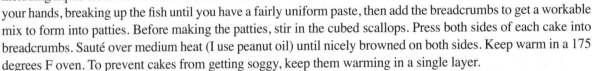
Fish, Scallop Cake

Mix everything but the scallops together, including liquid from the cooked cod. Mix with your hands, breaking up the fish until you have a fairly uniform paste, then add the breadcrumbs to get a workable mix to form into patties. Before making the patties, stir in the cubed scallops. Press both sides of each cake into breadcrumbs. Sauté over medium heat (I use peanut oil) until nicely browned on both sides. Keep warm in a 175 degrees F oven. To prevent cakes from getting soggy, keep them warming in a single layer.

I think two things elevate these cakes from merely good to amazing: the scallops and the briefly boiled garlic. The trick here is to boil unpeeled cloves of garlic for 45 seconds before peeling and chopping. This technique subdues the sometimes harsh flavor of raw garlic and adds a subtle flavor that's not normally associated with it. For whatever reason, Scott's fish cakes are the best, and they definitely outshine the crab cakes served in local eateries – even, I hate to admit, my own. You owe it to yourself to make this recipe. I would happily serve it as the main course at a dinner party, and to anyone on earth. Go for it this week!!

Scott served an unusual, exceptionally tasty tartar sauce with his cakes, incorporating chipotle peppers and canned adobo sauce. You can find the recipe on the next page.

SCOTT'S CHIPOTLE TARTAR SAUCE

½ cup mayonnaise
1 Tbsp. lemon juice
1 Tbsp. sweet pickle relish
1 scallion, minced finely
2 chipotle peppers, seeds removed, minced
1 tsp. capers
1 tsp. adobo sauce from can

Mix these things together, let stand in refrigerator for at least an hour, then serve proudly! Tomato salad, corn on the cob, or corn off the cob sautéed in butter with mushrooms and peppers are all grand accompaniments. These recipes can be halved or doubled, or whatever. Just give them a try.

My neighbor Gunjan Laborde, an accomplished weaver, yoga teacher, painter and occasional cook, served my wife and me a simple, delicious dinner of plain baked cod, tomato and mozzarella salad with basil, and corn on the cob that you also should try.

GUNJAN'S ROAST COD *(for 5)*

2 lbs. cod fillets (or striped bass)
2 Tbsp. olive oil
Salt and pepper

Preheat oven to 500 degrees F – yes, 500 degrees. Arrange cod in a single layer on a baking surface anointed with olive oil. Further anoint the cod, sprinkle with salt and pepper, and bake for 10 minutes. It should just start to flake at this point, so if it doesn't, give it a few more minutes in the oven. And there you have it: simple, delicious, pure sea flavor. I would sprinkle this with chopped parsley and garnish it with lemon.

I would accompany this with boiled new potatoes dressed with parsley and butter; I love to mush fish, potatoes and raw/cooked tomato all together! If you catch your own fish or have access to really fresh fish, you must try this ultra-simple technique. Remember that any leftovers can be made into fish cakes.

OYSTER AND SMOKED SALMON SCRAMBLED EGGS *(for 2)*

¼ cup minced smoked salmon
6 oysters
1 scallion
2 Tbsp. butter
Oyster juice
4 eggs or 1 cup Egg Beaters

Mix, scramble and enjoy this food fit for a king! Even Scott couldn't do better than this, but I do fear he will take up clam chowder soon (I am making quahog chowder for 150 people tomorrow), thereby threatening my last bastion of culinary supremacy. To this I say, "Bring it on!"

Oyster, smoked salmon, eggs

Great Mates: Bluefish and Tomatoes, Clams and Sweet Corn!

September and October are great months here on Cape Cod, boasting many crystal-clear days and warm temperatures, but with a slight cool snap in the air that indicates what is to come. The austerity of winter may be looming, but the cornucopia of harvest is upon us, coming from both the land and the sea. Sweet corn is at its sweetest, tomatoes are ripe and bursting with flavor, the fishing is at its best, and you can dig clams without freezing your tail. From this cornucopia come the meals I anticipate most every year. For me, there is an affinity between fish (especially fried snapper blues) and ripe tomatoes, and an equally grand compatibility between clams and corn. Who doesn't love steamers and corn at a New England clam boil?

In late August, when the "snap" in the air first occurs, the "snapper blues" (young-of-the-year bluefish, now 6 to 9 inches long) arrive in the harbors and inlets, feeding voraciously in anticipation of winter. You can sometimes catch them on almost every cast by using a small spoon, fly, or attractor-and-fly rig.

For over a month now, I have been enjoying – in fact, reveling in – pan-fried snapper served with raw or sautéed tomatoes several times a week. You should before it is too late, and it will be too late in a couple of weeks.

Snappers are a "snap" to clean. You merely take them in hand and make a diagonal cut behind the head and gill covers, cutting through the backbone. At this point, you should pull the head down, removing it from the body along with the entrails, and "Bob's your uncle!" You have a perfect little delicacy ready to be coated with seasoned flour and pan-fried to achieve immortality.

SEASONED FLOUR FOR 8 SNAPPERS

½ cup all-purpose flour
I tsp. salt
½ tsp. freshly ground pepper
¼ tsp. cayenne (optional, but necessary for me)

Snapper and tomato

Put this mixture, or one of your own devising (I often use half flour/half cornmeal) into a plastic bag, then toss in four fish and shake the bag until they are coated. Remove the fish and cook in hot oil over medium heat until nicely brown and crisp on both sides. Keep the fish warm in a 175 degrees F oven as you fry the next batch. I usually use peanut oil, though canola oil also works fine. Butter is delicious, but you must watch it carefully to keep it from burning.

I often cut a couple medium-sized tomatoes in half, dip the cut edges in the leftover seasoned flour, and sauté them in the same pan as the fish, either simultaneously or when the fish are keeping warm in the oven. When the breading on the tomatoes is nicely browned, I turn them over for a short time to cook through.

Serve this combination with a glass of orange juice, a piece of toast and a cup of coffee, and you will be set to take on the day, even if it doesn't get any better than breakfast. But who knows, you might get lucky.

Forty or so years ago, a 12-year-old boy won a weekend bluefishing derby held in Provincetown. There were valuable prizes given in several categories: biggest fish, most fish, etc. At the Sunday afternoon award ceremony, our enterprising 12-year-old showed up with 184 snapper blues to claim the "most fish caught" prize. The organizers of *the derby had not mentioned a minimum size for the fish, so he got the prize. A few years later, a giant bluefin tuna tournament held in Provincetown was won by a 16 year old who took an 800-pound tuna off Race Point from a dory, beating out the sports with $25,000 vessels. I don't know if it was a rowing dory, but I do know it had the lowest horsepower of any boat in the tourney, and it still caught the biggest "horse mackerel" (as bluefin tuna were sometimes known in those days). I think he did it on a hand-line. If this guy is still alive, I hope he will step forward. I'd like to shake his hand, especially if the "snapper kid" and the "horse mackerel" slayer are one and the same.*

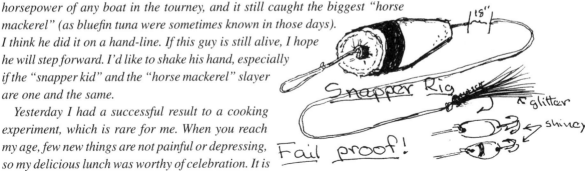

Yesterday I had a successful result to a cooking experiment, which is rare for me. When you reach my age, few new things are not painful or depressing, so my delicious lunch was worthy of celebration. It is hard to celebrate alone, but I did, and if you try the following recipe, you will too.

SQUID AND TOMATO SAUCE FOR PASTA *(for 1 lb. pasta)*

3 cups good tomato sauce
1 cup chopped raw squid
Pepper flakes and optional parmesan for sprinkling
1 lb. cooked spaghetti or linguini

Make up individual plates for four servings, putting cooked pasta covered with mixed sauce and raw squid on each plate. Cook each plate for 3 minutes in the microwave oven. Remove and keep warm in a preheated 175 degrees F oven as you cook the additional portions.

I had mine with plenty of parmesan and an adequate sprinkling of pepper flakes. It was delicious and worth celebrating. I am fortunate to have a grand tomato, basil, garlic, and onion harvest that I have been compressing into sauce for winter meals and reminders of the glory of late summer and autumn.

If you want to celebrate the mating of clams and corn, I strongly advise going to page 103 of my cookbook, "Cooking the Catch," and preparing the clam and corn fritter recipe. I also advise following any of the clam sauce recipes and serving the results accompanied by sweet corn and a tomato and basil salad.

These wonderful fresh foods – corn, snappers, and real garden tomatoes – are available briefly each year, so get out there and enjoy them while you can. I do not intend to go to my grave having missed a single season of these grand culinary blessings.

Who's Afraid of Mr. Flood?

I have written more than 120 of these columns in the past several years with more than 350 recipes (maybe 400) and must work harder to come up with something possibly new or at least interesting every month. This gets harder and harder to do. On the other hand, it may be time to start over with basic techniques and revise, update, or just repeat past recipes while still eagerly seeking the new and unusual. I do not think there are many totally new and unique recipes, only re-presented ideas passed down to us by our mentors. People have been cooking for hundreds of thousands of years, so the odds are not good that your creation is unique.

Cooking changed when sautéing pans became available, probably in the Bronze Age, making frying possible–perhaps my favorite way to eat fish, followed by sautéing. Frying to me means immersion in deep fat, whereas sautéing means browning in a thin film of fat, preferably butter.

The first metal pans made many new recipes possible that could not have been used in either direct-roasting or boiled-in-skin containers to which you added heated rocks. The next change came millennia later with the arrival of the microwave oven, which will nicely steam a fish but outrage many traditional cooks, who will be aghast. I know that old Mister Flood, a New York character and self-proclaimed "seafooditarian," written about by the great Joseph Mitchell more than 50 years ago, would explode if he heard of microwaving fish.

"I've made quite a study of fish cooks, and I've decided that old Italians are the best. Then come old colored men, then old mean Yankees, and then some old drunk Irishmen. They have to be old; it takes almost a lifetime to learn how to do a thing simply. Even the stove has to be old," states Mr. Flood. I know he would be repelled, perhaps violently, by a nuked fish fillet. So I will not present such a recipe at this time, but will in the future if any reader asks that I take this risk. I chickened out.

So instead, I will present a classic French recipe that even Mr. Flood might approve of; though it is of French origin, it is simple and classically delicious.

FLATFISH MEUNIÈRE (for 2)

¾ to 1 lb. flatfish fillets, or one whole, skinned 2 lb. fish
Salt and freshly ground black pepper
1 Tbsp. olive or vegetable oil
¼ cup (1/2 stick) butter
Juice of ½ lemon
Flour for dredging
Chopped fresh parsley for garnishing
2 wedges of lemon (use the other half of the lemon you got the juice from)
Note: This dish should be served hot, so warm a couple plates in a 175 degrees F oven for at least 15 minutes.

Season the fish with salt and pepper. Heat a skillet big enough to hold your fish for 3 to 4 minutes over medium-high heat and add the oil and half the butter. When the butter foam subsides, add the fillets or whole fish, which you have dredged in flour, shaking off the excess. Cook until golden on both sides, no more than 2 ½ minutes per side. Remove to warm serving plates, or serving platter if using a whole fish, and keep warm in a low oven. Turn burner down to medium and add remaining butter to the pan. Cook until butter foams, for 1 or 2 minutes. Add the lemon juice and stir, scraping the bottom of the pan to release flavorful browned bits. Pour sauce over warm fish and serve immediately! This is marvelous! A version of this, based on a Mark Bittman recipe, is eaten by Julia Child in the movie Julie and Julia. Meryl Streep portraying Julia did the actual eating.

You may use this classic technique with almost any fish fillet with white flesh with grand results as long as you adjust cooking times for the thickness of the fillet. Remember, no more than 10 minutes for each inch of thickness.

After you have made this a few times–I know you will if you do it once–you may try the following variation by one of my culinary heroes, Mark Bittman, who writes, "Add a teaspoon of capers, rinsed, to the skillet along with the lemon juice (you can also add a couple of minced anchovies if you like). Cook 30 seconds and pour over the fillets or whole fish." I say try it both ways, you will not be sorry! I promise!

We are going to move from a recipe that seems complex to one that is truly simple and delicious and does not appear in the French lexicon. In fact, it comes from my threatening and respected son-in-law, Scott Britton, who has taken over as culinary leader in our sometimes-dysfunctional but always-hungry family. I shouldn't say he is threatening, for he is a gentle soul, but I think he has earned his new status. Well, even Ted Williams got old, alas.

GRILLED OR BAKED SHELLFISH WITH BRITTON'S DIPPING SAUCE
As many clams and oysters as you have
A charcoal grill or an oven preheated to 400 degrees F

Scrub your oysters or clams and either put on the grill or arrange on baking sheets or roasting pans. Cook until they gape open, remove with tongs or gloves, and eat with either melted butter or Scott's marvelous dipping sauce.

Scott's Dipping Sauce
1 stick melted butter
Juice of ½ lemon
Zest of whole lemon
1 clove of garlic (blanched for 45 seconds) and minced
1 Tbsp. Sriracha or other Asian garlic and pepper sauce, or Tabasco (if you want it hotter)

There will be no shellfish left if you use this sauce, a welcome change from standard cocktail sauce. Boiled shrimp would be good here too. You can't go wrong here unless you burn yourself on a shell.

Remember, if you want instructions or recipes to microwave fish, write to me. I may be braver next month.

I was lying in bed last night thinking about this column and thought of cooking shellfish until they open on a metal slab over a fire, as they do in the Carolinas. I thought it might be fun and delicious to wrap bacon around a scallop, put it on a stick, and roast it as if it were marshmallow. I will try it; it will be good, I am sure – kind of a grown-up marshmallow. Let's go for it. Mr. Flood would approve, I think.

Grilling Clams + oysters

Can Quahogs be Dangerous?

I cannot yet stop writing about quahogs and their preparation. This versatile, available, delicious, noble, and sometimes dangerous animal has fascinated me since I dug my first one in 1963. Last week they contributed to my near demise. I was the other contributor, having eaten quahogs as the main ingredient of five consecutive meals, including one breakfast. Clams scrambled with eggs, or clam fritters, are fine breakfast fare. My own gluttony added to the problem I had on Monday night after my five quahog meals. I suffered a bout with congestive heart failure, probably brought on by stupidity and gluttony. I ate all those quahogs and forgot to take my diuretic medication, which probably brought on this life-threatening attack. Like the two British kings who "died of a surfeit of lampreys," I almost left on a "surfeit of quahogs," or actually on the salt in the clams.

However, the meals that brought on the "Angel of Death" in the form of a quahog were delicious. I will present several of these recipes here with a warning to not eat them for consecutive meals.

The trouble started when I decided to cook up a half-bushel of quahogs my daughter Amanda, a fine estuarine predator, had given me. I ended up with several quarts of clam meats and several quarts of clam broth, and I was off on a slippery, salty, delicious slope toward perdition.

I looked at these fine meats and decided to make a simple soup using onion, leftover mashed potatoes, clams, broth and ½ cup of evaporated milk, a kind of imitation chowder.

QUICK CLAM SOUP (for 2)

1/3 cup chopped clam meats
1 cup clam broth
1 medium onion, chopped
1 Tbsp. butter (or more)
2 cups leftover mashed potatoes
Chopped scallion greens or chives,
*   optional for a tasty garnish*
½ can evaporated milk (or cream)
Black pepper

Melt the butter in a saucepan and sauté the onion over medium heat until soft. Add clams, clam broth, and mashed potatoes and stir until smooth, simmer for 5 minutes, add evaporated milk and black pepper, and "Bob's your uncle" – a very simple semi-chowder.

Serve this stuff in heated cups with a garnish of chives or scallions and ½ teaspoon of butter, and your guests will think you are a gourmet.

My next clam meal was dinner with a slightly tarted-up white clam sauce for spaghetti, one of my all-time favorites.

SIMPLE QUAHOG FRITTERS

1 pint chopped or ground quahog meat
1/8 tsp. paprika
½ tsp. chopped parsley, chives or scallions
1 tsp. salt
½ tsp. black pepper
1 ½ tsp. sugar
¼ cup milk
¼ cup clam broth
1 cup flour
1 tsp. baking powder
Couple dashes of hot sauce
1 egg, beaten

Beat egg, add all other ingredients and mix thoroughly until you have a thick batter. If too thick, add more milk.

You can cook little balls by dropping a teaspoon at a time in deep fat at 375 degrees F, until golden brown. I usually cook little patties by dropping batter into shallow fat or oil and browning on both sides.

Serve these morsels with tartar sauce and lemon quarters.

SPAGHETTI WITH WHITE QUAHOG SAUCE

2 dozen shucked or steamed cherrystone
   clams, chopped
½ cup clam broth or reserved juice from
   shucking
4 Tbsp. olive oil
2 Tbsp. butter
2 or 3 cloves minced garlic
¼ cup chopped onion
½ cup chopped sweet red pepper
¼ cup Italian parsley
¼ cup fresh basil leaves
¼ tsp. crushed hot pepper
Freshly ground black pepper to taste
¼ cup dry white wine (optional)

Melt the butter in the olive oil over medium heat in a skillet large enough to hold a pound of pasta. Add onions, sweet red pepper, basil, parsley, and garlic, and sauté until veggies are soft; be careful not to burn the garlic (which will ruin the dish).

Now add the clam meats and broth, or clam meats and liquid, wine if you are using it, cover and cook over low heat for 10 minutes. Uncover and add 1 pound of spaghetti that you have cooked al dente, and stir until totally blended, add black pepper, stir and serve.

I like to garnish this with additional chopped parsley, freshly chopped oregano and grated Parmigiano-Reggiano. This is a splendid dish, "to die for." I nearly did.

I still had plenty of clams left, so my thoughts moved to fritters and clam cakes, which I ate for breakfast the next day.

FANCIER QUAHOG AND CORN FRITTERS

1 pint chopped or ground quahogs
1 small onion, minced
½ cup minced sweet red pepper
1 Tbsp. minced celery
1 Tbsp. minced Italian parsley
1 to 2 cups corn, cut from cob
2 cloves minced garlic (or pressed)
1 ½ cups all-purpose flour
1 ½ tsp. baking powder
½ tsp. ground cumin
¼ tsp. black pepper
¼ tsp. pepper flakes (or a couple of shakes of Frank's hot sauce)
1 cup half-and-half
2 eggs, beaten
Clam broth or juice, as needed
1/4 cup ground linguica, optional

Shuck or steam clams open and chop finely. Save broth or juice.

Mix all the dry ingredients, add the chopped veggies, corn, and parsley. Add eggs and mix well. Add all the half-and-half and enough clam liquid to make a thick batter. Heat oil in skillet, drop batter in hot oil by the spoonful, cook until nicely browned on both sides, and serve proudly.

My fifth meal down the slippery slope toward perdition was a fine clam chowder that almost did me in.

Unlike Kings Henry and Edward, I did not succumb to a surfeit of seafood. If I had, you wouldn't be reading this now.

Add a Little "Ginger" to Your Life

I sometimes fall into a rut and repeatedly prepare the same fish dishes – simple, classic, delicious recipes. Delicious they may be, but a foray into new tastes can be both satisfying and exciting. This comment is not meant to apply to marriages.

I decided to add a little "ginger" to my culinary life by preparing the following dishes from the cookbook of one of my hero cooks, David Waltuck, called "Staff Meals from Chanterelle." The recipes are for simply prepared fish served with a Chinese sauce or gravy; this presentation is odd in New England but delicious, as I hope you will see. I do not claim these or any recipes as my own. I will quote directly from Waltuck's cookbook.

Do not be put off by the long list of ingredients, all of which are available in most supermarkets. Whenever I do Asian cooking, I arrange all my ingredients before beginning and recommend that you do the same.

Waltuck says the gingery sauce is typically served over a whole fish that has been slashed to the bone with a sharp knife and then fried in oil until it is so extravagantly crisp, you can practically eat the crunchy bones. Amazingly, however, the flesh remains wonderfully moist. For our staff meal, I usually serve the sauce with the sautéed fish fillets, which are easier and faster to prepare.

FISH WITH GINGER SCALLION SAUCE

4 white fish (bass, cod, haddock, hake, etc.) fillets, about 8 ounces each
1 cup all-purpose flour for coating fish
8 dried shiitake mushrooms
2 cups chicken stock
¼ cup sugar
1/3 cup rice wine or cider vinegar
2 ½ Tbsp. oyster sauce
2 tsp. soy sauce
1 Tbsp. fresh lime juice
1 Tbsp. Thai fish sauce (Nam pla)

1 Tbsp. cornstarch
2 Tbsp. cold water
1 tsp. hot red pepper flakes
1 ½ Tbsp. grated fresh ginger
1 medium onion sliced lengthwise
1 small sweet red pepper, cored, seeded and chopped into narrow strips
3 scallions, trimmed and cut into ¼" lengths
2 Tbsp. canola or other vegetable oil (I like peanut)
Coarse (Kosher) salt to taste
Flour for breading

Place mushrooms in boiling water to cover. Let soak for 30 minutes to soften. Trim stems from mushrooms and slice the caps into strips. Save the soaking water.

Combine the chicken stock, shiitakes, sugar, vinegar, oyster sauce, soy sauce, lime juice and fish sauce in a small non-reactive saucepan and bring to a boil over high heat. Reduce the heat to low and simmer, uncovered, for about 20 minutes.

Mix cornstarch with water. Mix until smooth and whisk into sauce until the sauce thickens. Add pepper flakes and ginger and simmer for 1 minute more. Add the onions, bell pepper, and scallion until just heated through, another 1 to 2 minutes; the vegetables should be crisp. Remove from heat and taste for seasoning. Keep warm while you prepare the fish.

Coat fish fillets all over with flour and shake off excess. Heat the oil in a large skillet over medium-high heat. Lightly salt fillets and add them to skillet. Sauté until lightly browned and cooked through, 2 to 3 minutes per side.

Transfer hot browned fillets to a platter or individual plates and spoon sauce over them to serve.

You must try this; it is surprisingly easy and nearly fantastic in flavor. I would serve this with white rice and a stir-fried vegetable like bok choy, spinach or peapods cooked with garlic, oil and salt. Your family or guests will applaud your efforts and possibly worship you if you prepare the recipe on the next page. I would not count on the worship for no one is a hero at home; however they will brag about you to their friends.

CRISPY FISH WITH SPICY SWEET-AND-SOUR SAUCE

6 white fish fillets: bass, flounder, cod, haddock, hake, etc. (6 to 8 oz. each)
Coarse (Kosher) salt, to taste
2 Tbsp. peanut or canola oil
1 clove garlic
¾ tsp. grated fresh ginger
2 cups chicken stock or canned low-sodium chicken broth
2 Tbsp. white wine or rice vinegar
2 Tbsp. ketchup
4 tsp. sugar
1 Tbsp. good soy sauce (Kikkoman)
¾ tsp. Chinese chili paste or other hot sauce
2 tsp. cornstarch
3 Tbsp. cold water
1 cup all-purpose flour

Heat 2 Tbsp. oil in a large skillet over medium heat. Add the garlic (I squash it first) and ginger and cook until aromatic but not browned (about a minute). If garlic shows any sign of burning, toss it.

Stir (or pour) in chicken stock, vinegar, ketchup, sugar, soy sauce and chili paste and increase the heat to high. Bring to a boil, then reduce the heat to medium low and simmer, uncovered, until the flavors have blended and the sauce has reduced slightly, about 10 minutes.

Mix cornstarch with water until in suspension; stir this into the simmering sauce and stir until the sauce thickens, less than a minute. Remove from heat and taste for seasoning. Set aside, covered to keep warm, as you cook the fish.

Coat each fillet with flour seasoned with a little salt, and shake off excess. Preheat oven to 175 degrees F; line a baking sheet with paper towels.

Pour ¼ inch of oil into a large, heavy skillet and set it over medium-high heat. When a drop of water sizzles rapidly on contact with the oil, add fillet to oil without crowding. Fry until golden brown on both sides, 2 to 3 minutes per side. Remove browned fish with a slotted spoon and put on the prepared baking sheet to drain; put in oven to keep warm as you finish frying the remaining fish.

Arrange on a platter or plates, garnish if you wish (scallions and cilantro would be nice) after pouring sauce over fish. The same accompaniments as the first recipe will work here.

This sauce works with chicken tenders or scallops that have been coated with cornstarch or flour and fried. You can fry fish for adults, chicken for picky kids and scallops for gourmets.

Please try these recipes and enter a better, more fulfilled existence.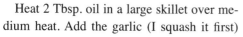

Chapter Eleven:
NOVEMBER

The month of Thanksgiving, the opening of the oyster season here on Cape Cod. Families gather to eat and share another year's stories. My son-in-law Scott and I continue our contention for top fish and shellfish cook, and my stepdaughter Francie makes super scalloped oysters. I have never made scalloped scallops. I will save that for my next book, should I live so long.

Herring gulls were once called Cape Cod turkeys, as was the codfish. I have eaten and enjoyed the eggs of both, and eaten baked stuffed cod, but never a roast stuffed gull and probably never will.

Do not fail to try the Lobster Cantonese recipe. If you cannot face cutting up the live lobster, substitute shrimp. Either way, you will not be sorry.

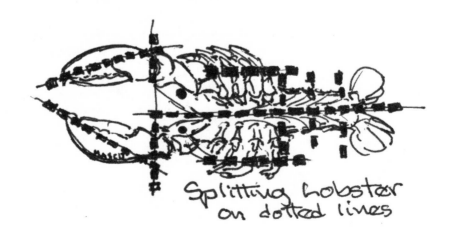

Splitting Lobster on dotted lines

Dear Pops,

I need information and an illustration, if possible, on filleting and deboning American shad.

Thanking you in advance,

Bob Dajda

I don't know how to do it, so I looked it up online. Apparently, deboning shad is a disappearing skill, one that involves at least eleven fairly precise cuts. There is supposedly a video somewhere demonstrating this skill, but I have yet to find it. There is enough information available to get you started, at least to the point of producing shad fingers for frying. Google "How to debone a shad" and take it from there.

Here is an idea about how to avoid the entire bone problem: Eat the bones!

SIX-HOUR BAKED SHAD WITH ONIONS AND BACON

1 whole shad (about 3 lbs.)
Juice of one lemon
Salt and pepper
1 large red onion sliced
3-4 sprigs fresh thyme or marjoram
4 slices bacon

Clean and scale fish (remove head and tail if you wish) and remove red flesh from around backbone inside the cavity.

Set oven at 200 to 225 degrees F. Lay out large sheet of aluminum foil, oil center lightly and spread half the onions on oiled area. Salt, pepper and lemon the fish inside and out, stuff remaining onions and herbs inside fish, and lay it upon the onion bed. Put bacon strips on top of fish and seal fish in aluminum foil packet. Bake for 5 or 6 hours.

Transfer packet to serving platter, split side of packet (a lot of liquid will come out) and carefully slide out fish. You can now remove the meat from the bones with a spoon and fork. Serve the meat with the juice and new potatoes. The remaining bones are now edible.

I must admit I have never tried this, though I've eaten and enjoyed shad flesh and roe frequently. If I had a spare shad, I know I would give this recipe a shot. If you do, let me know how it was.

Hey, Pops –

I heard you have a great recipe for "shell-less stuffed quahog a la Penikese."

Peter

SHELL-LESS STUFFED QUAHOGS A LA PENIKESE

1 part (2 cups) chopped or ground clams
1 part crumbled stale white bread or breadcrumbs
1 part chopped onions, green pepper (chopped garlic and linguica are optional in this part)
2 cloves garlic (recommended)
3 Tbsp. chopped parsley
Salt (be careful: clams are salty) and pepper
1 stick of butter
1 Tbsp. lemon juice (optional)
Tabasco or cayenne pepper to taste

Sauté the onion, garlic, and sweet peppers in melted butter over medium heat until translucent, but do not brown. Mix cooked vegetables with clams and breadcrumbs or cubes and add parsley, ground pepper, Tabasco or cayenne. Mix thoroughly with your hands. Put this mixture in an ovenproof pan (Pyrex is good) in a layer no more than 1½ inches deep. Bake in a 350 degrees F oven for about 45 minutes; it should be beginning to brown on top. Do not dry out! Serve with melted butter, lemon quarters and your favorite hot sauce, and there you have it.

This mixture is also good for stuffing a chicken, capon, turkey or whole fish. I think you should try them all! I have, and I am a pretty happy old guy.

Life After Sushi...

I know this column is called "Cooking the Catch," but this month we are going to talk about eating uncooked fish. Men and women have eaten raw shellfish, clams, oysters and scallops from time immemorial, so why not finfish as well?

I think many writers underestimate the sophistication of readers of outdoor magazines, but I think they are broad-minded in many ways. They also tend to be quite hip (as some say) and willing to try new things; the popularity of sushi and sashimi proves this.

Let's start by describing how raw fish is served and the names by which it is referred.

Pickled herring: we all know what this is, and it is raw. Gravlax (salmon cured with sugar and dill), lox (smoked fish) and caviar are also raw.

Sashimi, a Japanese specialty, is raw fish that can be made from many species. Tuna is probably the most popular type of sashimi, and fugu, a poisonous blowfish, is the most expensive. Sashimi is usually served with soy sauce, wasabi (a pale green, grated root that resembles horseradish) and pickled ginger.

Sushi, another Japanese treat, is vinegar-flavored semi-sweet rice combined with other ingredients. Often the rice is wrapped in seaweed (nori) and includes raw fish. Smoked eel sushi is my favorite.

All of these things, when done correctly, are delicious.

Recently, my talented (at least in the kitchen) son-in-law, Scott Britton, introduced me to raw fish prepared in the Italian style known as "crudo," which means "raw" in Italian. It was delicious! Crudo consists of carefully sliced or cubed pieces of fresh, raw fish briefly marinated in good virgin olive oil (the best you can afford), then garnished with flavors of your choice (often citrus juice or herbs) and sprinkled with coarse sea salt. Mario Batali and Joe Bastianich introduced this dish to the U.S. through their New York restaurant about seven years ago, where it became wildly popular. Now it is widely emulated around the country.

I was recently given some day-old yellowfin tuna steaks, and on the same day I caught some bluefish. My daughter Liz, wife of "Scott the Star," invited us over for dinner. I once vowed I would never turn down a dinner invitation from Scott, so I was compelled to accept. I told them about the fine fresh fish I had come into, and they asked if I would bring it over. Because I had intended to share the tuna with them anyway, I did, and Scott prepared them raw as "crudo." He carefully sliced and arranged the bluefish and tuna on a platter, bathed them in super olive oil and dappled them with sea salt and black pepper. I was blown away by how delicious they were – I have rarely eaten anything better. My hat is off to Scott once again!

I do not think I could improve upon this dish in any way, but I will try nonetheless. When I do, I will serve it on a bed of fresh field greens or baby spinach leaves and garnish it with lemon slices.

"CRUDO" APPETIZER *(for 4)*

½ lb. bluefish fillet (absolutely fresh)
½ lb. tuna as fresh as you can get
¼ cup extra virgin olive oil (more if needed)
Coarse sea salt to taste
Freshly ground black pepper
2 lemons quartered
Greens for presentation bed
Chopped parsley garnish

Carefully slice the fish into uniform pieces and marinate in olive oil for at least one hour, but no more than three hours.

Spread greens on a dish and arrange fish slices on top. Pour any extra oil over fish and greens. Sprinkle with salt and pepper, garnish with parsley and lemon, and serve. Sit back and wait for the applause.

Striped bass, fluke, black sea bass, scup, bonito and Spanish mackerel could all be used in this recipe. Sliced sea scallops would also be delicious.

The recipe as presented provides a basic example and a good starting point. Feel free to add flavorings of your choice, such as herbs and spices, sliced onions, capers, and various chopped pickles.

According to Erica Duecy in the Nation's Restaurant News, "At Il Grano, a contemporary Italian restaurant in West Los Angeles, chef-owner Salvatore Marino serves a daily crudo tasting plate featuring several selections, depending upon market availability. A recent crudo plate comprised a diver scallop on spinach leaf with olive oil, lemon and fleur de sel (sea salt); a slice of Pacific red snapper over mixed micro-greens; a piece of Japanese wild stone sole with micro celery; a slice of yellowtail with baby arugula; and a piece of octopus with fish roe vinaigrette." You could replace any of these fish with the fish we catch locally, marinate them in olive oil, season them up and serve.

SEA SCALLOP CRUDO WITH BACON AND LEMON *(for 2)*

½ lb. sea scallops, sliced crosswise
2 slices of bacon, fried crisp and crumbled
¼ cup olive oil
1 lemon
sea salt
Pepper, freshly ground

Marinate scallops in olive oil for one hour. Arrange scallops on greens, sprinkle with bacon, salt and pepper, then squeeze lemon juice over everything. There you have it – enjoy!

Scallops are ideal for any crudo recipe; they won't fall apart, and they maintain their texture and flavor even when not absolutely fresh.

BAY SCALLOPS WITH LIME JUICE & TOASTED SESAME *(for 2)*

½ lb. bay scallops
¼ cup good virgin olive oil
Sea salt
Pepper
2 limes

Marinate scallops in oil for one hour, then arrange on two plates. Put sesame seeds in a hot, dry skillet and heat, shaking the pan to prevent burning. Continue until the seeds begin to pop and smell delicious. Remove from heat and sprinkle over scallops, then squeeze the limes over all. You will not regret it!

Crudo provides an excellent outlet for your imagination, and I ask that you give it a shot. Personally, I think hot pepper is good in the marinade, as well as garlic, which you can blanch in boiling water for 45 seconds before crushing or mincing it. Toasted almonds would give flavor and texture. The possibilities seem endless! As I wrote this column, I marinated some chopped quahogs with chopped tarragon and hot pepper, and sprinkled them with a bit of sea salt. My wife and I ate them with a dash of lemon juice – delicious, and something I have never eaten before! ◄►

Grand Lobster and Two Remarkable Toasts!

Last week I made a truly delicious, almost wonderful lobster dinner. When it comes to cooking seafood, modesty is not one of my virtues. The dish I prepared came from the simple, classic Chinese cookbook by Joyce Chen published in 1962. It is called, not surprisingly, the "Joyce Chen Cook Book."

When this book appeared, I was a novice cook and culinary explorer. It was one of the first cookbooks to demystify Chinese cooking for the ordinary American cook, and it provides many simple, easily prepared dishes for home consumption that are just as good as or better than your local Chinese emporium.

I first tasted this marvelous dish at Joyce Chen's restaurant in North Cambridge. I had two unforgettable experiences at her restaurant at a wedding reception for a couple of international lovers; the bride was the daughter of the American consul in Bahrain, and the groom was the son of Chinese diplomats and a graduate of the Harvard Business School. The guest list was international in flavor, with many academics, rich folk, and other wise "high-toned" individuals in attendance.

The two experiences I will never forget were, first, the lobster in meat sauce, Cantonese-style, and second, the toast made by the best man, who proudly began his declamation by saying:

"I was the first man to sleep with the bride and the last man to sleep with the groom."

There were gasps, choking coughs, and finally, mostly laughter. The diplomat father of the bride was aghast, ashen and outraged, and the bride's mother was laughing uproariously. I can say that all in attendance were amazed – a real show-stopper of a toast introduction!

The only other event of extraordinary import at the reception was the serving of the following lobster dish:

LOBSTER IN MEAT SAUCE, CANTONESE-STYLE

1 live lobster, 1½ to 2 lbs.

½ cup ground pork (about ¼ lb.)

3 Tbsp. cooking oil

2 or 3 slices ginger root

2 cloves crushed garlic

1 ½ Tbsp. fermented black beans, minced (bottled black bean sauce may be used)

2 tsp. dry sherry

½ tsp. salt

¼ tsp. MSG

½ tsp. sugar

1 ½ Tbsp. cornstarch

1 beaten egg

1 scallion, sliced

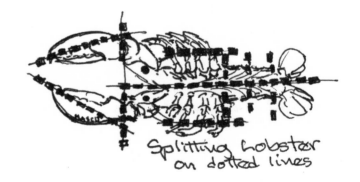

Splitting lobster on dotted lines

Cut lobster into 14 pieces as shown. Break tomalley* into smaller pieces in a bowl. Mix cornstarch in ¼ cup cold water. Pour oil into a wok, large skillet, or a saucepan over medium-high heat. Chop garlic and black beans together and add to hot oil along with the ginger slices, pork and tomalley. Stir for 3 minutes. Add lobster and sherry and give a few stirrings, then add ¾ cup water, salt, soy sauce, MSG and sugar. Cover and bring to a boil, reduce to an active simmer, and cook for 4 minutes. (The lobster should have turned red and the meat should be white.) Stir in the cornstarch dissolved in water and thicken the sauce by stirring. Now, add raw beaten egg and stir well. Garnish this with chopped scallions and serve with white rice. You will be overjoyed, loved and praised. I promise!

* As of July 2008, the FDA has issued a recommendation not to consume the tomalley of Atlantic (Maine) lobsters,

---

given the tomalley's tendency to build up high levels of toxins and other pollutants. This advisory applies only to tomalley and not to lobster meat.

SHRIMP TOAST

2 strips bacon
1 lb. raw shrimp, shelled and deveined
5 water chestnuts or ½ cup minced celery
1 tsp. dry sherry (cheap stuff is fine)
¼ tsp. MSG
1 tsp. salt
10 slices white bread (day-old is better)
Enough oil for 1-inch depth in a skillet

Grind, finely chop, or process shrimp and bacon into a paste. Mince water chestnuts and add to shrimp and bacon, along with MSG and sherry. Set aside.

Cut crusts from bread. Divide shrimp mixture into 10 portions and spread evenly on each piece of bread. (Dip your knife in cold water to aid spreading.) I cut each bread slice diagonally at this point.

Heat oil in skillet to 350 degrees F. Test oil temperature by putting a piece of bread crust into it; if foam forms around the crust, the oil is hot enough for frying the toasts. Fry bread-side down until edges are light brown. Turn to fry other side.

Drain on paper towel and serve hot. I like to garnish them with parsley, minced scallions or cilantro when serving. If you wish, you can add a teaspoon or so of any of the herbs directly to the shrimp paste before frying. These things are terrific! They can be kept warm in the oven or reheated should any be left over, which is very unlikely.

If you like, you can confidently substitute shrimp or scallops for the lobster in the first recipe. Your guests will rave! Vegetarians can substitute tofu or chopped mushrooms for the pork with good results, but pork is best.

The groomsman's toast was made less shocking by his explanation of the circumstances of his bed-sharing: he once shared a crib in infancy with the bride, and he shared a two-man tent with the groom on a pre-wedding camping trip. Personally I think he should have left the whole thing up in the air for our personal "prurient" imaginings!

When or Where Does Soup Become Chowder?

I think a true, authentic clam chowder contains but four main ingredients: clams, onions, potatoes, and milk in some form — whole, evaporated, or cream. Salt, pepper, a bit of thyme or butter may be added, but nothing else. A tugboat captain I once knew told me that my chowder, made with the above ingredients, was chowder "the way God meant it to be!" This was the finest compliment I ever received.

I heard an old lady from Nantucket say she heard of someone who put celery and cream and possibly other adulterants in her chowder. She would have probably expired if someone put tomatoes in chowder. She was possibly more conservative than I on this topic.

After much thought, I have decided to try to develop more tolerance for other forms of chowder, without giving up my basic beliefs. Now that my column is being read in our New York and New Jersey edition, I may have to include Manhattan Clam Chowder in the fold along with clam and fish chowders prepared in the New England way. I have presented a recipe for this tomato-based "chowder" but called it clam soup in the past. Will I be accused of selling out? Possibly, but not by my tugboat captain friend who has unfortunately died. Maybe the lady on Nantucket has also. So here goes, I'll chance it.

MANHATTAN CLAM CHOWDER (for 6)

12 large hard-shelled clams (quahogs)
½ lb. salt pork or slab bacon in ¼" diced pieces
2 medium onions in 1/4" dice
4 carrots, diced
2 stalks celery, diced
½ green pepper, diced
3 Tbsp. chopped parsley
1 16-ounce can diced tomatoes
Water to add to tomato and clam juice to make 2 quarts
6 peppercorns
1 bay leaf
½ tsp. thyme
2 medium potatoes in ½" cubes
Tabasco (optional, but good)
Oyster crackers for serving

Put ½ cup of water in pan with cover and steam clams over medium heat until all are open. Save clam juice.

Render salt pork or bacon in a four-quart saucepan until slightly browned. Put onions in pan and sweat (cook gently) until translucent. Add the carrot, celery, green pepper and parsley and cook another 10 minutes.

Mix clam broth and tomatoes to make 2 quarts of liquid, add water if necessary. Pour over vegetables and rendered pork, add bay leaf, peppercorns and thyme. Bring to a simmer, add diced potatoes and simmer until potatoes are cooked, about 30 minutes.

Chop, grind or process clams until pea-sized and add to the chowder, simmer for 6 or 7 minutes, do not boil.

You now have a Manhattan Clam Chowder. Some people add ½ teaspoon of caraway seeds at this point, but I wouldn't. This chowder, not New England chowder, but chowder to many, nonetheless, is delicious. Serve with crackers and optional hot sauce.

Somewhere around the Massachusetts and Rhode Island border, the milk disappears from clam chowder and a clear chowder is made, and then somewhere around Niantic, Connecticut, tomato begins to appear in the chowder. This Rhode Island clam chowder has even fewer ingredients than my New England Clam Chowder.

RHODE ISLAND CLAM CHOWDER

1 pint quahog meats and liquid (18 to 24 clams)
¼ lb. salt pork
2 quarts water
6 medium potatoes (P.E.I., Maine, boiling potatoes) in ¼" cubes
2 medium onions, diced
Salt, if needed, and freshly ground pepper when serving
Tabasco or other hot sauce, optional

Steam clams open, save liquid, and chop into ¼-inch bits with a chef's knife. Dry out the salt pork in a skillet over medium heat until all fat is rendered and pork is lightly browned. Remove cracklings with a slotted spoon and set aside.

Mix saved clam juice and water to make two quarts in a four-quart saucepan, add potatoes and cracklings, simmer for 8 to 10 minutes. Potatoes should not be mushy.

Cook the onions in the pork fat over medium heat until translucent, about 8 minutes. Now add clams and onions to the potato broth, scraping in all fat, and cook at a boil for 4 or 5 minutes. Now rest the chowder for at least an hour before serving; overnight is even better. If the chowder is too thin, it can be boiled down. It is probably best to pour off the liquid if you wish to boil it down so the vegetables will not go to mush, and return it to clams and veggies before serving. This is clammy and delicious. If chicken soup is Jewish penicillin, I think clam soup or chowder must be Yankee penicillin.

I like to include chowder or some other fish soup in holiday celebrations. If not in the actual Thanksgiving or Christmas dinner, I make it in the days before or after the main event, and almost always on Christmas Eve for the feast of the seven (minimum) or thirteen (there is no maximum) fishes, and you should too!

Real Chowder Ingredients

Will This Family Food End in Disaster?

Well, it has happened again. My culinarily gifted son-in-law served me a dinner (ignoring my fear of quahogs) that was so good I probably cannot do better. I would like to say that I was getting used to it, even comfortable with it, but I am not. The menu was exotic while using common ingredients: Clams Oreganato, Oysters Rockefeller, Aunt somebody's cooked tomatoes, and a Porcini, Wild Mushroom and Sea Scallop Soup. It was an outstanding, unusual meal, with the crumbed cooked tomatoes as a separate, delicious course. I would probably have served everything at once, but Scott, being both more elegant and aware of individual flavors, served the meal in sequential exquisite courses. I may be getting to dislike this feeling of inferiority, and maybe even him. I will overcome these feelings because I swore, as part of my vow at his wedding, that I would never turn down a dinner invitation from him, but I am having second thoughts. When I get over my fit of pique, I may even give you another of his recipes. But for now I will present some very good, but not exquisite, recipes from meals made and served in my kitchen by increasingly modest me.

I made a spaghetti sauce of haddock, shrimp and homemade tomato sauce last week that was so good I had the leftovers for two consecutive breakfasts. I got the tomato sauce recipe from Kenny Shopsin's unique, rudely titled "Eat Me" cookbook published by Knopf. It is also listed on page 51 of this cookbook for your referral.

SPAGHETTI WITH HADDOCK AND SHRIMP *(for 2 or 3)*

½ lb. spaghetti or linguini
2 cups marinara sauce (see p.51)
12 small shrimp
½ lb. haddock (or other white-fleshed fish)

As you boil the pasta, following package directions for al dente, heat the marinara to a steady simmer. Five minutes before the pasta is cooked, add the whole fish fillet to the sauce, followed by the shelled shrimp. By the time the pasta is cooked, the fish and shrimp will be cooked. Drain the pasta and pour the sauce on top. Garnish with a little chopped parsley and serve.

The Italians do not like this, but I serve mine with optional grated cheese. I also like a little coarsely ground black pepper on mine.

I make a point of watching for frozen uncooked shrimp at the supermarket and always have some in my freezer for fancying up simple dishes or quick appetizers. They are incredibly convenient to have at hand. They thaw very quickly in water. Get some, you won't be sorry.

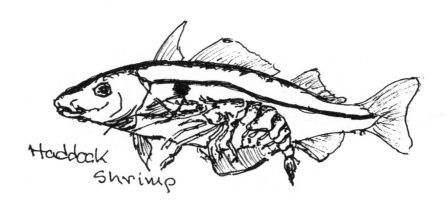

Haddock
Shrimp

I was hoping to find monkfish for the shrimp and marinara sauce. I think that monkfish cut in 1-inch cubes would be very good as would striped bass. While looking for monkfish, I came upon some fresh whole sardines that were flown over from Portugal, where they are eaten as frequently as we eat hot dogs. I consider a grilled, lightly salted Portuguese sardine one of the world's great culinary treats. These sardines are not tiny as those in the cans, but about 9 or 10 inches of plump goodness. I bought two fine sardines to grill for my breakfast.

I gutted and gilled the sardines, leaving the head on, and sprinkled them with sea salt (coarse) to sit overnight. This is done in Portugal as well. In the morning, I preheated my oven broiler and a small broiling pan in which I put a Tbsp. of olive oil. I brushed most of the salt off the fish, scored them on both sides and broiled them for 4 minutes per side, about 4 inches from the broiler flame, until the skin began to parch. I removed the broiling pan from the oven and carefully put the grilled sardines on a throne of crusty homemade bread on a plate and poured the delicious oil from the pan over them. Probably nobody, not even son-in-law Scott, had a better breakfast than I did that morning. So there!

I can't bring myself to call Scott and ask for his Oysters Rockefeller recipe yet, so in homage to his, I will give you one I have used and remember as spectacularly good. Here goes:

MY VERSION OF OYSTERS ROCKEFELLER *(for 6 as an appetizer)*

12 oysters
4 Tbsp. unsalted butter
¼ cup minced celery
½ cup minced flat-leaf parsley
¼ cup chopped scallions
½ bunch watercress
¼ lb. spinach
1 ½ tsp. anchovy paste
Cayenne pepper to taste
2 Tbsp. Pernod (I think you can get it in nips)
½ cup unseasoned breadcrumbs

Melt butter in a skillet until bubbling, add celery and cook, stirring until softened, about 1½ minutes. Stir in parsley and scallions, cook 30 seconds, add watercress and spinach mixing to coat with butter. Cook until wilted; then add anchovy paste, cayenne and Pernod. Add breadcrumbs and mix thoroughly. Arrange opened oysters on a broiler pan (you may place them in a layer of rock salt should you wish). Put a spoonful of the spinach mixture on each oyster. Boil in preheated broiler until bubbly and oysters curl.

Take that, Scott. I remember these being as good as yours, but I wouldn't bet on it.

Winter Whip Ups?

On Thanksgiving Eve I was at a loss for what I, my wife, and my 95-year-old mother-in-law should have for dinner, so I agreed with mother-in-law Irma when she said, "A piece of haddock would be nice!" What piece she did not say, so off to the fishmonger (a good word) I went for a pound and a half of haddock fillets so we would have a bit of fish leftover for fish cakes, which my wife's mother loves. I often make a bunch and freeze them, two to a bag, as a gift for her on Mother's Day.

I was uninspired, but had on hand a mashed potato and turnip dish (four parts potato to one part turnip) and some Brussel sprouts. I also found half of both a red and green sweet pepper in a vegetable drawer, so dinner would be mashed potato and turnip reheated, steamed Brussels sprouts with butter (or olive oil), salt, pepper and a pinch of nutmeg, and haddock fillets baked on a bed of peppers and onions. Things were looking up!

BAKED HADDOCK FILLETS WITH ONIONS AND PEPPERS *(for 3)*

1 ½ lbs. haddock fillets (skinned)

1 medium onion

½ green pepper (sweet)

½ red pepper (sweet)

4 Tbsp. olive oil

¼ cup bread or cracker crumbs

Salt and pepper

Preheat oven to 415 degrees F. Cut the peppers and onions into strips for sautéing. Put 2 Tbsp. olive oil in a skillet or oven-proof casserole that can be put on direct heat and cook gently until soft but not browned. Now salt and pepper the haddock fillets, anoint with oil and lay them on the sautéed onions and peppers.

Sprinkle a layer of breadcrumbs or cracker crumbs on the fillets and drizzle olive oil over all, put the whole works in the oven for 15 minutes and there you have it, a fine fish course, in its own sauce, enough sauce to use some on your warmed-up mashed potatoes. Garnish this dish with parsley and a quartered lemon and you have something good enough for anyone on earth, I promise!

Here we are in the coldest month of the year with little freshly caught fish available unless we want to go ice fishing or sit on a cold pier fishing for smelt – or we can get some younger, generous, hot-blooded youths to gather fresh treasures for us. You catch the winter fish, and I will be delighted to cook them for you, but if this does not work I can resort to canned or, as the Queen would say, "tinned" fish. I did this one day last week, making myself a delicious lunch: canned smoked herring on a mixed green salad containing sweet onions, tiny tomatoes, and sliced cucumber as well as lettuce and spinach dressed with vinaigrette. You could use any number of dressings; I bet poppyseed would be good. The smoked herring will stand up to any of the commercial dressings. Add a few croutons and a slice of crusty bread, a glass of wine or soda, and there you have it: a "gourmet" lunch.

QUICK GOOD LUNCH *(for 2)*

1 can smoked herring (6.7 oz.), 2 cans sardines, 1 can tuna or any canned fish you like

Mesclun or lettuce

10 grape tomatoes

½ sliced cucumber

Some sliced sweet onion

¼ cup vinaigrette or a bottled dressing of your choice

Croutons (optional)

Arrange all this stuff prettily on a small platter with the fish on top. Either dress the whole works or serve the dressing on the side, which many people think makes it less fattening – another mystery – but a great lunch.

While on the subject of canned fish, I must mention a book from my cookbook collection (I have over 250 and continually acquire more, though more critically as I grow older and more knowledgeable) called "BEST RECIPES From the Backs of Boxes, Bottles, Cans and Jars," and that is what it contains. In this book I found a very simple recipe for salmon loaf, something my mother made when I was a lad that I still enjoy. The following recipe is simple and good, better if you make the easy sauce that follows.

SALMON LOAF

1 16 oz. can salmon, drained, deboned
½ cup dry breadcrumbs
½ cup mayonnaise
½ cup finely chopped onion
¼ cup chopped celery
¼ cup chopped green pepper
¼ cup minced parsley
1 egg, beaten
1 tsp. salt
½ tsp. pepper
Hot sauce to taste (optional)

Combine all ingredients thoroughly but lightly. Butter a shallow baking pan and put in salmon mixture shaped into a loaf. Bake at 350 degrees F for 40 minutes. Remove from oven, allow to cool slightly, slice and serve with the following sauce.

CUCUMBER SAUCE

½ cup mayonnaise
½ cup sour cream
½ cup finely chopped cucumber
2 Tbsp. finely chopped onion (I like to use a scallion for color)
½ tsp. dill weed (or 2 Tbsp. chopped fresh dill)

Mix everything and serve.

BAKED FISH FILLETS JOSE *(for 4 to 6)*

1 package Ortega Taco dinner (7 oz.)
2 lbs. fish fillets (cod, haddock, striped bass – whatever)
½ cup butter

Heat taco shells, mix with seasoning, and crush thoroughly or grind in blender or food processor until fine. Dip fish in butter and then in crumbs to coat with crumbs. Bake in a preheated 425 degrees F oven for 15 to 20 minutes (probably 15 is enough), serve with taco sauce.

An avocado and onion salad goes well with this, and maybe some Spanish rice.

These recipes are good and unpretentious, and help empty the cabinets. Maybe next month I will tune things up and go for Coquille St. Jacques (scallops in a white sauce). We can do it!

Chapter Twelve:
DECEMBER

The days start getting longer this month, a good thing, so we should celebrate the growing length of daylight with festive holiday meals, particularly the Feast of the Seven Fishes, a wonderful Italian traditional meal for Christmas Eve. You can show off most of your seafood cooking skills in one grand burst.

New Year's Eve is another great occasion for serving fish. I suggest oysters and clams, raw on the half-shell, cold shrimp, pickled herring, scallops wrapped in bacon and broiled, and gravlax with pumpernickel bread and butter. A little beer and sparkling wine will not hurt, either.

Celebrate another year and the grand seafood we are fortunate enough to enjoy.

HAPPY HOLIDAYS!

Hi Pops,

Many years ago when I was a kid, my dad "Pep," as his many friends called him, would take me along with my Uncle Bob and friends to go eeling on Cape Cod's Green Pond when it would freeze over. It would be so cold, but, man, I loved it. Listening to my dad and uncle talk about fishing for sea trout ("salters" my dad called them) or hunting for deer on the island with buddies from the Beagle Club and the Skeet Club, all while catching big, thick eels and cooking linguica on a hibachi. Special times I'll cherish. Sadly, my dad passed away a few years ago. He left me all of his fishing gear along with the eel spears. A couple of the spears have a tine or two broken off. I'm wondering if there is anyone who could fix them? I know they are the old-type spears, but I'd like to try eeling again and bring my brother and son along. I'm sure my dad would get a smile, as I never see anyone eeling any more. Also, he used to marinate them in a Portuguese style. Do you know this recipe? Or maybe you know of a different one? Thanks, Pops and OTW for a great magazine and a fantastic fishing show.

Sincerely,
Steve Pimental

Eeling with your father and uncles sounds wonderful. Not so much the cold, but the idea of grilling linguica on a hibachi out on the frozen pond. What could be better?

I may have someone who could repair your spears. The R.A. Ribb Company in Harwich, MA, makes fine clamming gear and does repairs to clam rakes, so I am reasonably sure they could help you, and if they will not, they can probably recommend someone who will. This is a very good company.

There is a classic marinade for ocean catfish (wolffish) called "vinho D'Alhos" (literally wine of garlic) in Portuguese that also works wonderfully with eel. Every cook has his or her particular recipe, but all have salt, pepper, cumin, vinegar, and garlic as part of the final potion. The Portuguese trap fishermen in Provincetown, Massachusetts, with whom I worked 40 years ago referred to marinating as "galvanizing." They would often "galvanize" tuna. Here are two recipes, one from Mary-Jo Avellar, author of *"The Provincetown Portuguese Cookbook,"* the other from one of my heroes, Howard Mitcham, author of the great *"Provincetown Seafood Cookbook."*

VINHO D'ALHOS, MARINADE SIMPLE

1 16 oz. bottle cider vinegar
1 cup pickling spices
1 clove garlic (I like 4 cloves) sliced
2 Tbsp. onion powder (I slice a small onion thinly)
1 cup water
2 Tbsp. saffron (way too expensive), or substitute cumin or turmeric (optional)

VINHO D'ALHOS ALA MITCHUM

2 cups water
1 cup vinegar
Salt and pepper
4 crumbled bay leaves, a variety of spices of your choice, including a tsp. of ground cumin; avoid oregano here
6 cloves garlic, crushed
1 sliced onion
¼ cup mixed pickling spice

Wolffish or eel should be cut in 2½-inch pieces and marinated overnight in the mixture of all the ingredients. Other fish should marinate for no more than 45 minutes or they will soften.

Remove eel from marinade, rinse and pat dry. Bread the eel in any breading you prefer and fry it slowly in bacon fat or some other oil. Sauté slowly until nicely browned on all sides. Do this over medium heat so that you do not burn the breading before the eel is cooked. This is a marvelous peasant dish too good for most upscale restaurants.

Celebrate Shellfish for Fame and Fun

I am writing this between Christmas and New Year's Eve, still smarting because I received no seafood for Christmas. Not a shrimp, lobster, eel, or piece of smoked salmon. Not even a can of sardines! (My culinary threat son-in-law, Scott, did give me a dozen oysters a few days before Christmas, so I guess he is off the hook.) I am probably a better person for my deprivation, since it is supposedly better to give than to receive.

I have always admired the Catholic (particularly Italian) tradition of eating seafood, ideally seven species, on Christmas Eve, a fasting day. So for a winter solstice celebration of my own, I headed to my fishmonger in search of treasures. My fishmonger was out of scallops and cleaned squid, so I settled for a few shrimp, some mussels and a lonely-looking octopus to put in a seafood risotto that would accompany three steamed lobsters. I already had Scott's "gift" oysters and my own smoked bluefish at home. I thought I could come up with a fine meal, though I would only have six varieties of seafood because of the scallop shortage.

I decided on a smoked bluefish dip and a paté, followed by the steamed lobster, seafood risotto, and salad. This turned into a grandly festive meal; the red lobster with white meat beside the dark green spinach salad made a Christmassy presentation indeed!

I steamed three 1½-pound lobsters for 12 minutes after the pot was full of steam. Cook yours any way you like, but avoid overcooking them. Pay attention! Almost all of my cooking disasters have been caused by inattention.

I made stock with the octopus I brought home: 5 cups of water, a stalk of celery, an onion, 8 peppercorns, 2 cloves of garlic, ½ cup of parsley, and a glass (6 oz.) of dry white wine. I simmered this for an hour until the octopus was tender, strained it, and it was ready. You can also make a stock from fish bouillon or lobster bisque base.

This risotto recipe is from the basic Italian cookbook, "The Silver Spoon", published by Phaidon. Some people call this book "The Joy of Cooking" of Italy. All serious lovers of Italian food should own a copy.

RISOTTO AL FRUTTA DI MARE (for 4)

(Seafood and Rice)
4 Tbsp. olive oil
1 onion chopped
1 or 2 cloves garlic (crushed)
1 lb. mixed seafood, such as octopus, cuttlefish, squid or
  scallops, chopped to pencil eraser-sized pieces
4 to 5 cups fish stock (or clam juice)
¾ cup dry white wine
2 Tbsp. tomato paste
A scant 2 cups of risotto rice (arborio or carnaroli)
½ lb. mussels (shelled or whole)
½ lb. shrimp
1 Tbsp. minced flat-leaf parsley
Salt and pepper
Cayenne pepper (optional) to taste

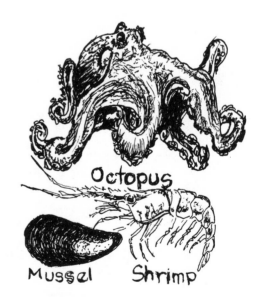

Octopus

Mussel   Shrimp

Heat the oil in a heavy-bottomed 4-quart pan, add the onion and garlic, and cook for about 10 minutes over low heat until lightly browned, being careful not to burn the garlic. Meanwhile, bring the stock to a boil in another pan. Add the seafood to the onion and garlic and sprinkle (I pour) the wine over everything. Cook until nearly evaporated, then salt and pepper the seafood. (Be careful with the salt, especially if using clam juice for your stock.) Put in 3 Tbsp. (1/2 cup) water and the tomato paste and cook very gently on low heat for about 10 minutes. Stir in all the rice until the liquid is absorbed. Raise the heat to medium and add stock a ladleful at a time, stirring constantly at first. Continue to add stock in about ½-cup doses, stirring very often until all stock is absorbed and the rice is creamily cooked. Add the shrimp and mussels for the last five minutes of cooking. Sprinkle the whole works with parsley and serve.

I know that some of you will be daunted by the risotto recipe, but I urge you to try it – your life will be changed and the world will be a better place! Your lobsters should be steaming as you are preparing the risotto. You will assemble the following salad ahead of time on individual plates.

BABY SPINACH WITH GOAT CHEESE AND WALNUT SALAD (for 4)
4 handfuls of baby spinach leaves
1/3 cup toasted chopped walnuts
2 Tbsp. goat cheese per plate (to taste)
Balsamic vinegar
Virgin olive oil
Salt and freshly ground pepper

Lightly toast walnuts in a tablespoon of olive oil in a skillet. Arrange, in whatever amount you choose, spinach leaves on plates, top with crumbled or cubed goat cheese and toasted walnuts. Sprinkle with balsamic vinegar and drizzle with olive oil just before serving.

SCALLOPS IN SNAIL BUTTER (for 2 or 3)
1 lb. scallops (bay or sea)
¼ lb. softened butter (unsalted is best)
¾ cups packed flat-leaf parsley
4 cloves garlic
2 cups fresh ½-inch square croutons
Salt and freshly ground black pepper
Juice of one lemon

Put garlic, parsley and butter in a blender with a little salt and pepper. Blend until nearly smooth, scraping down sides. Heat oven to 500 degrees F. Spread croutons in a 9 x 13-inch casserole dish and toast in oven until lightly browned. Remove from casserole dish.

Spread garlic, parsley and butter sauce in warm casserole dish. Arrange scallops (whole bay scallops, or cut sea scallops in quarters) and croutons in a single layer on butter sauce and bake for 4 minutes, stir ingredients to coat everything, and bake for 4 minutes more. Sprinkle with lemon juice, stir, correct seasoning and serve – satisfaction will be yours. You can cut butter and garlic amounts in half and omit the croutons, and you will not be sorry. What could be easier? Go for it! ◀━◀

A Path to Fame and Fortune?

I recently read a quotation, the author of which I have forgotten, saying in effect that, "The only reason people write cookbooks is to increase the well-being and happiness of mankind." This was one of my reasons for writing a cookbook. The second was money. I am going to write about a relatively simple, elegant meal that will increase both your well-being and happiness should you choose to prepare it. I urge you to do so!

I prepared this for my wife, myself, and a dear friend for our New Year's Eve Dinner. We started with an assortment of cheeses and raw oysters, accompanied by champagne (the least expensive — I say that to avoid being taken for a snob). The main meal was a spinach, goat cheese and orange salad dressed with oil and vinegar, a plain cheese risotto and sautéed shrimp, scallops and sesame-coated tuna. Dessert was a Tarte Tatin (a one-crust caramelized apple tart made in a skillet) and vanilla ice cream. The champagne ran out, and white wine was substituted. It could hardly have been better, I say with pretend modesty.

The oysters were purchased from Wellfleet. The cheeses were French. The tuna, shrimp and scallops were quickly sautéed in hot brown butter flavored with garlic and ginger just before serving, an easy process, but one that needs careful attention, for shrimp and tuna are easily overcooked – this is especially true of shrimp in American cookery. The risotto, the only dish needing much work, was prepared ahead and kept warm over hot water. Instead of risotto, you might serve plain white rice or pasta dressed with oil and garlic. The Tarte Tatin I had made in the afternoon.

SAUTÉED SEAFOOD FOR NEW YEAR'S EVE
(or any special occasion or just for the hell of it)
(for 3 people)

1 lb. fresh tuna 1" thick

12 large shrimp (not giant)

3 large sea scallops (or more)

Salt and pepper

4 Tbsp. butter

2 cloves garlic (crushed)

2 slices of fresh ginger (1/8" thick)

½ cup sesame seeds

¼ cup half-and-half (optional for moistening tuna before coating)

Parsley and scallion (minced) for garnish

Sliced lemon for garnish

Shell, devein and dry shrimp on paper towel; dry scallops also. Cut tuna steak in 1-inch-wide, 3-inch-long pieces. Salt and pepper shrimp, scallops and tuna pieces. Now moisten tuna in cream and dip in sesame seeds to coat both sides. Set all seafood aside.

Crush garlic and slice fresh ginger. Melt butter over medium heat in a skillet big enough for all the seafood pieces. (I used two 8-inch skillets.) Add garlic and ginger and cook for a couple of minutes to flavor the butter. Do not burn the garlic; remove ginger and garlic from pan when garlic begins to brown. You can do all this ahead of time.

At serving time, heat butter on medium-high heat until it just begins to brown. As the butter is heating, arrange salad on a serving plate (1/4 of plate). When butter is hot, put scallops in first, allow them to caramelize on one side before turning, about 2 minutes. Add shrimp and coated tuna pieces to pan and sauté for 1 minute; turn everything over and sauté for 1 to 2 minutes longer.

Place risotto (or pasta or whatever) on plates opposite the salad. Remove seafood and arrange on the empty quarter of the plates. Garnish with parsley, scallions, and lemons and serve – beautiful and delicious.

I served melted butter and a soy-based dipping sauce. The soy-based sauce is especially good with the tuna, while lemon and butter is great with the shrimp and scallops.

If you have a guest who likes tuna less rare, cook it a bit longer. I feel this is a mistake, but the guest should get his or her wishes met. I often must remind myself of this courtesy. This is a great dinner!

DIPPING SAUCE FOR SEAFOOD

2 Tbsp. soy sauce
1 Tbsp. fish sauce (or nuoc cham or nam pla)
1 Tbsp. dark sesame oil
1 ½ tsp. rice vinegar or lemon juice
1 Tbsp. minced fresh ginger or 1 tsp. ground ginger
½ tsp. sugar
½ tsp. crushed, minced garlic
1 Tbsp. chopped scallion (optional)

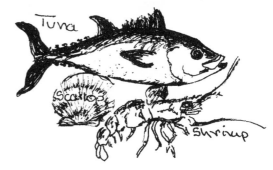

Mix all these together and have at it. Delicious! You may add chopped hot pepper or hot sauce. If the sauce seems too strong, add water a teaspoon at a time.

Here is another shrimp appetizer that my family is crazy about.

SPICY SAUTÉED SHRIMP

1 lb. small shrimp (thawed and dried)
2 cloves crushed garlic
2 slices ginger
2 Tbsp. peanut oil
½ Tbsp. Chinese chili garlic paste
Salt
2 Tbsp. minced scallion

Salt shrimp lightly. Heat 2 Tbsp. oil in a wok or large skillet. Toast garlic and ginger in oil until garlic begins to color, remove before it burns, add shrimp, garlic and chili paste to hot oil and stir over high heat until the shrimp are barely cooked, all pinkish and opaque. Serve as-is or with above dip. I eat them "feathers and all." Some of my wimpier relatives shell them.

Another very simple dip to eat with seafood is diluted oyster sauce. This may be the easiest recipe I have ever offered.

OYSTER SAUCE DIP

¼ cup oyster sauce
Water to taste

How's that for easy?

These recipes could make you famous, but remember, don't listen only to your family because no one's a hero at home. ◄●►

Never Sniff a Gift Fish in Public

I find it difficult to come up with a new idea for a Christmas holiday column each year, having done the Italian seven-fish dinner for Christmas Eve and a couple on my family's limited Midwestern seafood options for the holidays. So this year I will suggest some gifts to give to seafood cooks and consumers along with promoting my plan to make shellfish wrapped in bacon a holiday tradition. I would be overjoyed to receive a bushel of oysters for the holidays or a half-bushel of littlenecks, and so would any serious "foodies" you know; a pound or two of bay scallops make an opulent gift as well. I often get shrimp and, less often, lobsters as gifts. All of these are great last-minute shopping ideas. For eaters, but not cooks, some cooked frozen shrimp from supermarkets are good. Until the last year or so they were invariably overcooked; this is no longer always so. I would not turn down a "nice" piece of swordfish either.

I have often heard people ask for a "nice piece of fish." Who would want anything else? What kind of fishmonger would admit to selling anything else? Who would request a mediocre piece of fish? Hmm...

If a bushel or a half-bushel of oysters seems like too much, do not hesitate to give me, or any other deserving person, a dozen or two. Remember, those of you fortunate enough to receive such a gift, that your shellfish will be much easier to open if they are well chilled and handled gently rather than roughly treated at room temperature – you do not want to frighten them, or they will "clam up."

Smoked salmon makes a grand gift. I sometimes buy some from Russ and Daughters, a fine New York fish purveyor you can find online – they also have grand pickled herring, a holiday treat at my house. Good smoked salmon is costly but worth the price.

I enjoy making scrambled eggs with smoked salmon and scallions or chives. I enjoy eating these eggs even more. Some supermarkets have bits and pieces trimmed from whole fillets for very little money, about $5 a pound rather than $20 plus for the fancy stuff, so for $1.25 you can get enough lox (smoked salmon) to make:

SCRAMBLED EGGS WITH SALMON (for 4)

6 eggs
¼ lb. smoked salmon bits chopped
2 Tbsp. chopped scallion greens or chives
1 Tbsp. water
Salt and pepper
2 Tbsp. butter

Melt the butter; when it begins to bubble, put in the chopped salmon, mix to coat with butter, add the scallions, pour in the beaten eggs and a tablespoon of water. Now, rather than stirring, pull the eggs away from the sides of the skillet to the center as they set. When they form a moist clump in the center of the pan, they are ready to serve. If you have not added salt and pepper, do it now, sprinkle with additional chopped onion tops or chives, and serve. You will not be sorry, I promise. This is a good dish for Christmas morning with a glass of champagne.

Cooking equipment is always well received by "foodies." I own many frying pans and skillets, perhaps a dozen that I actually use. I have two skillets designed for fish cooking; one measures 16" by 10½", the other 14" by 9", that I find almost indispensable. The oval shape is ideal for lining up fillets to pan fry and for small, whole fish. The smaller skillet has a metal handle so I can sear a large, thick fish steak or two and finish cooking it in the oven without the surface charring.

SEARED ROAST SWORDFISH STEAK

½ lb. thick (1 to 1½") swordfish steak for each person
Spice rub of your choice or a premixed blackening blend
Olive oil (not virgin) or peanut oil to coat a skillet that can be put into the oven

Preheat oven to 415 degrees F. Heat oil in skillet until just beginning to smoke. Sear the spice-rubbed steaks for about one minute on each side and put skillet and fish into the hot oven for 10 to 12 minutes. Serve with a dab of butter (flavored, if you wish) and some quartered lemons on the side and a parsley garnish.

Add buttery mashed potatoes and a green vegetable (green beans, peas or spinach) and you have a memorable dinner – not much work and lots of pleasure and praise from your lucky guests.

An oval, ovenproof skillet will make a prized Christmas gift for any fish cook!

Why should "Angels on Horseback," oysters or scallops wrapped in bacon and broiled until the bacon is barely crisp, be served seemingly only at wedding receptions or big cocktail parties? I think we should have them at Christmas and New Year's. I wonder how this name came to be; perhaps the bacon resembles a saddle – beats me. I don't care greatly what they are called, but I am delighted to eat them.

These treats are usually broiled, but can be prepared with less fuss by roasting them in a 500 degrees F oven.

You can, and may, marinate the oysters, scallops or shrimp in white wine, garlic (crushed), and salt and pepper. This is not essential but adds a little kick to the flavor of the shrimp especially. Most of the shrimp we find frozen in supermarkets is farm raised in fresh water and rather bland in flavor compared to shrimp netted in saltwater and therefore need a little boost; garlic will do it.

When I make "Angels on Horseback," I precook the bacon until about half done, some of the fat released but still flexible enough to wrap whatever I am wrapping. I pin the bacon with a toothpick. Remember to use thinly sliced bacon and never use maple flavored! That's an order. This precooking of the bacon makes it crisp faster in the final cooking, thus reducing the chance of overcooking of the seafood.

Beyond the oyster, clams, scallops, and shrimp, try some swordfish cubes, monkfish chunks, or shark steak pieces – you and your guests will not be sorry that you did, and you will be more famous than you were already.

I have another suggestion for a fine Christmas gift for your favorite cook: my first cookbook, "Cooking the Catch," which is available through "On The Water" magazine's website, www.OnTheWater.com. If you follow my suggestions, we will both be richer for it.

Happy Holidays – go for the "Angels on Horseback"! Cheers!

Bring an Oyster to Christmas Dinner

I am writing this during an unseasonably warm late October, which makes it hard to believe that this column will appear just before Christmas. The bass and blues are still here and active, there were many false albacore in the Canal only two weeks ago, my wife cut armloads of flowers this morning, and I still have a few precious tomatoes ripening on the vine. Life is good – odd, but good.

I have had some new culinary experiences in the past month, all good, that I will pass on to you. New experiences are increasingly rare the older one gets, but no less interesting – good or bad.

I associate Christmas feasts with seafood, especially shellfish and preserved finfish, such as pickled herring, smoked bluefish or salmon, and finnan haddie (lightly smoked haddock).

Once again, my son-in-law has come up with a few fine recipes that I highly recommend for holiday consumption. He is gaining in the family seafood-cooking department; although I think my clam chowder still gives me an edge, he is chipping away. I may just have to keep him out of my column! That would be a great loss to you, but it could come to that. Or maybe I should just retire my number (#1) and leave the arena to him.

Scott gathered oysters this month and shared them with his in-laws. A truly noble fellow, indeed!

SCOTT'S BROILED OYSTERS WITH CHIPOTLE PESTO

3 dozen oysters, shucked
3 chipotle peppers
1 bunch cilantro
1 large clove garlic (blanched 45 seconds)
2 Tbsp. toasted pine nuts
¼ cup breadcrumbs
2 or 3 Tbsp. olive oil
Salt and pepper
3 or 4 limes

chipotle on oyster

Char peppers on a grill, under a broiler, or directly in the flames of a gas stove, until blackened all over. Put charred peppers in a paper bag for 10 minutes to facilitate peeling. This may seem like a lot of bother, but it is well worth it if fame and joy is your goal. Toast the pine nuts in a dry skillet until aromatic, shaking or stirring to avoid burning. Blanch unpeeled garlic in boiling water for 45 seconds and peel. This blanching reduces the harshness of raw garlic without sacrificing its flavor. Remove coarse bottom stems from the cilantro. Put the cilantro, peeled peppers, garlic, pine nuts and breadcrumbs into a food processor and blend. Gradually add olive oil until you have a lovely green paste. Season with a little salt and pepper.

Put a dollop of this magical pesto on each oyster, all of which have been arranged on a baking sheet. (You can make a bed of salt to rest them in if you wish to prevent capsizing; I don't bother.) Run the oysters under an oven broiler, about 3 inches from the flame, for three minutes. And there you have it! Squeeze a little lime juice on each gustatory jewel or urge your guests to do this themselves. The fame will be yours, and the joy will be shared when you and your lucky guests taste Scott's Wonders!

I wouldn't hesitate to treat the slightly less noble littleneck in the same way, nor should you.

Two weeks ago, my old friend "Predator Phil" and his friend Louis Fedick took me bluefishing for an hour and a half. We brought back over 30 pounds of bluefish, yielding slightly more than 10 pounds of fillets, which I smoked using Seth's dry brine and a slightly different technique than I have used in the past.

SETH'S DRY BRINE (for 10 pounds of fillets)

1 ½ lbs. kosher salt
3 cups (1 ½ lbs.) brown sugar
1 ½ Tbsp. chili powder
2 Tbsp. cumin
¼ tsp. hot pepper flakes
1 tsp. or more garlic powder, optional

Smoked the hard way.

Mix brining ingredients. I leave the skin on the fillets that will be smoked so they don't fall apart as easily. Put a layer of the salt and sugar mixture on the bottom of a vessel large enough to accommodate all of your fish. Lay fish skin-side down on salt, and put a liberal amount of salt sugar/mixture on first fish layer. Put a second layer of fish and more salt on top, alternating until all fish are covered with mix. Let fish sit at room temperature for at least an hour and a half, but no longer than two hours or your final product will be too salty. By reducing the brining and smoking times and finishing the fish in the oven, I wind up with fish that is not overly salty, overly smoked, or too dry, as I find many smoked bluefish to be.

After removing fish from brine and rinsing them, allow them to air-dry as you prepare your smoker. For abundant smoke and flavor, I use soaked hickory chips and green applewood trimmings on a bed of charcoal. I try to keep the temperature no higher than 200 degrees F.

Arrange your fish on racks or the grill itself and smoke for two to three hours. The fillets should be golden brown and a white fluid should be oozing out between some muscle segments.

Now move the fillets to a cookie sheet or other large tray and bake for 15 to 20 minutes in a 300 degrees F oven, being careful not to dry them out. Cool to room temperature and enjoy. I wrap and freeze those I don't eat or give away, so I always have a supply on hand – so should you.

In the following recipe, you can use smoked bluefish or you can smoke your own haddock to make creamed finnan haddie. If you smoke your own haddock, do not make a spice mix. Instead, use plain salt, brine for two hours, smoke for two more, and use the following recipe from Howard Mitcham, found in his wonderful "Provincetown Seafood Cookbook."

CREAMED FINNAN HADDIE

Take 2 pounds of finnan haddie fillets and remove bones and skin. Flake or dice the meat and place it in a saucepan of boiling water for 5 minutes, then drain in a colander (skip this boiling if using smoked bluefish). Melt a half stick of butter in a skillet and add 2 Tbsp. of flour. Remove from fire and add 1 cup of milk and 1 cup of light cream (or evaporated milk, my addition to the recipe), ½ tsp. salt, a little fresh ground pepper, a pinch of nutmeg and a dash of cayenne pepper. Stir the sauce until it thickens (back on the heat), then add the haddock and cook a few minutes longer. Ladle over toast on hot plates and serve at once. This is great for breakfast, luncheon, 4 o'clock tea, supper, dinner or a midnight snack, and if you wake up hungry at 2 a.m., it is good even then. You can spark up this cream sauce by adding chopped or sliced onions, celery, chopped hard-boiled eggs, fresh dill or mint leaves, capers, etc.

I say give it a try – you won't be sorry!

Remember that fresh seafood makes a great last-minute gift. Who would be disappointed by a couple of lobsters or a peck of oysters or some precious bay scallops? A side of smoked salmon isn't to be sneezed at, either. Happy Holidays! Welcome in the New Year with seafood and hope!

Feast of the Seven (at Least!) Fishes

Every year, I am delighted by thinking about and partaking in the traditional Italian Christmas Eve "Feast of the Seven Fishes." Christmas Eve is a fasting day in the Catholic calendar, so this feast became a tradition on the night of the Christmas vigil awaiting the birth of the Christ Child. The tradition is Southern Italian in origin, but being a seafood lover myself, I think that it should be observed and preserved throughout the Christian world. I think it should also be extended to the "heathens" in the true spirit of Christmas. We could probably get more participation by calling it a "seafood orgy" rather than a vigil, but regardless, let's plan one. I will have one at my house.

There are many theories about why the number seven is most widely required – too many, in fact, to go into (they range from the seven days of the week to the seven hills of Rome) – but that is beside the point. My point is the food.

Most Italians expect certain fish to be included, with bacala (salt cod), shrimp, oysters, eels, and smelt among them. Squid are often included, clams are critical, and you'll usually find a piece of swordfish or fresh cod. Now that is plenty to work with.

My feast will begin with clams and oysters on the half-shell, followed by a few sautéed and boiled shrimp, and a salt cod (bacala) soup.

SAUTÉED SHRIMP WITH GARLIC AND CHILIES

1 lb. medium shrimp (shells on)
2 small hot chilies (or ½ Tbsp. Chinese chili garlic paste)
2 Tbsp. peanut oil
2 cloves garlic (peeled and crushed flat)
1 tsp. salt (sea salt, preferably)

Heat skillet or wok, add oil and heat until almost smoking. Put in garlic cloves and whole chilies and brown both. Remove garlic before it burns, but chilies may burn. Toss shrimp in hot oil until opaque and turning pink, no more than two minutes. Remove and serve hot.

Serving these hot, spicy shrimp with the raw shellfish and relatively bland boiled shrimp is a great way to start. Have lemon, ground pepper and cocktail sauce close at hand.

So, three varieties down! Now onto the soup, which takes three days. Do not despair, it is easy!

CHRISTMAS BACALA SOUP (for 12)

2 lbs. salt cod
2 medium onions (coarsely chopped)
2 Tbsp. olive oil
1 28 oz. can tomatoes, chunked (preferably Italian)
1 can tomato paste (6 oz.)
5 medium boiling potatoes
½ tsp. baking soda
2 Tbsp. minced, flat-leaf parsley
Salt and pepper to taste
Tabasco, served on the side

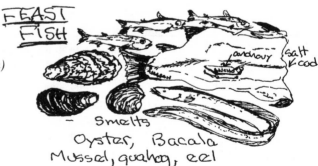

Soak salt cod for at least 24 hours. Some say two days, but I think one day is long enough. Change soaking water four times. Sauté onion chunks in oil over medium heat, stirring occasionally, for about five minutes until they just begin to brown. Add potatoes, tomatoes, tomato paste, baking soda and fish. Bring the whole works to simmer for 20 minutes. Do not season yet. Let the mixture cool to room temperature and then refrigerate for at least one day; two is all right. Stir once or twice as it ages.

To serve, reheat, test for salt and pepper, and then add Tabasco, crushed red pepper or cayenne to taste. I serve without adding hot spice, letting guests add it at their own discretion. This stuff, served in a shallow soup dish with crusty bread on the side, is ambrosial.

From here we will move on to a little pasta. The mention of crusty Italian or French bread to soak up seafood sauces brings to mind mussels marinara and clam sauce with linguini. There are so many possibilities out there that they cannot be put into one column, but I have a suggestion involving a little shameless self-promotion: Buy one of my cookbooks. In the book, you will find five recipes for mussels marinara and clam sauce for spaghetti. This book is also a grand Christmas gift. Shameless, right?

EASY ANCHOVY AND PARSLEY SAUCE FOR PASTA
1 lb. pasta of your choice
1 can anchovies in oil (I use 2 cans)
2 Tbsp. olive oil
2 Tbsp. butter
1 medium onion, finely chopped
½ cup chopped Italian (flat-leaf) parsley
2 large cloves garlic (minced)
1/3 cup white wine (desirable, but optional)

Over medium heat, heat the oil and melt the butter in a skillet or pot large enough to hold the pasta. Add the anchovies and the oil from the can and mash with a fork. Add onions and sauté until they become opaque, then add garlic and sauté one minute longer. You do not want the garlic to burn. The anchovies should have kind of melted by now. Toss in half the chopped parsley, add optional wine, and cook another minute. Now stir in a pound of pasta that you have cooked separately, and stir. Serve on a heated platter or right from the skillet and garnish with remaining parsley. Terrific!

PAN-ROASTED SMELTS
1 lb. smelts
3 garlic cloves, minced and mashed
3 Tbsp. butter
2 Tbsp. olive oil
½ cup dry white wine
1 cup flour
½ tsp. dried oregano
2 Tbsp. minced parsley
Salt and pepper
Lemon juice

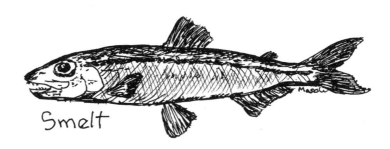
Smelt

Heat oil and butter in a frying pan large enough to hold fish in a single layer. Dredge the fish in flour seasoned with salt and pepper. I shake them up together in a plastic freezer bag. Add garlic and oregano to melted butter and oil over medium-high heat, then add fish and brown for about 1½ minutes per side. Splash in the wine, lower heat, cover pan and simmer slowly for 6 minutes, turning fish over after 3 minutes. Remove the fish to a heated dish, pour pan juices over it all, and garnish with parsley and lemon. Then rejoice!

I think you should also have some fried calamari, breaded fried eel, and Italian braised swordfish. You can find recipes in my book. Bona Natale! Mangé!

I have been trying to fit Italian dishes into the lyrics of The Twelve Days of Christmas – you know, "a partridge in a pear tree" and all of that. I have only got "lobster ravioli" so far. Maybe next year. Merry Christmas!

Putting the Fish Back in Christmas

This holiday celebrating the birth of Christ always gets me thinking about the connection between fish and the son of the Christian god. In early Christian art, the symbol of Christ is a fish because he was the fisher of souls for their salvation and because the initial letters of the Greek word for fish, IXOYC (ichthos), formed an acrostic which could be read as "Jesus Christ, Son of God, the Savior." Because of this Greek root, the scientific study of fish is called ichthyology. Perhaps fish are the holiest of creatures, which would explain why some pursue them religiously. Christians were also spoken of as fish living in the waters of baptism.

Jesus seemed to have a definite interest in fish and the sea, both catching fish and "walking of the waters." He also chose them as the entrée at his miracle meal when performing the miracle of feeding the 5,000 with loaves and fishes.

I have often wondered how the fish were prepared and presented. My wife and I came up with the same idea in trying to answer this puzzle: sardines. No, not the canned sort, but the kind sold grilled as street food all around the Mediterranean that are eaten on bread like our sub rolls. Rolls would save a lot of slicing and don't fall apart like sliced bread. These sardines are delectable, wonderfully flavored by their own salty oil and are a snap to prepare on a grill or under a broiler.

Fresh sardines have only become available in this country in the past ten years, being flown in twice a week from Portugal. You can find them in some markets or order them through your fishmonger.

GRILLED SARDINES

6 sardines per person
6 rolls
Enough coarse salt to cover fish
Olive oil

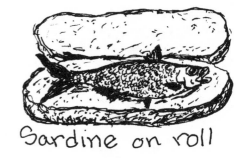

Sardine on roll

Cover the fish in coarse (Kosher or sea) salt for one hour. Dig them out and brush off all but a little salt, anoint them with oil, and grill them over charcoal (best) or in the oven for about three minutes per side about three inches from the flame. The skin should be beginning to char when you remove them.

Serve these grilled sardines on a Portuguese roll or a sub roll; you want something more substantial than a hotdog bun. Mackerel is a good alternative if sardines are unavailable.

Split a roll and lay a fish on it. Break the skin should you wish to skin it. I eat the skin happily. Pick the meat off the fish with your fingers or teeth, then turn the fish over and eat the second side. Keep using the same roll as you eat the rest of your serving of fish. The sardine oil will saturate the bread, and you can eat the utterly delicious roll.

My wife and I think this divine dish may have been served at the miraculous feeding of the 5,000. It saves plates and is delicious. I think a repeat of the miracle at the wedding at Cana involving turning water into wine would have made this a truly grand meal; a little vinho verde would go well here.

I should get back to the celebration feast for the birth of the miracle worker. I grew up far from the sea, where fresh fish were rarely available and shellfish were nearly non-existent in the fresh form, but salted fish were, as were barreled oysters. My father always bought a 2-gallon wooden keg of salt herring, and sometimes a keg of salt mackerel. If times were good, there would be oysters, as well.

The herring would be desalted and pickled with onions, the mackerel desalted, coated with seasoned flour and baked or fried. It seemed that we rarely finished the mackerel, which were eventually fed to my father's chickens, giving the breakfast eggs a strange low-tide maritime flavor, unique in Michigan, for a spell.

I strongly recommend digging, collecting, or even buying several dozen oysters and littlenecks to store in your fridge over the holidays, a fine treat for unexpected or expected guests. They will keep beautifully for a couple of weeks and will always be ready; besides, they are some of the better things of life, suitable for celebrations.

Some enterprising souls even make wreaths and ornaments and mildly interesting gifts out of their shells.

SIMPLE PORTUGUESE STEAMED MUSSELS (for 6+)

4 dozen scrubbed mussels
3" linguica, diced
1 tsp. ground cumin
1 14.5 oz. can diced tomatoes (basil, oregano, and garlic flavored)
1 cup cheap red wine
Tabasco to taste

Put everything in a pot and bring to a brisk simmer for at least two minutes, or until mussels are open and alcohol has burned off.

Serve with Portuguese rolls and the rest of the wine – a grand simple dish. Serve in a white bowl and garnish with parsley and it will look like Christmas. So does a cold, boiled lobster on a bed of mesclun dressed with vinaigrette. Very festive and even regal if you throw in a few raw oysters on the side.

Another fairly cheap, easy, and delicious appetizer that will strengthen your culinary fame is little finger-sized pieces of swordfish coated with seasoned flour, or a simple batter, and fried. I buy the relatively cheap swordfish trimmings to cut these morsels. These fried gems are great, especially if served with the following tartar sauce.

EASY TARTAR SAUCE

½ cup mayonnaise
1 ½ Tbsp. sweet pickle relish
1 ½ Tbsp. horseradish
¼ tsp. sherry vinegar (or red wine)

Mix, and "Bob's your uncle". Dip a piece of hot fried swordfish in this and eat it and be gleeful. I certainly am at holiday feasts, especially Christmas.

Why Seven?

It is hard to realize that another year has passed and that it is time, once again, to write of my favorite culinary event of the year: the traditional Italian Christmas Eve Feast of the Seven Fishes. I wonder why the number seven is so prominent in our culture: seven deadly sins, lucky seven, seven seas, etc.

I like to serve seven fishes. (I allow oysters, shrimp, clams, and mussels honorary fish status for the holiday, but you do not have to.) You can serve more or even fewer, more is better.

I am going to start with raw oysters and littleneck clams on the half shell, along with a smoked bluefish pate. There are three fishes already. If I sauté a few shrimp in garlic and chili, we will have four before we reach the main meal.

For those of you who do not want to open oysters or clams by hand, you can put them on a baking sheet and heat them in a 300 degrees F oven until they pop open. Remove them from the oven and serve them with melted butter and a few lemon quarters. Almost as good as raw, better to some.

For the main course I will serve a whitefish fillet or two, haddock, cod, pollock, etc., cooked in a tomato sauce to which I will add a few scallops and mussels. The fish will be served beside a mess of spaghetti dressed with the scallop, mussel and tomato sauce. I might put a few squid rings in the sauce for its last five minutes in the oven; I could throw in a few shrimp at the same time.

This will be served with a Christmas green and red salad of dark lettuce and grape tomato vinaigrette with a few snow-like flecks of white onion thrown in, "just for pretty," as my mother would have said.

ITALIAN STYLE BRAISED SEAFOOD FOR CHRISTMAS EVE (for 6)

3 lbs. white fish (haddock, cod, halibut, monkfish, pollock)

12 sea scallops

12 shrimp

12 mussels

1 quart Italian tomato sauce (homemade or bottled marinara is good)

¼ cup chopped olives (optional)

Preheat oven to 415 degrees F. Place fish fillets in a single layer in a large baking pan that you have lightly anointed with olive oil. Salt and pepper the fish. Pour tomato sauce around fish without submerging them. Cover the exposed fish with breadcrumbs (Japanese-style panko breadcrumbs are very good) and drizzle with oil. Bake in oven for five minutes, add scallops and mussels, bake five minutes more and add shrimp (shelled) and calamari, if you are including some. Bake five minutes longer until everything is done and the sauce is bubbling.

While the fish is baking, you should have 1 pound of linguini or spaghetti boiling. When you remove the fish from the oven, keep it warm. Drain the pasta and add it to the roasting pan from which you have removed the fish, mix thoroughly and pour the whole works onto a platter large enough to hold the pasta with the fish alongside. Bring the shrimp, scallops and mussels to the top for showing off. Sprinkle the whole thing with minced Italian parsley and serve proudly!

I would serve Parmigiano-Reggiano with this despite what some Italians would say ("No cheese with seafood") and also ground red pepper.

A salad on the side, some crusty bread and a glass of pinot grigio and you will have at least a Merry Christmas Eve dinner and a growing reputation as a seafood cook.

I can't come up with a fish dessert; maybe fish-shaped Christmas cookies?

SPICY GARLIC AND GINGER SHRIMP APPETIZER

1 lb. medium or small shrimp (shell on)
2 Tbsp. oil (peanut is best)
1 or 2 bulbs garlic, squashed
2 slices ginger root
1 Tbsp. Chinese chili garlic paste or Sriracha sauce
2 Tbsp. chopped scallion for garnish

Heat oil in wok or frying pan; when the oil is nearly smoking, add ginger slices and crushed garlic. Do not allow garlic to burn. When it turns brown, add chili paste or sauce and the shrimp. Stir fry until shrimp become opaque and somewhat pink. Remove shrimp from oil and serve garnished with chopped scallions.

I eat the shrimp as my hero Howard Mitcham, author of "The Provincetown Seafood Cookbook," would say, "feathers and all!" Spicy and delicious! The shrimp cry out for a swig of cold beer or soothing eggnog.

For the less adventurous, smoked bluefish pate on crackers will have to do, and do very well indeed!

SMOKED BLUEFISH PATÉ

½ lb. smoked bluefish
1 smallish onion, grated
½ lb. cream cheese
1 tsp. Worcestershire sauce
1 lemon for juice
Dash of Tabasco or other hot sauce
1 or 2 Tbsp. horseradish sauce or 1 Tbsp. grated prepared horseradish
1 or 2 Tbsp. whiskey or cognac, optional
2 Tbsp. green part of scallion minced with some parsley

Mix the whole mess together in a bowl and, with the back of a fork, crush it together until nearly smooth. Chill and serve with crackers – so good!

Only one thing is missing for me in this menu and that is:

CHICKEN-FRIED EEL

A quantity of 1" to 1 ½" thick eel cut 3" or 4" long
Breading for fried chicken
Enough oil to provide ¼" depth in your skillet
1 egg beaten with ½ cup of milk
Lemon and parsley

Dip eel pieces in milk and egg and in breading mixture of your choice and set aside to dry for five minutes. Heat the oil over a medium flame and sauté eel slowly until nicely browned on all surfaces. Unlike most fish, fried eel should cook slowly and will not dry out. When eel is done, about 20 minutes, drop some whole parsley stems in the hot oil. They will crisp up almost instantly. Serve this crisp parsley with the fried eel, garnished with lemon, and you will have a dish to celebrate!

But alas, eel is scarce and getting scarcer, but I would eat one if I could get it; my stomach often dominates my inclinations toward conservation. This is an eternal problem for our species, but then again Christmas comes but once a year!

"Fasting" Can Be Feasting

Thirteen, eleven, nine, seven... these are not necessarily lucky numbers everywhere, but they are if you have the good fortune to share a Christmas Eve feast in an Italian household. They represent the number of types of fish and shellfish served at a Feast of the Seven (or nine, etc.) Fishes served on Christmas Eve.

Christmas Eve is a day of fasting in the Catholic Church. The Italians see fasting as abstaining from meat. They assuage the pain of this fasting by forcing themselves to eat seafood. This seems a very sensible idea to me.

The most common number of species eaten at the feast is seven, one for each day of God's creation proceedings. Another number represents the stages of the cross, and thirteen provides a species for each of the Apostles and one for Christ, diners at the Last Supper. I think you aim for seven and go from there depending on your wallet, appetite, and the amount of effort you want to put into this feast.

In order to serve such a multitude of dishes at a single meal, it behooves one to serve some dishes that can be prepared ahead of time or that require little or no preparation (raw oysters, clams on the half shell).

Every family has its own traditional menu, but all families include most of these seven foods: calamari, scungilli (whelk), baccala (salt cod), shrimp, clams, mussels and a finfish (cod, haddock, etc.)

The shrimp can be precooked and served cold; a scungilli or calamari salad can be made ahead and chilled. The salt cod can be prepared as a soup with potatoes and onions and reheated at mealtime. This leaves the clams, mussels, and fish to cook at mealtime. I would steam the mussels, make white clam sauce, and simply roast or broil the fish.

Some sort of greens, like kale, broccoli rabe, or spinach, are served along with the seafood. You also should have plenty of wine and crusty Italian bread to round out the "fast." I am so full I can hardly go on, but Italians traditionally serve a bunch of pastries along with anisette. A brave and noble race, indeed.

Many Italians used to insist that eel be included in the feast, so the price and demand for fresh eel soared just before the holidays. New England fishermen accumulated thousands of eels in the autumn, keeping them in live cans to ship to New York and Boston to sell at a premium at Christmastime. Alas, this is no more, because we have greatly overfished our eels. If you insist on eels for your feast, you will either capture them yourself or pay dearly.

Eels are served smoked, breaded and fried like chicken, or in a marinara sauce to be served over pasta. Eels are delicious every way but raw, as far as I know.

Some Italians want battered and fried smelt, steamed lobster, or broiled octopus in marinara sauce. Another popular salad is tuna (canned) and white beans. This list could go on indefinitely.

Instead of serving seven individually prepared items, some people make a cioppino (pronounced "Joe Peeno") says my mentor and culinary hero, Howard Mitcham, author of the classic "Provincetown Seafood Cookbook". The following recipe is based on his excellent rendition of this peasant triumph.

CAPE COD CIOPPINO (for 6 or 7)

The Zuppa

2 quarts fish stock
2 cups dry white wine (vinho verdi, good)
2 cups sliced mushrooms
2 onions chopped
¼ cup minced fresh parsley
6 scallions
6 cloves garlic
2 ½ cups canned tomatoes
1 can tomato puree (8 oz.)
1 bay leaf
½ tsp. basil
½ tsp. oregano
Salt (to use carefully after all shellfish have cooked)
½ tsp. black pepper
A big pinch of pepper flakes

The Seafood

2 live lobsters (about 2 lb. each)
5 haddock fillets
5 flounder fillets
6 squid and tentacles, cleaned and diced
2 doz. mussels
2 doz. steamer clams
2 doz. littleneck clams
1 lb. shrimp (fresh or frozen) in their shells

You may leave some ingredients out or substitute crab for lobster, conch for squid, octopus for whatever. Just make sure you have plenty of seafood and a lot of variety.

You will need a large heavy-bottomed pot, a large skillet and a medium pot with a lid for steaming shellfish.

Chop lobster into large chunks (or omit). Heat 1 cup olive oil in the skillet, add onions, scallops and garlic, sauté until onions are soft and golden brown; add the parsley and mushrooms and stir.

Add tomatoes, the puree and spices, herbs, and condiments. Stir frequently and cook at a simmer for 30 minutes until sauce thickens and loses its acidic flavor. If acidity persists, add a Tbsp. of white sugar. Transfer this sauce to the large pot and add a quart of fish stock.

Meanwhile, scrub shellfish. Put 2 cups dry white wine in a pot that will hold them all. Put shellfish in pot and steam (covered) for 10 minutes or until all shells are open. Remove shellfish and pour liquid into big pot of sauce. If using lobster, heat ½ Tbsp. olive oil in skillet and sauté the lobster chunks and claws for about 10 minutes. Add to big pot, stir gently and thoroughly, and add the fish pieces – do not stir, cook 10 minutes more, add shrimp and remaining fish broth to cover all ingredients, cook 10 more minutes in covered pot. Add clams and mussels, cover for 1 minute, and serve in bowls. Accompany with bread fried in garlic-flavored olive oil – and *mangé*!

You can omit some of the fish stock, leaving a seafood-laden tomato sauce thick enough to serve over pasta. I prefer it served as a zuppa. Hurrah for cioppinno, and Merry Christmas!

Index